AGRICULTURAL PRICE ANALYSIS AND FORECASTING

John W. Goodwin
University Professor
University of Arkansas

WILEY

John Wiley & Sons, Inc.
New York   Chichester   Brisbane   Toronto
Singapore

ACQUISITIONS EDITOR Whitney Blake
MARKETING MANAGER Debra Riegert
PRODUCTION SUPERVISOR Ingrao Associates and Katie Erdman
DESIGNER Karin Kincheloe
MANUFACTURING MANAGER Susan Stetzer
ILLUSTRATION COORDINATOR Jaime Perea

Recognizing the importance of preserving what has been written, it is a policy of John Wiley & Sons, Inc. to have books of enduring value published in the United States printed on acid-free paper, and we exert our best efforts to that end.

Library of Congress Cataloging in Publication Data:

Goodwin, John W.
    Agricultural price analysis and forecasting / John W. Goodwin.
      p. cm.

    Includes index.
    ISBN 0-471-30447-6
    1. Agricultural prices—Mathematical models. 2. Agriculture
—Economic aspects—Mathematical models.   I. Title.
HD1447-066 1994
338.1-3.0112—dc20   93-21449
                                   CIP

For:
Leo V. Blakley

Professor Emeritus
Oklahoma State University

A Superb Price Analyst, my
Professor, my Mentor, and my
very good Friend

Foreword

Most junior or senior students in Agricultural Economics will see very little that is new to them in this book. There may be a manner of presenting information that is different. There may be a merger or a combination of economic models that has not been encountered previously. But almost all undergraduates at this level will have encountered the economic concepts, the individual economic models, and the economic theory in a variety of other courses.

What *is* likely to be new to many Agricultural Economics undergraduates is the concept that economic theory is more than intellectual gymnastics. Economic theory can actually be *used* with real numbers to solve real problems! Indeed, economic theory provides the framework within which real information may be organized and analyzed. Economic theory provides us with the only means we have for evaluating the accuracy and reliability of business information.

The objective of this textbook has been to provide undergraduate students with a means for acquiring skills in the *application* of economic theory. The ability to utilize and apply economic theory in a problem-solving framework is a highly marketable skill. This skill is sought not only by agribusiness firms, but also by the business community at large, by government agencies, and by financial institutions.

The materials in this book were developed from the author's class notes in a senior-level course in agricultural price analysis and forecasting. These materials have been classroom tested with four sets of undergraduate students—the most effective editors that any academic author can find. Each set of these students has provided valuable assistance in identifying segments of the text that require either clarification or strengthening. Since some parts of the text have been rewritten at the urging of each of the four sets of students, there may well be segments that will require still further revision.

Instructors may find the absence of discussions of the Commodity Futures Markets to be peculiar. However, the recent addition of financial futures, currency futures, petroleum futures, wood products futures, and options for all of these items plus agricultural commodities has caused the futures markets to become a subdiscipline in and of themselves. There are several recent texts that treat these issues in depth. Further, most universities have independent courses in the area. Therefore, the inclusion of futures markets in this text would appear to be redundant.

John W. Goodwin
Fayetteville, Arkansas
June 1993

Contents

Agricultural
Price
Analysis
and
Forecasting

CHAPTER 1

Introduction

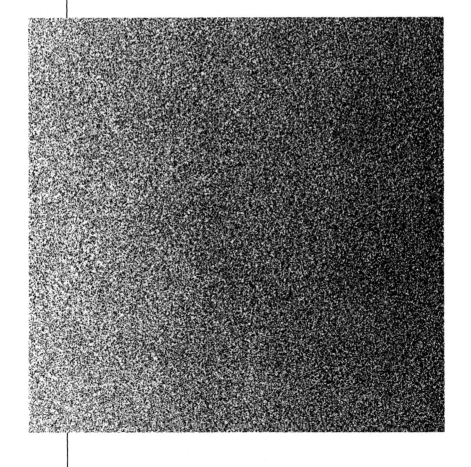

The analysis and forecasting of agricultural prices is one of the most demanding and potentially one of the most rewarding areas in agricultural economics. The tools of price analysis have a very broad range of application. And while those applications have proved to be extremely useful to those who are concerned with the business end of agriculture, the analytical tools of agricultural price analysis are by no means restricted to agricultural applications.

The tools of price analysis are just as relevant to the oil, automotive, or steel industries as to agriculture. The only difference in price analyses for these industries is the database—the tools are the same. The experience of the Organization of Petroleum Exporting Countries (OPEC) in the mid-1980s provides a vivid example of the applicability of the tools of price analysis to the oil industry. While the Sheiks of Araby upon occasion may have appeared to have acquired the ability to *amend* the laws of supply and demand for short periods of time, the facts are that there is no way that they (or any other group) can *repeal* those laws. It doesn't matter how closely held the ownership of a given product or commodity may be. The fact that market demand is less than perfectly elastic (i.e., that the demand curve exhibits some slope) means that increased quantities of product can be sold if and only if prices are reduced. When Iran and Iraq both increased oil production (exceeding their assigned production quotas) in order to finance their efforts to destroy one another, the quite predictable result was an erosion of world prices for crude oil.

Why do we study prices in general and agricultural prices in particular? What functions are performed by the price system in our market driven capitalistic economy that make it necessary for us to devote an entire body of courses to the analysis and study of prices? In almost *any* economy, prices are the economic messenger boy for the entire system. Even in a "command" economy with administered prices that prevailed in the old Soviet Union, Eastern Europe and parts of Asia, prices play a significant role. But in our free-wheeling, open, market economy, the role of prices is crucial.

We depend upon market prices for a number of very important economic functions. Among them are to:

1. Fix standards of value
2. Organize production
3. Distribute products (both geographically and among consumers)
4. Ration products (over time)
5. Provide for maintenance and growth in the economy

FIXING STANDARDS OF VALUE —————————

In the process of maximizing their satisfaction, consumers cast their dollar votes in the form of prices they are willing to pay in the market place. In this fashion, prices have determined the relative values (or fixed the standards of value) among commodities. Fords and Chevrolets provide exactly the same transportation service as do Mercedes. Then why is the Mercedes so much more expensive? A pound of pork provides a level of nutrition almost identical with that of a pound of beef. Yet in the United States, beef is more expensive than pork, and both beef and pork are more expensive than chicken. In Argentina, precisely the reverse is true. Why?

In casting their dollar votes in the market place, consumers are sending a message regarding the relative levels of satisfaction they realize from various sorts of consumption. These votes are counted by producers who are committed to maximizing the profit or return to the resources they control. On the basis of the apparent consumers' desires, producers organize (or *allocate*) these resources in such a manner that they produce the products that maximize the returns to their owned resources. In other words, *the standards of value, as fixed by the price system,* provide the information necessary for the organizational types of managerial decisions made by producers.

ORGANIZING PRODUCTION —————————

How do prices organize production? Let's go back to the three production management models to which you were probably introduced in your initial exposure to microeconomic principles. The simple production function (other terms for this relationship include the *transformation function* and the *Factor–Product* model) showed you how producers used the prices of inputs and outputs to determine the levels of variable resources to use and the level of output to produce and offer for sale (Figure 1.1). The profit maximizing criterion was that the manager would select that level of variable resource usage that equated the marginal cost of the variable input with the value of the marginal product. If the price of the product or the variable resource should change, the manager of the production unit would adjust the use of that resource and the output of the product to reflect that change.

The *Factor–Factor* model showed the manner in which managers utilize resource (or factor) prices to determine the least cost combination of resources to use in the production of given levels of output (Figure 1.2). For any given level of output, managers will utilize that combination of

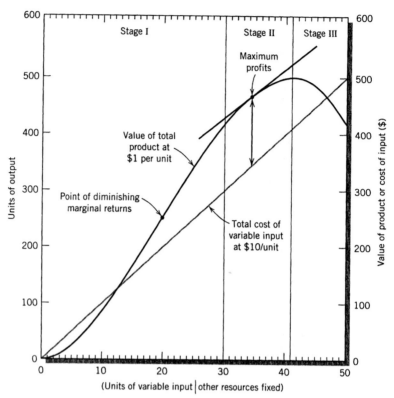

FIGURE 1.1.   The Factor–Product Model—resource and product prices as organizers of production.

variable resources where the marginal rate at which one factor of production may be substituted for another is equal to the inverse ratio of factor prices. If the price of one of these factors of production should change, the manager will substitute the now relatively lower-cost factor for the higher-cost factor. This substitution will continue so long as a dollar spent on one resource will replace more than a dollar's worth of the other. When the marginal rate of factor substitution is exactly equal to the inverse ratio of factor prices, the new cost minimizing combination of factors has been achieved.

The final production management model—the *Product–Product* model (another name for this is the *Production Possibilities* curve)—is concerned with the revenue-maximizing combination of products to produce with a given resource outlay (Figure 1.3). The management criterion in this case is that managers will shift resources from one product to another so long as a dollar lost from a reduction in the output of one product is replaced with more than a dollar gained in the output of the other. That is, managers will substitute one product for the other up to the point where the marginal rate of product transformation is exactly equal to the inverse ratio of product prices.

These three models can be combined and interrelated in various combinations and permutations to solve a wide variety of production management problems. But in every case, the determining factor is a set of price relationships that are used to organize production.

DISTRIBUTION OF PRODUCTION _____

After resources have been allocated and the production process completed, the product must be distributed among the various consumers of that product. Since the concept of demand by definition involves purchasing power as well as desire for products, the decisions as to who

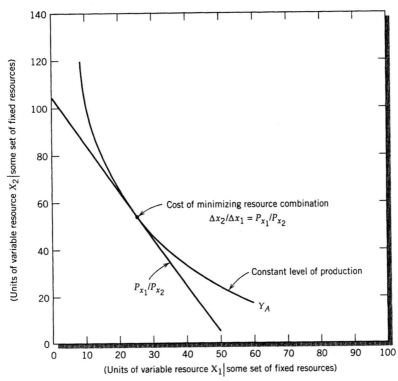

FIGURE 1.2. The Factor–Factor Relationship—resource prices as organizers of production.

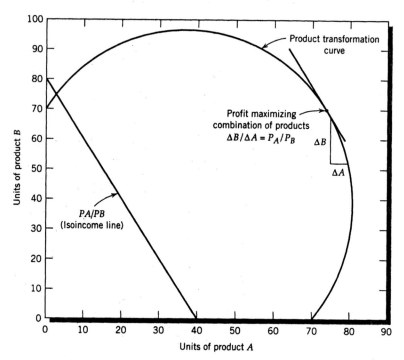

FIGURE 1.3.   The Product–Product Relationship—product prices as organizers of production.

gets what are made on the basis of who is willing to pay the necessary price. To a very significant degree, the income at the consumer's disposal will determine how much he will buy.

At very high prices, only a few people with high levels of income will be either willing or able to purchase goods. However, as the production of a good increases, the price falls and consumption of the good is spread over a larger and larger group. This is very much like the flow of water through the various levels of basins in Figure 1.4. As prices decline to the levels that lower-income consumers can afford, not only do more and more people participate in consumption, but those people previously engaged in consuming the good in question can increase the level of consumption in which they indulge. Thus, the product-distributing function of price is shown. At very high prices, only those few persons who have high incomes and who derive a large degree of satisfaction from consuming the product are willing to make these purchases. As price declines, the number of people participating in the market grows larger.

Another dimension of the distributional role of price is the dimension of geographic distribution. Typically, market prices are lowest at the point of production. At points away from the point of production, prices will be higher in order to pay the cost of transportation from the point of production to the point of consumption. This is the reason that rough rice prices at Stuttgart, Arkansas, are likely to be lower than at New Orleans. Wheat prices are likely to be lower at Enid, Oklahoma; Fargo, North Dakota; or Wichita, Kansas; than at Charlotte, North Carolina. Lettuce is likely to be less expensive at Salinas, California, or Yuma, Arizona, than in St. Louis. Soybeans are likely to be cheaper at Decatur, Illinois, than at any of the Great Lakes ports. And ready-to-cook whole bird prices for chicken are likely to be lower at Fayetteville-Springdale, Arkansas, than in New York or Washington, DC.

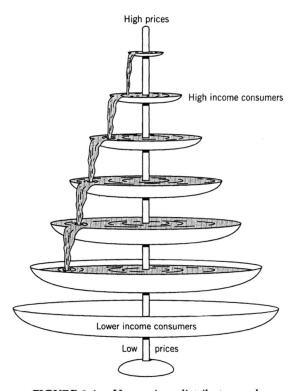

FIGURE 1.4. How prices distribute goods.

SHORT-RUN RATIONING
OF PRODUCTS _____

The short-run rationing of the product as performed by the price system simply means that the use of the product is spread over a longer period of time. This price function is particularly important in the case of agricultural commodities, since the production of many of these goods tends to be highly seasonal in nature. Wheat, for example, is harvested in the summer months. The use of the wheat harvested each summer must be spread over the months until the next crop is harvested. Through the early 1970s, when wheat export markets were increasing, the general price pattern was that wheat price would normally be low at harvest time and then increase through the fall until about mid-October when export commitments were generally completed (Figure 1.5). Prices generally tapered off through November, when the corn harvest increased availability of all grains. In December, wheat producers began to make plans to hold a part of their wheat inventories until after January 1 in order to spread their incomes over two tax years. This action reduced

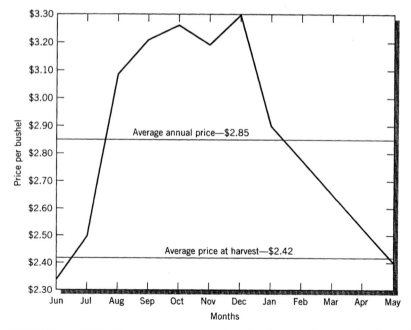

FIGURE 1.5.   WHEAT: average price received by farmers, by months, United States, 1971–75 crop years.

SOURCE: *Agricultural Prices, 1976 Annual Summary,* CRB, SRS, USDA, July 1976.

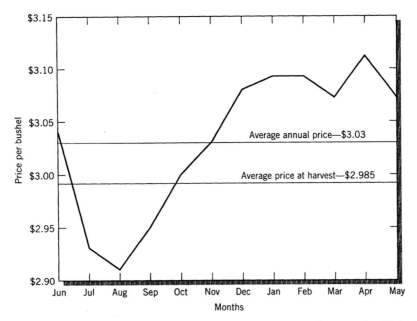

FIGURE 1.6. WHEAT: average price received by farmers, by months, United States, 1986–90 crop years.

source: *Wheat Situation and Outlook Report*, ERS-USDA, WS-293, May 1991.

the volume of wheat going to market. The price would normally rise fairly rapidly during this period, and then fall rapidly after the first of January as producers released wheat to generate the cash needed for spring farming operations (and as Commodity Credit Corporation crop loans on wheat began to mature). Wheat prices would generally decline through the new harvest, which began in June.

During the latter half of the 1980s, when wheat export markets were declining—largely as a result of U.S. monetary and fiscal policy—quite a different seasonal wheat price pattern was evident (Figure 1.6). Prices were still low at harvest time. But since wheat was priced very competitively with corn, December was no longer the peak price month. Rather, wheat prices exhibited a seasonal price pattern very comparable with that for corn, with a generally increasing price from one harvest to the next. It should be pointed out that the dollar axis scales on Figures 1.5 and 1.6 are different. The overall range of average monthly prices was reduced substantially between the two periods. During the period between 1971 and 1976, when wheat was priced as a food grain, the range in average monthly prices was almost $1.00. During the 1986–90 period, when wheat was priced as a feed grain, this range was reduced to about 20 cents.

PROVIDING FOR ECONOMIC
MAINTENANCE AND GROWTH ————————

If product prices are not high enough for the replacement cost of capital equipment to be covered, then the products produced by that capital equipment will gradually disappear. If costs are just barely being covered, then there will be no funds to plow back into the business for purposes of expansion. Thus, the dollar votes that consumers cast in the form of prices are the determining factor in what products are to be available and in what quantities. There are numerous examples in the American economy in which prices have not provided for maintenance and growth. American steel manufacturing, for example, has been and is being replaced largely by offshore manufacturing. American electronics, likewise, have been replaced largely by Japanese firms. American-based frozen citrus concentrates are under siege by low-cost Brazilian products. Hog lard was replaced by vegetable shortenings, and meat-type hogs replaced the lard-types that were dominant in the U.S. swine industry well into the 1950s.

Economists are fond of statements that describe economic relationships as if those relationships were carved in stone. But those statements are invariably couched in terms of the *ceteris paribus* assumption that holds all other factors constant. The reality is that the *ceteris paribus* assumption is an ideal mechanism for providing protection for the gluteal muscles of economists. We economists know full well that all other factors are in fact *not* constant. Indeed, *most* other factors *do* change with some frequency. It is these changing *ceteris paribus* conditions that give rise to the dynamic nature of our economy. And it is the dynamics of our economy that provide the source of the price movements that create many of the entrepreneurial opportunities in a capitalistic (or market) economy such as ours. Anticipating these price movements can yield some enormous benefits to the astute and can extract some enormous penalties from those who are unaware.

The *ceteris paribus* assumption does provide a useful framework for analysis. The initial analysis can be conducted under this assumption, and then as the *ceteris paribus* conditions are relaxed one by one, the impact associated with each can be identified. Thus, as changes occur, the probable price impact of various sorts of changes can be anticipated.

The analysis of *how* and *why* prices change is fundamental to the anticipation of *when, in what direction,* and *by how much* prices are likely to change as a result of a change in some condition. Any time a farmer plants a crop, some *anticipation* (or *forecast*) of the price that is likely to be received at harvest time has implicitly been included as a dimension of that decision. Any time an oil company begins to drill a well, the decision to drill the well involves some *expectation* (or *forecast*) of the price that is likely to be received for any oil discovered. The decision of a steel mill to purchase iron ore involves an implicit expectation of steel prices. And the decision to purchase a saloon keeper's license involves some anticipation of both liquor costs and cocktail prices.

The purpose of this book is to examine not only why and how prices change, but also to provide some approaches and techniques for anticipating or forecasting when prices are likely to move, the probable direction of such price movements, and the estimated magnitude of change. The focus of our effort will be upon agricultural commodities, primarily because there are decades of agricultural price and production information that are publicly available. But the same approaches and analytical techniques can be used with the data internally available to most nonagricultural businesses.

The analytical chapters of the book include an appendix that provides guidance to utilizing computer assistance in the analytical processes. These analyses can be conducted very effectively in the absence of computer expertise, but the presence of that expertise reduces the time required to complete the analysis. Time can become critical in the fast-moving worlds of both product and commodity marketing, and familiarity with the computer tools available can be enormously useful.

CHAPTER 2

Price Determination versus Price Discovery

In Chapter 1, we discussed the economic functions performed by prices in our free-wheeling, market-oriented economy. We saw how prices:

1. Fixed standards of value
2. Organized production
3. Distributed products
4. Rationed products in the short run
5. Provided for economic maintenance and growth

If prices perform all of these important functions, then obviously, the process by which prices are determined must be a fairly important process to be understood by the participants in the market place.

Almost any course in microeconomic principles introduces the whole process of price determination. Market prices are determined by the interaction between the forces of supply and demand, subject to the constraints imposed by the conditions of competition in that market. For example, most farm products are produced and sold under conditions approaching pure competition (polyopoly). The conditions necessary for the existence of pure competition are:

1. The number of buyers and sellers are sufficiently large that no individual buyer or seller can affect the market price.
2. The product is sufficiently homogeneous that it cannot be identified as to source once it gets to the market.
3. There are no artificial barriers to entering into or exiting from the market.

Under purely competitive conditions, the market supply function represents the horizontal summation of that portion of the marginal cost function that lies above the average variable cost function for all of the individual firms in that market (Figure 2.1). The equilibrium quantity exchanged and equilibrium price are determined at the intersection of the market supply and demand functions—the price at which consumers are willing to purchase exactly the same quantity as producers are willing to offer for sale.

Since the individual firm can sell as much or as little as wished without affecting market price, the manager of the firm is not aware of the market demand function with its downward to the right slope. The manager may realize that increased market quantities are associated with reduced market prices, but as far as the management of the business is concerned, the demand faced is a horizontal line at that market

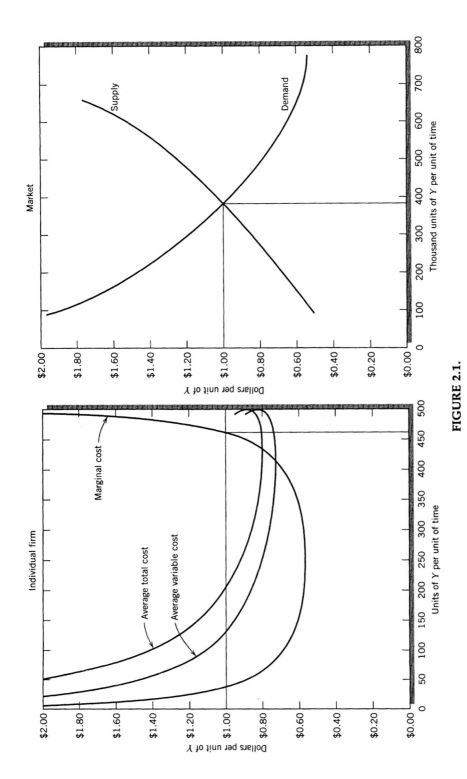

FIGURE 2.1.

15

price level. That is, every unit sold brings the market price. If the manager expands sales, that firm is such a small part of the total that the market can't tell whether or not the firm is there—the price is unchanged. Likewise, if he reduces sales, the price is unchanged. The market price, therefore, defines both the average revenue per unit of product sold and the marginal revenue generated by a one-unit change in the level of sales. If the manager's objective is to maximize profits, he wants to sell every unit that adds more to receipts than it adds to costs. Thus, in Figure 2.1, the manager will produce where marginal costs and marginal revenues are equal, selling about 465 units of Y at a price of $1.00 per unit. As prices rise or fall (as a result of a change in some *ceteris paribus* condition having caused one of these market functions to shift), the producer will respond to these changes by adjusting output along the marginal cost curve. This equating of marginal cost and marginal revenue yields the maximum profit possible for any given level of market price.

The cost structure for the firm in Figure 2.1 is fundamentally determined by that firm's production function and the prices for *variable* resources (Figure 2.2). The production function has its basic shape because of the *fixed* resources such as land, machinery, technology, and the like. Figure 2.2 shows the cost structure under conditions in which the variable resource X_1 is priced at $10.00 per unit. With the product Y priced at $1.00 per unit, the several physical product functions are identical with the value of product functions (that is, with Y priced at $1.00, the curves appear the same when measured in product units as they would appear if measured in monetary terms. We can see that the various profit maximizing criteria are met. Beginning in the lower-left corner of Figure 2.2, profits are maximum where the *value of marginal product* (VMP) and the *marginal factor cost* (MFC) are equal. The diagrams to the right of this one show profits to be maximum where the *value of total product function* (VTP) has the same slope as does the *total factor cost* (TFC) and where the *total revenue* (TR), *total variable cost* (TVC), and *total cost* (TC) functions have equal slopes. All of these profit maximizing positions occur at precisely the same level of output as does the point where *marginal cost* (MC) and *marginal revenue* (MR) are equal.

Short-term production decisions have been shown to be made upon the basis of the prices of products and variable resources. The adjustment to a change in the market price of the product Y would be shown by a change in the slope of the total revenue function and a corresponding change in the level of the horizontal line defined by the marginal revenue function. This can be traced back to a change in the level at which the variable resource X_1 is employed. That is, a change in the price of the product simply entails a rescaling of the Y axis for the production function and the marginal and average physical product

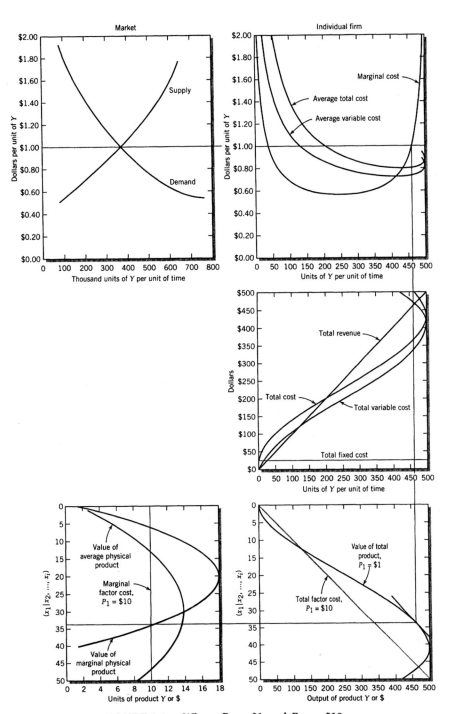

FIGURE 2.2. Where $P_Y = \$1$ and $P_{X1} = \$10$.

functions. The total factor cost would have a different slope relative to this revised scale, and the horizontal line defined by the marginal factor cost would be correspondingly raised or lowered. (Another way of stating this is that if X_1 is priced at $10.00 and Y is priced at $1.00, the TFC has a slope of $10Y$ per unit of X_1 employed. If the price of the product should rise to $2.00 per unit, the TFC would have a slope of $5Y$ per unit of X_1 employed. The position of the MFC would drop from $10Y$ to $5Y$ since the ratio of resource prices to product values has declined by half.)

A change in the cost of a variable resource shows up in quite a different manner. In the two physical product diagrams in the lower part of Figure 2.2, the change in resource prices is reflected by a change in the slope of the TFC and in the position of the horizontal line defined by MFC. An increase in variable resource prices would cause a retrenchment to a lower point on the production function. But the cost of variable resources is a *ceteris paribus* condition for the cost structure of the individual firm and hence for that firm's willingness and ability to offer products for sale at a given series of prices. That is, resource costs are a *ceteris paribus* condition for both the individual supply function and for market supply.

Suppose that variable resource prices have risen from $10 per unit to $15 per unit (Figure 2.3). The result would be the aforementioned changes in the slope of the total factor cost and the level at which the marginal factor cost traces out a horizontal line. But there would be a repositioning of the entire TVC and TC curves. The impact of this repositioning would be an upward shift in the cost structure for the individual firm and a resulting move upward to the left in the supply functions both for the firm and for the entire market. A new price would be determined (at $1.20 per unit of Y in the case of Figure 2.3) and the volume of sales would be reduced both for the firm and for the entire market.

In the case of our example of the firm operating in a purely competitive market, the equilibrium positions shown in both Figures 2.2 and 2.3 are unstable. The market price determined by the forces of supply and demand is in each case above the minimum point on the average total cost curve. The average total cost curve includes a "normal" return to all fixed resources. Thus, economic profits are being earned. The existence of economic profits would not only encourage existing firms to expand via increased investments in fixed resources as well as increased usage of variable resources, but also, new firms would be encouraged to enter into production of the good in question. As a result of this, the market supply function would shift to the right and a new market price would be determined. Resources would continue to flow into the industry until the market price fell to the level at which all fixed resources were earning exactly the return that those resources could expect in the next best

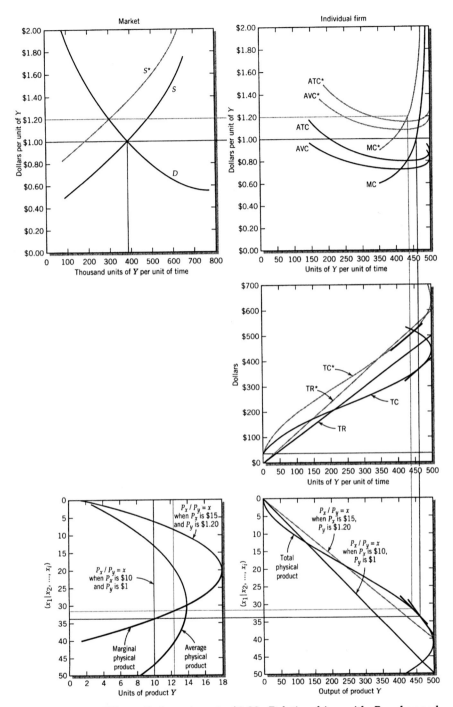

FIGURE 2.3. Where P_Y has risen to \$1.20. Relationships with P_{X1} changed from \$10 to \$15 per unit. (Dotted lines are associated with the higher prices.)

19

alternative use. At this point, the equilibrium achieved would be stable until some new disequilibrating factor arose.

All this information regarding the process by which prices are determined in a purely competitive market and how producers facing that market adjust to the economic realities is important for agricultural producers, processors, and marketing agencies to understand. But once they have achieved that understanding, their problems are far from solved. That understanding has provided nothing more than a *framework* or a *context* within which these businesses can *search* for solutions to their problems. Once the process by which prices are *determined* is understood, the problem facing the agricultural businessman—be he farmer, processor, provisioner, or marketer—becomes the problem of *discovering* or anticipating the price that *has been, is being,* or *will be* determined.

How do buyers and sellers arrive at specific prices in a given market at a given time? There are several processes that cover most of the pricing systems used today:

1. Individual negotiation,
2. Trading on organized exchanges or through auctions,
3. Formula pricing,
4. Group bargaining, and
5. Administrative decisions, including those made in both the private and public sectors.

The most primitive price discovery process is, of course, the process of individual negotiation on a case-by-case basis. Anyone who goes through a market in one of the less-developed countries such as Mexico immediately discovers that every transaction is an exercise in price discovery. The question in the buyer's mind is, "How much will they take?" That in the seller's mind is, "How much will they give?" Through a process of offer and counteroffer, the two parties ultimately reach an agreed-upon price—*if* there is an overlap between their divergence of opinion regarding the relative worth of the item in question. In the United States, this process of individual negotiation has largely disappeared except for cases of major items such as real estate or automobiles that most individuals purchase very infrequently. For frequently purchased items, the process is too time consuming and hence too expensive and inefficient.

Trading on organized exchanges or through auction markets has tended to replace the individual negotiation process of price discovery as the volume of products exchanged has increased. While a transaction-by-transaction private treaty process of negotiation might be appropriate when only one animal (or one bushel of grain, apples, or soybeans) is to be sold, this process would become burdensome if several hundred or even thousands of units of the product were to be marketed. Historically, auction markets have been widely used to discover the prices for livestock. But with increasing specialization and ever-growing sizes of livestock consignments, smaller and smaller proportions of animals are being sold through auctions each year.

As the volume exchanged increases sufficiently, centralized markets tend to be replaced with direct selling to chain stores or processors. With direct selling, prices tend to be established on the basis of formulas or collective bargaining procedures. Many slaughter cattle, for example, are sold "on the rail" with the price to the producer to be determined by the wholesale carcass market with a system of formulae based on carcass grade and carcass yield used to establish price premiums and discounts.

Group bargaining conducted by producer associations and cooperatives such as Riceland Foods for rice or Union Equity for wheat have tended to replace the centralized grain exchanges located in places such as Kansas City and Chicago, even though these central markets may still serve as a basis for pricing. Frequently, the bargaining agent will negotiate a system of formula premiums and discounts from a central market, the premiums and discounts determined by grade and quality standards.

The price discovery process in the case of some commodities such as fluid milk has been replaced by formulas and administrative decisions made by public agencies. Price-support loan rates are also established in this manner, even though actual market prices are still established (or "discovered") on the basis of transactions, particularly when supplies are small enough to force prices above the loan rate.

When agricultural producers (or for that matter, any other group) complain about the inequities in the laws of supply and demand, the fundamental supply–demand relationships that *determine* prices are typically *not* relationships about which they are concerned. Rather, their concern is based upon the imperfections in the mechanisms for *price discovery*. People can easily observe the maneuvering of packer buyers and commission house salesmen in a terminal livestock market or of floor traders in a futures market exchange and draw entirely erroneous conclusions. Imperfect mechanisms for price discovery can temporarily cause the general level of prices for a commodity to get out of line with the underlying supply–demand forces that ultimately determine prices. These circumstances can result in price differentials between markets, and between grades and classes of commodities that will generate complaints from both producers and consumers. While these price discovery imperfections need to be corrected when possible, we must recognize that the mechanisms that allow us to *discover* prices do not *determine* prices. This confusion of the difference between price determination and price discovery was the crux of the issue among some cattlemen in their effort to terminate the futures trading of cattle during the middle 1980s.

The processes of price discovery are fundamentally the same as the processes of price forecasting. The primary difference in these two processes is in the *time* dimension. People who are in some phase of the business of agriculture go through some process of forecasting prices in order to make decisions such as the timing of buying or selling products or in order to make decisions regarding how much (if any) of a product is to be produced. That forecast may be as simple as assuming that the current soybean price is the best estimate of the next crop's price. It may be as complex as the detailed analysis we will be discussing throughout this book. But almost any business decision implicitly involves a price forecast of some sort.

The processes of price discovery are basically the processes of price forecasting, telescoped in time. In our market system, the processes of price discovery are primarily the responsibility of the marketing agencies, which oversee and conduct the buying and selling of commodities. Middle-men, when buying and selling farm products, are attempting to forecast the value those products will command when they ultimately reach retail consumer markets. They are estimating the forces of the imperfectly competitive markets between the farm and retail levels and the processing costs that determine the margins to be subtracted from retail values in order to derive an estimate of demand (and the appropriate price) at some lower market level.

If prices are to be *forecast*—essentially the same process as that by which prices are *discovered*—the place that one must obviously begin is with the forces that *determine* prices. But if those forces are to be identified and adequately analyzed, the dynamic factors that tend to obscure those forces must first be stabilized. In the 1970s and 1980s, one of the factors that has tended to obscure the patterns of supply and demand for farm products (and for that matter, for *any other* product) has been the continuing tendency for the value of the dollar to decline as a result of inflationary increases in the general level of prices. Chapter 3 discusses the use of index numbers for correcting raw price data for changes in the value of the dollar.

CHAPTER **3**

Correcting for Inflation—the Use of Index Numbers

One of the most pernicious problems in the post-World War II U.S. economy—and particularly since the OPEC countries began to do their thing in the early 1970s—has been that of inflation. In the simplest terms, inflation occurs when there are too many dollars chasing too few goods. That is, when money supplies increase more rapidly than does the general availability of goods, the result is an increase in the general level of prices and a consequent decline in the value of the monetary unit.

The term *general price level* refers to the weighted average of prices arising from all business transactions during some specified period of time. When the general price level "rises," a dollar buys less than it bought previously. That is, the dollar has lost purchasing power. The dollar is reduced in value as a result of an increase in the general price level. The value of the dollar, therefore, is the reciprocal (or the inverse) of the general price level.

The problem of inflation is particularly bothersome in the analysis and forecasting of prices for agricultural goods. Producers of these goods for a variety of reasons tend to be highly responsive to positive price movements and somewhat less responsive to negative price movements. Thus, if the value of a good is perceived to be increasing, there will typically be a fairly predictable increase in output. But because of some very important differences between *price* and *value*, it is easy for market participants who are observing changes in market price to be misled regarding what is actually happening to the value of products.

The price of a good is measured by the ability of that good to command the monetary unit. In other words, the numbers of dollars per bushel, per pound, per bale, and so on, commanded by the good in question defines its nominal price. That nominal price ignores any changes that may have occurred or may be occurring in the value of the monetary unit.

The value of a good, by way of contrast, is measured by the ability of that good to command other goods in exchange. While the monetary unit may be utilized as a vehicle for measuring the ability of a good to command other goods in exchange, changing values of the currency are the same for all goods. Thus, changes in the purchasing power of money are of no consequence when the value of a good is measured in terms of its ability to command other goods.

One of the more convenient approaches for making comparisons of prices over long periods of time is through the use of index numbers. In the simplest of terms, an index number is fundamentally a percentage and is interpreted in precisely the same manner as a percentage. Table

3.1 shows the nominal prices for three commodities—No. 2 Yellow Corn at St Louis, the season average U.S. price for Middling grade $1\frac{1}{16}''$ cotton, and the price for crude oil at the well head over the 1960–1990 period. If 1967 is selected as the base period, the 1967 price for each of these commodities is arbitrarily defined to be 100 percent, and the prices for each year over the entire period are "indexed" to this base price. Corn, for example, with an index price value of 159 in 1986 was priced at 159 percent of the 1967 base price. Cotton in that year was priced at 214 percent and crude oil at 646 percent of the base year prices.

If the nominal prices for all goods increased (or decreased) at similar rates, the relative abilities of these goods to command other goods (i.e., their values) would be fairly stable. But Table 3.1 illustrates the fact that prices for different goods inflate at very different rates. As a result, the relative values of those goods are highly instable. A bushel of corn, for example, in the base year of 1967, commanded a price of $1.16—40 percent of the price of a barrel of oil and the price of 4.67 pounds of cotton lint. That is, in 1967, a barrel of oil priced at $2.92 could have been acquired for 2.5 bushels of corn or for 11.76 pounds of cotton lint. By 1981, 12.17 bushels of corn or 52.53 pounds of cotton lint were required to acquire that same barrel of oil. These relationships are reflected by the reality that the 1967-based self-index value for corn in 1981 was 225 and for cotton was 244, while that for crude oil was 1088. That is, corn and cotton prices had a bit more than doubled while oil prices had increased by almost a thousand percent!

The self-indices of prices for corn, cotton, and crude oil are useful for purposes of examining what has happened to the *price* of a product over time. And while these self-indices can be used to compare the ability of one good to command another good, they aren't particularly useful for purposes of comparing the value of one good relative to all other goods that consumers might be purchasing.

Let's assume, for example, that there are only three goods—the three in our example—and that during some base period such as 1967, the typical consuming family of four purchased the following combination of these goods:

880 bushels of corn @ $1.16 per bushel

500 pounds of cotton @ 24.83 cents per pound

100 barrels of crude oil @ $2.92 per barrel

At the prices that prevailed in the base year of 1967, the cost of this "typical" family purchase would have been $1,436.95. Using the information in Table 3.2, we can make a similar calculation for each of the other years in our 1950-86 period. If we set the cost of this "market basket" of goods equal to 100 in the 1967 base year, we can calculate the index value of the cost of this market basket of goods over time.

TABLE 3.1.   Prices for Corn, Cotton, and Crude Oil, with Index Values for Those Prices, Selected Markets, United States, 1960–1990

Year	Season Price for #2 Yellow Corn at St. Louis* ($/bu)	Average Price Middling $1\frac{1}{16}''$ Cotton, United States (cts/lb)	Price for Crude Oil at Well Head ($/bbl)	Self Indices of Price (1967 = 100)		
				Corn	Cotton	Crude Oil
1960	1.14	30.96	2.88	98	125	99
1961	1.15	33.67	2.90	99	136	99
1962	1.26	33.52	2.90	109	135	99
1963	1.28	33.18	2.89	110	134	99
1964	1.34	30.73	2.88	116	124	99
1965	1.37	29.60	2.86	118	119	98
1966	1.41	22.08	2.88	122	89	99
1967	1.16	24.83	2.92	100	100	100
1968	1.23	22.90	2.94	106	92	101
1969	1.33	22.15	3.09	115	89	106
1970	1.45	23.55	3.18	125	95	109
1971	1.19	31.52	3.39	103	127	116
1972	1.85	33.14	3.39	159	133	116
1973	2.87	67.10	3.89	247	270	133
1974	3.07	41.69	6.74	265	168	231
1975	2.70	57.99	7.67	233	234	263
1976	2.25	70.88	8.14	194	285	279
1977	2.23	52.74	8.57	192	212	293
1978	2.51	61.58	8.96	216	48	307
1979	2.73	71.48	12.64	235	288	433
1980	3.35	82.99	21.59	289	334	739
1981	2.61	60.48	31.77	225	244	1088
1982	2.98	63.08	28.52	257	254	977
1983	3.45	73.11	26.19	297	294	897
1984	2.75	60.51	25.87	237	244	886
1985	2.37	60.01	24.08	204	242	825
1986	1.68	53.16	12.51	145	214	428
1987	2.19	63.13	15.40	189	254	527
1988	2.72	57.67	12.57	234	232	430
1989	2.59	69.78	16.05	223	281	550
1990	2.70	82.91	20.22	233	334	692

Source. Corn and Cotton Prices from *Agricultural Statistics*, USDA, GPO, 1972 and 1991 issues. Oil Prices and CPI from *Statistical Abstract* of the U.S., 1972, 1980 and 1992 issues.
* Average Price for Crop Year beginning September of that year for corn, beginning August for cotton.

These index values may be interpreted in a variety of ways. First of all, they can be interpreted to mean the amount of money that would be required in any given year to purchase the combination of goods that would have been purchased by $100 in 1967. That is, a total of $332.38 would have been required in 1985 to purchase the combination of corn, cotton, and crude oil that could have been purchased for $100 in 1967.

A second interpretation, since we have assumed that we are in a three-commodity world, is that a dollar would have been required in 1985 to purchase what 30 cents would have purchased in 1967.

$$(100/332.38 = 0.30) \tag{3.1}$$

That is, the value of the 1985 dollar was only 30 cents in terms of 1967 dollars.

The index values of the market basket of goods in our three commodity world represents the general price level. As pointed out earlier in this chapter, *the inverse of that general price level defines the current value of the dollar* relative to the purchasing power of the dollar during the base year.

The index values of the "market basket" of goods, since these values represent the general price level, can be used to "adjust" (or "deflate") the nominal (or "raw") prices for changes in the value of the monetary unit. The $2.35 nominal price for corn in 1985 was almost exactly double the $1.16 nominal price in the 1967 base year. But in our three-commodity 1967-based world, the general price level in 1985 with an index value of 332.38 had more than tripled since the base year. Thus, the "real" price (i.e., the *value* of corn in terms of its ability to command other goods in exchange) could be calculated:

$$(\$2.35/332.38) \times 100 = \$0.71 \tag{3.2}$$

The interpretation of this "real" price is that in terms of 1967 dollars, the price of corn in 1985 was 71 cents per bushel—45 cents less than in 1967. That is, corn lost a substantial portion of its value in terms of its ability to command other goods.

THE IMPORTANCE AND LIMITATIONS OF THE BASE YEAR IN INDEX NUMBERS ___

You will undoubtedly have noticed that we have consistently used 1967 as a base year in our discussion of index numbers. The 1967 base year has been selected simply for convenience since many of the governmentally published price indices—most notably the Consumer Price Index

TABLE 3.2. Prices for Corn, Cotton, and Crude Oil, with Estimated Cost for a "Market Basket" of these Goods with Index Value of that Market Basket, and Deflated Prices for Products

Year ($/bu)	Price for #2 Yellow Corn at St. Louis* ($/bu)	Season Av. Price Middling 1 1/16" Cotton, U.S.* (cts/lb)	Crude Oil Prices at Well ($/bbl)	Total Cost for 880 bu Corn, 500 lb Cotton and 100 bbl Oil ($)	Index of Value of Market Basket of Goods (1967 = 100)	Deflated Prices		
						Corn ($/bu)	Cotton (cts/lb)	Crude Oil ($/bbl)
1960	1.14	30.96	2.88	1446.00	100.63	1.13	30.77	2.86
1961	1.15	33.67	2.90	1470.35	102.32	1.12	32.91	2.83
1962	1.26	33.52	2.90	1566.40	109.01	1.16	30.75	2.66
1963	1.28	33.18	2.89	1581.30	110.05	1.16	30.15	2.63
1964	1.34	30.73	2.88	1620.85	112.80	1.19	27.24	2.55
1965	1.37	29.60	2.86	1639.60	114.10	1.20	25.94	2.51
1966	1.41	22.08	2.88	1639.20	114.07	1.24	19.36	2.52
1967	1.16	24.83	2.92	1436.95	100.00	1.16	24.83	2.92
1968	1.23	22.90	2.94	1490.90	103.75	1.19	22.07	2.83
1969	1.33	22.15	3.09	1590.15	110.66	1.20	20.02	2.79
1970	1.45	23.55	3.18	1711.75	119.12	1.22	19.77	2.67
1971	1.19	31.52	3.39	1543.80	107.44	1.11	29.34	3.16
1972	1.85	33.14	3.39	2132.70	148.42	1.25	22.33	2.28

Year								
1973	2.87	67.10	3.89	3250.10	226.18	1.27	29.67	1.72
1974	3.07	41.69	6.74	3584.05	249.42	1.23	16.71	2.70
1975	2.70	57.99	7.67	3432.95	238.91	1.13	24.27	3.21
1976	2.25	70.88	8.14	3148.40	219.10	1.03	32.35	3.72
1977	2.23	52.74	8.57	3083.10	214.56	1.04	24.58	3.99
1978	2.51	61.58	8.96	3412.70	237.50	1.06	25.93	3.77
1979	2.73	71.48	12.64	4023.80	280.02	0.97	25.53	
1980	3.35	82.99	21.59	5521.95	384.28	0.87	21.60	5.62
1981	2.61	60.48	31.77	5776.20	401.98	0.65	15.05	7.90
1982	2.98	63.08	28.52	5789.80	402.92	0.74	15.66	7.08
1983	3.45	73.11	26.19	6020.55	418.98	0.82	17.45	6.25
1984	2.75	60.51	25.87	5309.55	369.50	0.74	16.38	7.00
1985	2.37	60.01	24.08	4793.65	333.60	0.71	17.99	7.22
1986	1.68	53.16	12.51	2995.20	208.44	0.81	25.50	6.00
1987	2.19	63.13	15.40	3782.85	263.26	0.83	23.98	5.85
1988	2.72	57.67	12.57	3938.95	274.12	0.99	21.04	4.59
1989	2.59	69.78	16.05	4233.10	294.59	0.88	23.69	5.45
1990	2.70	82.91	20.22	4812.55	334.91	0.81	24.76	6.04

Source. Corn and Cotton Prices from *Agricultural Statistics*, USDA, GPO, 1972 and 1991 issues. Crude Oil Prices from *Statistical Abstract of the U.S.*, 1972, 1980, and 1992 issues.

* *Av.* Price for Crop Year Beginning September of that year for corn, beginning August for cotton.

(CPI)—for many years were reported for a 1967 base. The 1967 base year for the Consumer Price Index arose from the fact that 1967 was the year of the Bureau of Labor Statistics Survey of Household Consumption Expenditures. That survey was repeated for 1982–84, and more recent published estimates of the Consumer Price Index and related indices have been reported for the 1982–84 base period.

The Consumer Price Index and other published indices are constructed in essentially the same manner as was our index value for the market basket of three commodities in Table 3.2. The major difference is that there are a great many more than three commodities involved in the Survey of Household Consumption Expenditures, which defined the "market basket" of consumer goods upon which the construction of that index depends.

There are several limitations associated with the base year for any series of index numbers that should be pointed out. First of all, the assumption that the typical consumer will regularly and dependably buy the same "market basket" of goods is most probably contrary to the facts. Most consumers will substitute one good for another within fairly broad ranges in response to changes in relative prices.

A second problem with a base year such as 1967 is that many of the consumer products that were commonly purchased in the 1980s did not exist in the 1967 base year. For example, microwave ovens, microwavable food products, videocassette recorders and videocassette tapes were all products commonly used by well over half the U.S. households in the 1980s, but none of them existed in 1967. While the emergence of these products has been captured in the 1982–1984-based CPI, no price index can fully reflect the dynamics of the continuing development of new products.

A third limitation imposed by any base period is that fact that most of us implicitly equate 100 percent (or an index value of 100) with "normal." We have already recognized that the value of any good—be it a commodity, a product, or a service—is the power of that good to command other goods in exchange. In our three commodity world, if corn prices should rise by 10 percent while the prices of the other goods increased by 30 percent, then the *value* of corn in terms of its ability to command other goods would have declined by a bit more than 15 percent.

$$(110/130 = 0.846) \qquad (3.3)$$

The value of any good, therefore, is the ratio of the price of that good to the prices of all items included in the general price level.

The difficulty with the assumption that the base period represents a normal situation can be illustrated by examining two of the commodities in our three commodity world over the 1966–90 period. If there were only two commodities—corn and crude oil—changes in the relative values of these commodities could be interpreted to represent the ability of these goods to command other goods (Table 3.3). We can see that over the 1966–90 period, the value or purchasing power of a bushel of corn has ranged from a high in 1973 of 0.74 barrels of crude oil to a low in 1981 of 0.08 barrels. We could select some "base" year (or set of years) that we might define as being "normal" and "index" the price ratio in the individual years to that base year. This indexing would be accomplished simply by dividing the value of the price ratio for any given year by the value of that ratio in the selected base year and multiplying the resulting value by 100:

$$\frac{\text{Price Ratio for Any Year}}{\text{Price Ratio in Base Year}} \times 100 = \text{Index} \tag{3.4}$$

The resulting index value would be interpreted in precisely the same manner as a percentage. The value of corn relative to the value of oil in the base year would be 100 with the other years being some percentage of that "normal" base year relationship.

The choice of a base period for an index can make a great deal of difference in what is typically inferred from the index. If, for example, one were the chief executive officer of Standard Oil or a member of the Saudi royal family, the preferred base period for an index of the relative values of corn and oil would be 1981—the period during which oil prices relative to the price of the alternative product were the highest. This is the period that oil producers would prefer to define as normal.

If, on the other hand, one were a corn farmer, the choice base period would be 1973—the year during which corn prices relative to the alternative product prices were at an all time high. If an index value of 100 is considered to be normal, then a 1973 base year suggests that either oil prices were scandalously high in the late 1970s and in the 1980s or corn prices were disgracefully low. But if 1981 is selected as the base year, the implication would be that corn, which is a primary source of human nutrition for most of the people in the Western hemisphere, was obscenely over priced until the early 1980s.

The facts are, despite the apparent differences in the three different base periods of Table 3.3, these three base periods show precisely the same thing. Index numbers by their very design present *relative* information. Semilogarithmic scales in graphs are designed to present information in a relative context. That is, one and ten have exactly the same proportional relationship as 10 and 100 and as 100 and 1,000. Figure 3.1 shows the semilograithmic chart of the crude oil based index value of corn as calculated in Table 3.3 for each of the three base years. These

TABLE 3.3. Price Relationships Between Prices for Corn and Crude Oil, United States, 1965–1990

Year	Price for #2 Yellow Corn at St. Louis* ($/bu)	Crude Oil Price at Well ($/bbl)	Barrels of Crude Oil per Bushel of Corn	Index of Value of Corn in Terms of Crude Oil		
				1967 = 100	1981 = 100	1990 = 100
1965	1.37	2.86	0.479	121	584	357
1966	1.41	2.88	0.490	123	597	365
1967	1.16	2.92	0.397	100	484	296
1968	1.23	2.94	0.418	105	510	312
1969	1.33	3.09	0.430	108	525	321
1970	1.45	3.18	0.456	115	556	340
1971	1.19	3.39	0.351	88	428	262
1972	1.85	3.39	0.546	137	666	407
1973	2.87	3.89	0.738	186	900	551
1974	3.07	6.74	0.455	115	555	340
1975	2.70	7.67	0.352	89	429	263

Year						
1976	2.25	8.14	0.276	70	337	206
1977	2.23	8.57	0.260	66	317	194
1978	2.51	8.96	0.280	71	342	209
1979	2.73	12.64	0.216	54	263	161
1980	3.35	21.59	0.155	39	189	116
1981	2.61	31.77	0.082	21	100	61
1982	2.98	28.52	0.104	26	127	78
1983	3.45	26.19	0.132	33	161	98
1984	2.75	25.87	0.106	27	130	79
1985	2.37	24.08	0.098	25	120	73
1986	1.68	12.51	0.134	34	164	100
1987	2.19	15.40	0.142	36	173	106
1988	2.72	12.57	0.216	54	264	161
1989	2.59	16.05	0.161	41	197	120
1990	2.70	20.22	0.134	34	163	100

Source. Corn Prices from *Agricultural Statistics*, USDA, GPO, 1972, 1980, 1972 and 1991 issues. Oil Prices and CPI from *Statistical Abstract of the U.S.*, 1972, 1980, and 1992 issues.

* Av. Price for Crop Marketing Year beginning September of that year.

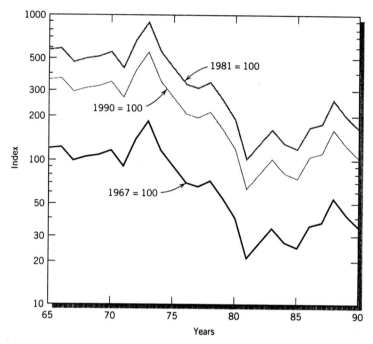

FIGURE 3.1.   Index Value of Corn in Terms of Crude Oil, Using Three Different Base Years, United States 1965–1990.

three different indices are exactly the same except for the point in time where the index has been defined to be 100. The distance from the peak value to the low value is exactly the same.

There are a set of fairly obvious reasons for the relative highs and lows in crude oil and corn prices. In 1973, corn prices were very high as a result of the Russian Grain Deal, which virtually liquidated U.S. inventories (and for all practical purposes, world inventories) of both food and feed grains. Oil prices doubled in the mid-1970s as a result of the OPEC oil cartel's action to restrict available supplies. The already doubled oil prices were tripled in the 1979–81 period when OPEC dropped the other shoe. The point is, drawing implications and conclusions on the basis of changes in relative values of two specific goods or groups of goods can be very hazardous—most especially when a base period is implicitly considered to be normal. There is an old adage about liars and figures that usually describes the intent of individuals and organizations that indulge in this practice.

DEFLATING PRICES TO ADJUST FOR INFLATION _____

There can be no doubt that the relative values of different goods over time can be obscured by changes in the value (or the purchasing power) of the dollar. There are a whole series of indices such as the Index of Wholesale Prices or the CPI that have been constructed to reflect the changes in the value of the dollar. Probably the most commonly used of these is the Consumer Price Index. The Consumer Price Index (CPI) is based upon a calculation of the value of a "market basket" of goods and services during some base period compared with the cost of that same combination of goods and services in some other year. Thus, a CPI of 339.80 in 1987 can be interpreted to mean that it cost $339.80 in 1987 to buy the consumer goods that could have been purchased for $100 in the base year of 1967. Alternatively, it could be interpreted to mean that only 29.4 cents was required in 1967 to buy what cost a dollar in 1987. That is, a 1987 dollar was worth only 29.4 cents in terms of 1967.

$$\frac{100}{339.8} = 0.294 \tag{3.5}$$

cents in terms of 1967 dollars. Since 1967, the general level of prices has more than tripled, making it very difficult to directly compare nominal prices over time.

The Consumer Price Index can be used to "correct" prices for changes in the value of the dollar, making year-to-year comparisons feasible. When you read about "real" prices or "real" income in the financial pages of your newspaper, the term *real* simply means that the prices or income have been adjusted to remove the effects of inflation. The real figures are in a constant-value dollar (i.e., a 1967 or a 1982–84 dollar) that purchases the same amount of goods and services in one period as another.

In terms of our corn, cotton, and crude oil prices, we can "deflate" the "raw" (or nominal) prices into terms of constant-value 1967 dollars simply by dividing the raw price by the CPI (Table 3.4). The 1984 price of corn in raw dollars was $2.75—more than double the 1967 base period price of $1.16. But the CPI for 1984 was 311.1, telling us that the general price level in 1984 was more than triple that of 1967. To correct the raw price for inflation and derive a real price in constant-value 1967 dollars, the calculation would be

$$\frac{\$2.75}{311.1} \times 100 = \$0.88 \tag{3.6}$$

Thus, the ability of corn to command other goods had actually declined by 12 percent, even though the raw dollar price had increased by 137 percent.

TABLE 3.4. Nominal Prices for Corn, Cotton, and Crude Oil, with Consumer Price Index and "Real" Prices for Corn, Cotton and Crude Oil, Selected Markets, United States, 1965–1990

Year at ($/bu)	Price for #2 Yellow Corn at St. Louis* ($/bu)	Season Av Price Middling 1 1/16" Cotton, United States* (cts/lb)	Crude Oil Price at Well Head United States ($/bbl)	Consumer Price Index (1967 = 100)	"Real" Prices #2 Yellow Corn at St. Louis* ($/bu)	"Real" Prices Seas. Av. Mid 1 1/16" Cotton, United States* (cts/lb)	"Real" Prices Crude Oil at Well Head ($/bbl)
1965	1.37	29.60	2.86	94.5	1.45	31.32	3.03
1966	1.41	22.08	2.88	97.2	1.45	22.72	2.96
1967	1.16	24.83	2.92	100.0	1.16	24.83	2.92
1968	1.23	22.90	2.94	104.2	1.18	21.98	2.82
1969	1.33	22.15	3.09	109.8	1.21	20.17	2.81
1970	1.45	23.55	3.18	116.3	1.25	20.25	2.73
1971	1.19	31.52	3.39	121.3	0.98	25.99	2.79
1972	1.85	33.14	3.39	125.3	1.48	26.45	2.71
1973	2.87	67.10	3.89	133.1	2.16	50.41	2.92
1974	3.07	41.69	6.74	147.7	2.08	28.23	4.56

1975	2.70	57.99	7.67	161.2	1.67	35.97	4.76
1976	2.25	70.88	8.14	170.5	1.32	41.57	4.77
1977	2.23	52.74	8.57	181.5	1.23	29.06	4.72
1978	2.51	61.58	8.96	195.4	1.28	31.51	4.59
1979	2.73	71.48	12.64	217.4	1.26	32.88	5.81
1980	3.35	82.99	21.59	216.8	1.55	38.28	9.96
1981	2.61	60.48	31.77	272.4	0.96	22.20	11.66
1982	2.98	63.08	28.52	289.1	1.03	21.82	9.87
1983	3.45	73.11	26.19	298.4	1.16	24.50	8.78
1984	2.75	60.51	25.87	311.1	0.88	19.45	8.32
1985	2.37	60.01	24.08	322.0	0.74	18.64	7.48
1986	1.68	53.16	12.51	328.4	0.51	16.19	3.81
1987	2.19	63.13	15.40	339.8	0.64	18.58	4.53
1988	2.72	57.67	12.57	354.5	0.77	16.27	3.55
1989	2.59	69.78	16.05	371.5	0.70	18.78	4.32
1990	2.70	82.91	20.22	391.3	0.69	21.19	5.17

Source. Corn and Cotton Prices from *Agricultural Statistics*, USDA, GPO, 1972 and 1991 issues. Oil Prices and CPI from *Statistical Abstract of the U.S.*, 1972, 1980, and 1992 issues.

* Average Price for Crop Year beginning September of that year for corn, beginning August for cotton.

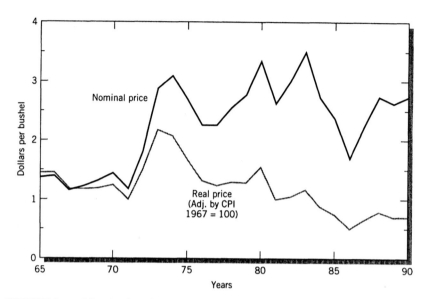

FIGURE 3.2. Nominal and Real Season Average Prices for #2 Yellow Corn at St. Louis, 1965–1990.

SOURCE: *Agricultural Statistics*, USDA, GPO, 1972, and 1991 issues.

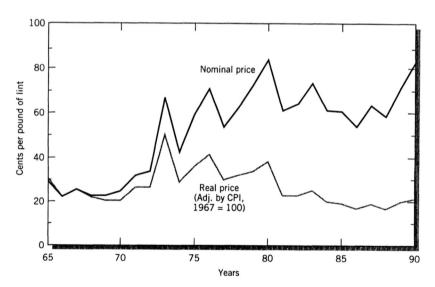

FIGURE 3.3. Nominal and Real Season Average Prices for Middling $1\frac{1}{16}$" Cotton Lint, United States, 1965–1990.

SOURCE: *Agricultural Statistics*, USDA, GPO, 1972, and 1991 issues.

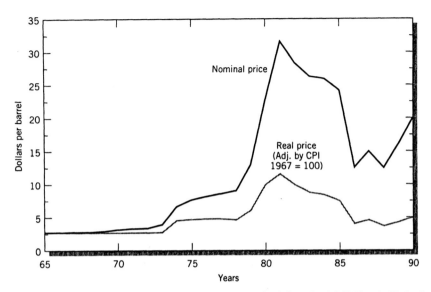

FIGURE 3.4. Nominal and Real Prices for Crude Oil at the Well Head, United States, 1965–1990.
SOURCE: *Statistical Abstract of the United States*, 1972, 1980, and 1992 issues.

When calculations deflating the 1965–90 price series for corn, cotton, and crude oil are charted, the full impact of inflation since the early 1970s in the United States can be clearly seen (Figures 3.2, 3.3, and 3.4). The difference in the raw price and the deflated price is the part of raw price that can be attributed to inflation. Except for the 1973–74 spike in corn and cotton prices associated with the Russian Grain Deal, real farm prices have generally trended downward. Real prices for crude oil, on the other hand, have generally trended *upward*, reflecting the reality that energy costs were a major contributor to worldwide price inflation.

THE BASE PERIOD REVISITED _____

It was suggested earlier that the motives for redefining the base period for indices of the general price level might sometimes be less than pure. This suggestion of impure motives may be validated simply by reviewing some of the political literature and press releases of many special interest groups. However, there *are* some defensible reasons for adjusting from an earlier to a more recent base period. It is the nature of the human animal to think in terms of the present rather than the past. A deflated or real price of $7.47 per barrel of crude oil in 1985—based on the 1967 base year—really doesn't have much meaning to the economically unsophisticated person in the 1990s when crude oil has a nominal price in the neighborhood of $20.00 per barrel. However, if one corrects the 1985 price to the 1990 value of the dollar,

$$\left(\frac{CPI_{1990}}{CPI_{1985}}\right)(Price_{1985}) = \left(\frac{(391.3)}{322.0}\right)(\$24.08) = \$29.26 \qquad (3.7)$$

the result is a 1985 price of $29.26 per barrel of crude oil—a real price that has much more meaning to the average American than does the 1967-based number.

An examination of 25 years of deflated price data shows precisely the same information, regardless of the base period. The ability of crude oil to command other goods increased rapidly from the mid-1970s through the mid-1980s. Since the mid-1980s, the ability of oil to command other goods has diminished. But if those data are presented in terms of current-value dollars, they are generally more meaningful to people who have limited experience with economic concepts. This is one reason that many federally published index numbers will be revised to a more recent base period, even though the foundation for these indices (Index of Prices Paid and Index of Prices Received by Farmers, for example) is rooted in a much earlier period.

THE PARITY RATIO _____

One of the more unfortunate applications of index numbers has been the development of the *parity ratio*. The parity ratio was developed during the 1930's in an effort to develop a framework for evaluating and promoting programs designed to provide some relief from the devastating impact of the Great Depression upon rural America. The Index of Prices Paid by Farmers and the Index of Prices Received by Farmers were developed for the base period 1910–14. The ratio of these two indices (the Index of Prices Received divided by the Index of Prices Paid) was defined as the parity ratio. A parity ratio of 100 suggested that the economic well-being of farmers was comparable with their well-being during the "normal" period of 1910–14.

There were fundamental problems with the parity ratio from the beginning. First of all, the 1910–14 base period was the period during which farm prices relative to farm costs were at an all-time high. Second, crop prices were abnormally high relative to livestock prices. Export markets for crops were especially favorable during this base period because of the armed conflicts in Europe that ultimately escalated into World War I.

The continued usage of the parity ratio has compounded the problems that were present from the beginning. Publicly funded agricultural research has dramatically increased the productivity of agricultural resources. If per acre yields are doubled, per unit prices for the crop could be reduced by half, or per acre costs could be doubled without reducing net returns per acre. But the parity ratio would be reduced substantially, erroneously suggesting—or at least grossly overstating—a deterioration in the economic well-being of farmers.

Many of the farm production inputs in the 1980s did not exist in the 1910–1914 base period. The Index of Prices Paid in the base period described a horse-powered agriculture that had a very high level of labor input per acre. Supplemental plant nutrients—where used—were limited to animal manure and green manure crops. Weed and insect control were largely from hand labor.

Oat-powered horses and mules have been replaced with petroleum-powered four-wheel drive tractors that allow a farm worker to farm at least ten times the acreage he could have handled during the base period. Hand labor for pest control has been replaced with chemicals. Chemical fertilizers have permitted much greater levels of supplemental plant nutrients, and hence, much higher yields. Improved crop varieties and improved genetic strains of animals have greatly enhanced yields. In short, the Index of Prices Paid by Farmers with a 1910–14 base period—even with the very substantial adjustments that have been made—is of questionable value today.

When we consider the Index of Prices Received by Farmers with a 1910–14 base period, problems similar to those observed in the case of the Index of Prices Paid become apparent. Soybeans, which were a major crop in the 1990s, were at best a botanical curiosity in 1910–14. A "parity" price with a 1910–14 base for soybeans is therefore ludicrous. The vast majority of beef produced in 1910–14 was a by-product of the dairy industry. No more than 20 percent of the beef production during the 1990s comes from the dairy sector. The list goes on and on.

With both elements of the parity ratio subject to the sorts of limitations outlined above, it becomes fairly clear that the parity concept in agriculture is of primarily historical interest. No matter how sympathetic one may be with regard to the very destructive deterioration of the American farm economy during the 1980s, the use of a parity ratio based on the 1910–14 period for purposes of promoting proposed solutions cannot be justified. When encountering those who adamantly advocate parity, it is well to remember that there are three types of people who do so: liars, pervaricators, and folks who simply do not tell the truth.

Appendix _____

The purpose of this Appendix to Chapter 3 is to provide information regarding the manner in which index numbers may be utilized with standard spreadsheet computer software to correct prices or income for changes in the value of the dollar. The instructions provided are in terms of the commands either for LOTUS 1-2-3 or for the Lotus mode of QUATTROPRO software. However, any spreadsheet software may be utilized in the manner shown.

Table 3A.1 shows the annual average values for the Consumer Price Index for both the 1967 and 1982–84 base periods. The last column of that table shows a ratio between the two indices. It will be noted that the ratio is almost constant, varying primarily in the third decimal place as a result of rounding. That is, the values in the 1967-based index are consistently almost exactly triple those for the 1982–84 index. Thus, if one desired to convert from the 1982–84 base period to the 1967 base period, all that would be necessary would be to simply multiply the 1982–84 values by 2.994 (the average value of the ratio for the entire 31-year period). Conversely, the values for the 1967 base can be converted to the 1982–84 base simply by dividing those values by 2.994. As additional information with regard to the values in the Consumer Price Index becomes available, it may be converted to either of these two base periods—or to any other—simply by utilizing the approach above.

Table 3A.2 presents the monthly U.S. Consumer Price Index for the 1960–93 period for the base year 1967 = 100. Table 3A.3 presents the same information for a 1982–84 base period.

Changing Base Periods

As discussed in Chapter 3, it may be useful to adjust price or income data into terms closer to the value of today's dollar. Assume that the need is to adjust the CPI data for the 1982–84 base period in Table 3A.4 to a 1992 base. This simply involves defining the 1992 value of 140.4 to be 100.0. The calculation would be:

$$\frac{CPI_{82\text{-}84\ =\ 100}}{140.4} \times 100 = CPI_{92\ =\ 100} \qquad (3A.1)$$

To convert the 1982 value to a 1992 base, the cursor should be placed on cell C1 (Column C, Line 1). Enter the following:

$$(+B1/140.4)*100 \qquad (3A.2)$$

and press ENTER. The result of this calculation (68.7) will appear in Cell C1. It means that only 68.7 1992-value cents would have been required in 1982 to purchase what required $1 in 1992.

TABLE 3A.1. Relationship Between Consumer Price Indices for Different Base Periods United States, 1960–92

Year	CPI 1967 = 100	CPI 1982–84 = 100	CPI 1967 / CPI 1982–84
1960	88.7	29.6	2.995
1961	89.6	29.9	2.997
1962	90.6	30.3	2.995
1963	91.7	30.6	2.994
1964	92.9	31.0	2.995
1965	94.5	31.5	2.999
1966	97.2	32.5	2.995
1967	100.0	33.4	2.998
1968	104.2	34.8	2.996
1969	109.8	36.7	2.993
1970	116.3	38.8	2.995
1971	121.3	40.5	2.996
1972	125.3	41.8	2.996
1973	133.1	44.4	2.998
1974	147.7	49.3	2.995
1975	161.2	53.8	2.995
1976	170.5	56.9	2.996
1977	181.5	60.6	2.995
1978	195.4	65.2	2.995
1979	217.4	72.6	2.996
1980	246.8	82.4	2.995
1981	270.4	90.9	2.974
1982	289.1	96.5	2.996
1983	298.4	99.6	2.996
1984	311.1	103.9	2.995
1985	322.2	107.6	2.995
1986	328.4	109.6	2.996
1987	338.9	113.6	2.983
1988	354.1	118.3	2.994
1989	371.2	124.0	2.994
1990	391.2	130.7	2.994
1991	407.9	136.2	2.995
1992	420.4P	140.4P	2.994

P preliminary

TABLE 3A.2. Consumer Price Index, United States, All Urban Consumers (CPI-U), All Items, by Months, 1960–1992 (1967 = 100)

Year	Jan	Feb	Mar	Apr	May	Jun	Jul	Aug	Sep	Oct	Nov	Dec	Ann Avg
1960	87.9	88.0	88.0	88.5	88.5	88.7	88.7	88.7	88.8	89.2	89.3	89.3	88.7
1961	89.3	89.3	89.3	89.3	89.3	89.4	89.8	89.7	89.9	89.9	89.9	89.9	89.6
1962	89.9	90.1	90.3	90.5	90.5	90.5	90.7	90.7	91.2	91.1	91.1	91.0	90.6
1963	91.1	91.2	91.3	91.3	91.3	91.7	92.1	92.1	92.1	92.2	92.3	92.5	91.7
1964	92.6	92.5	92.6	92.7	92.7	92.9	93.1	93.0	93.2	93.3	93.5	93.6	92.9
1965	93.6	93.6	93.7	94.0	94.2	94.7	94.8	94.6	94.8	94.9	95.1	95.4	94.5
1966	95.4	96.0	96.3	96.7	96.8	97.1	97.4	97.9	98.1	98.5	98.5	98.6	97.2
1967	98.6	98.7	98.9	99.1	99.4	99.7	100.2	100.5	100.7	101.0	101.3	101.6	100.0
1968	102.0	102.3	102.8	103.1	103.4	104.0	104.5	104.8	105.1	105.7	106.1	106.4	104.2
1969	106.7	107.1	108.0	108.7	109.0	109.7	110.2	110.7	111.2	111.6	112.2	112.9	109.8
1970	113.3	113.9	114.5	115.2	115.7	116.3	116.7	116.9	117.5	118.1	118.5	119.1	116.3
1971	119.2	119.4	119.8	120.2	120.8	121.5	121.8	122.1	122.2	122.4	122.6	123.1	121.3
1972	123.2	123.8	124.0	124.3	124.7	125.0	125.5	125.7	126.2	126.6	126.9	127.3	125.3
1973	127.7	128.6	129.8	130.7	131.5	132.4	132.7	135.1	135.5	136.6	137.6	138.5	133.1
1974	139.7	141.5	143.1	143.9	145.5	146.9	148.0	149.9	151.7	153.0	154.3	155.4	147.7
1975	156.1	157.2	157.8	158.6	159.3	160.6	162.3	162.8	163.6	164.6	165.6	166.3	161.2

Year													
1976	166.7	167.1	167.5	168.2	169.2	170.1	171.1	171.9	172.6	173.3	173.8	174.3	170.5
1977	175.3	177.1	178.2	179.6	180.6	181.8	182.6	183.3	184.0	184.5	185.4	186.1	181.5
1978	187.2	188.4	189.8	191.5	193.3	195.3	196.7	197.8	199.3	200.9	202.0	202.9	195.4
1979	204.7	207.1	209.1	211.5	214.1	216.6	218.9	221.1	223.4	225.4	227.5	229.9	217.4
1980	233.2	236.4	239.8	242.5	244.9	247.6	247.8	249.4	251.7	253.9	256.2	258.4	246.8
1981	260.5	263.2	265.2	266.8	269.0	271.3	274.4	276.5	279.3	279.9	280.7	281.5	270.4
1982	282.5	283.4	283.1	284.3	287.1	290.6	292.2	292.8	293.3	294.1	293.6	292.4	289.1
1983	293.1	293.2	293.4	295.5	297.1	298.1	299.3	300.3	301.8	302.6	303.1	303.5	298.4
1984	305.2	306.6	307.3	308.8	309.7	310.7	311.7	313.0	314.5	315.3	315.3	315.5	311.1
1985	316.1	317.4	318.8	320.1	321.3	322.3	322.8	323.5	324.5	325.5	326.6	327.4	322.2
1986	328.4	327.5	326.0	325.3	326.3	327.9	328.0	328.6	330.2	330.5	330.8	331.1	328.4
1987	333.2	334.4	335.9	337.7	338.9	339.5	341.0	342.8	338.6	339.5	339.8	345.8	338.9
1988	346.7	347.6	349.1	350.9	351.8	353.3	354.8	356.3	358.7	359.9	360.2	360.8	354.1
1989	362.6	364.1	366.2	368.6	370.7	371.6	372.5	373.1	374.3	376.0	376.9	377.5	371.2
1990	381.4	383.2	385.3	385.9	386.8	388.9	390.4	394.0	397.3	399.7	400.6	400.6	391.2
1991	403.0	403.6	404.2	404.8	406.0	407.2	407.9	409.1	410.9	411.5	412.4	413.0	407.9
1992	413.7	415.2	417.2	417.8	418.4	419.9	420.8	422.0	423.2	424.7	425.3	425.9P	420.4P
1993	426.9	428.4	429.9	431.1	431.7	432.3	432.3	433.5					

Source. U.S. Bureau of Labor Statistics, U.S. Department of Labor, as reported in *Basic Statistics-Price Indexes, Commodities, Producer, Cost of Living,* Standard and Poor's Statistical Service, Standard and Poor's Corporation, August 1974 and subsequent issues. Values since May 1988 calculated from reported values with the 1982–1984 = 100 base.

TABLE 3A.3. Consumer Price Index, United States, All Urban Consumers (CPI-U), All Items, by Months, 1960–92 (1982–84 = 100)

Year	Jan	Feb	Mar	Apr	May	Jun	Jul	Aug	Sep	Oct	Nov	Dec	Ann Avg
1960	29.3	29.4	29.4	29.5	29.5	29.6	29.6	29.6	29.6	29.8	29.8	29.8	29.6
1961	29.8	29.8	29.8	29.8	29.8	29.8	30.0	29.9	30.0	30.0	30.0	30.0	29.6
1962	30.0	30.1	30.1	30.2	30.2	30.2	30.3	30.3	30.4	30.4	30.4	30.4	30.3
1963	30.4	30.4	30.5	30.5	30.5	30.6	30.7	30.7	30.7	30.8	30.8	30.9	30.6
1964	30.9	30.9	30.9	30.9	30.9	31.0	31.1	31.0	31.1	31.1	31.2	31.2	31.0
1965	31.2	31.2	31.3	31.4	31.4	31.6	31.6	31.6	31.6	31.7	31.7	31.8	31.5
1966	31.8	32.0	32.1	32.3	32.3	32.4	32.5	32.7	32.7	32.9	32.9	32.9	32.5
1967	32.9	32.9	33.0	33.1	33.2	33.3	33.4	33.5	33.6	33.7	33.8	33.9	33.4
1968	34.1	34.2	34.3	34.4	34.5	34.7	34.9	35.0	35.1	35.3	35.4	35.5	34.8
1969	35.6	35.8	36.1	36.3	36.4	36.6	36.8	37.0	37.1	37.3	37.5	37.7	36.7
1970	37.8	38.0	38.2	38.5	38.6	38.8	39.0	39.0	39.2	39.4	39.6	39.8	38.8
1971	39.8	39.9	40.0	40.1	40.3	40.6	40.7	40.8	40.8	40.9	40.9	41.1	40.5
1972	41.1	41.3	41.4	41.5	41.6	41.7	41.9	42.0	42.1	42.3	42.4	42.5	41.8
1973	42.6	42.9	43.3	43.6	43.9	44.2	44.3	45.1	45.2	45.6	45.9	46.2	44.4
1974	46.6	47.2	47.8	48.0	48.6	49.0	49.4	50.0	50.6	51.1	51.5	51.9	49.3

Year													Annual
1975	52.1	52.5	52.7	52.9	53.2	53.6	54.2	54.3	54.6	54.9	55.3	55.5	53.8
1976	55.6	55.8	55.9	56.1	56.5	56.8	57.1	57.4	57.6	57.9	58.0	58.2	56.9
1977	58.5	59.1	59.5	60.0	60.3	60.7	61.0	61.2	61.4	61.6	61.9	62.1	60.6
1978	62.5	62.9	63.4	63.9	64.5	65.2	65.7	66.0	66.5	67.1	67.4	67.7	65.2
1979	68.3	69.1	69.8	70.6	71.5	72.3	73.1	73.8	74.6	75.2	75.9	76.7	72.6
1980	77.8	78.9	80.1	81.0	81.8	82.7	82.7	83.3	84.0	84.8	85.5	86.3	82.4
1981	87.0	87.9	88.5	89.1	89.8	90.6	91.6	92.3	93.2	93.4	93.7	94.0	90.9
1982	94.3	94.6	94.5	94.9	95.8	97.0	97.5	97.7	97.9	98.2	98.0	97.6	96.5
1983	97.8	97.9	97.9	98.6	99.2	99.5	99.9	100.2	100.7	101.0	101.2	101.3	99.6
1984	101.9	102.4	102.6	103.1	103.4	103.7	104.1	104.5	105.0	105.3	105.3	105.3	103.9
1985	105.5	106.0	106.4	106.9	107.3	107.6	107.8	108.0	108.3	108.7	109.0	109.3	107.6
1986	109.6	109.3	108.8	108.6	108.9	109.5	109.5	109.7	110.2	110.3	110.4	110.5	109.6
1987	111.2	111.6	112.1	112.7	113.1	113.5	113.8	114.4	115.0	115.3	115.4	115.4	113.6
1988	115.7	116.0	116.5	117.1	117.5	118.0	118.5	119.0	119.8	120.2	120.3	120.5	118.3
1989	121.1	121.6	122.3	123.1	123.8	124.1	124.4	124.6	125.0	125.6	125.9	126.1	124.0
1990	127.4	128.0	128.7	128.9	129.2	129.9	130.4	131.6	132.7	133.5	133.8	133.8	130.7
1991	134.6	134.8	135.0	135.2	135.6	136.0	136.2	136.6	137.2	137.4	137.7	137.9	136.2
1992	138.1	138.6	139.3	139.5	139.7	140.2	140.5	140.9	141.3	141.8	142.0	142.3P	140.41P
1993	142.6	143.1	143.6	144.0	144.2	144.4	144.4	144.8					

Source. Bureau of Labor Statistics, U.S. Department of Labor, as reported in *Basic Statistics—Price Indexes, Commodities, Producer, Cost of Living,* Standard and Poor's Statistical Service, Standard and Poor's Corp., August 1974 and subsequent issues. Values prior to 1984 calculated from values reported from previous base period (1967 = 100).

Since 1988, the U.S. Consumer Price Index has been reported in terms of the 1982–84 base. Thus, Table 3A.3 will be the easiest to bring up to date.

TABLE 3A.4.   Converting Base Periods

R o w	A Year	B CPI$_{82-84}$ = 100	C CPI$_{92}$ = 100
		Column	
1	1982	96.5	_____
2	1983	99.6	_____
3	1984	103.9	_____
4	1985	107.6	_____
5	1986	109.6	_____
6	1987	113.6	_____
7	1988	118.3	_____
8	1989	124.0	_____
9	1990	130.7	_____
10	1991	136.2	_____
11	1992	140.4^P	100.0

^{P} preliminary

To convert the 1983 and subsequent year CPI$_{82-84}$ = 100 values to a 1992 base, use the following commands.

With the cursor in Cell C1: Press Slash (/) to get the menu. Select "Copy," Press "Enter."

Move the cursor to Cell C2.

Lock the command to copy the formula in Cell C1 by pressing the period.

Move the cursor to Cell C11 (Cells C2 through C11 will be illuminated, indicating that the formula in Cell C1 will be used in all of these cells). Press "Enter."

The result of this procedure will be that Column C will contain the values for a 1992-based Consumer Price Index.

Deflating Price and Income Data

Correcting price or income data for changes in the value of the dollar is simply a matter of dividing the nominal value of price or income reported for any given period by the Consumer Price Index for that period. Table 3A.5 shows U.S. Per Capita Disposable Personal Income and the CPI$_{82-84}$ = 100 for the period 1980 through 1990.

TABLE 3A.5. Deflating Price or Income Data

| | | | Column | |
| | A | B | C | D |
R o w	Year	U.S. Per Cap Disposable Personal Income	CPI 1982–1984 = 100	Real or Deflated Income
1	1980	$ 8,421	82.4	_____
2	1981	9,243	90.9	_____
3	1982	9,724	96.5	_____
4	1983	10,340	99.6	_____
5	1984	11,257	103.9	_____
6	1985	11,861	107.6	_____
7	1986	12,469	109.6	_____
8	1987	13,140	113.6	_____
9	1988	14,123	118.3	_____
10	1989	14,973	124.0	_____
11	1990	15,695	130.7	_____
12	1991	16,318P	136.2	_____
13	1992	17,301P	140.4P	_____

Source. Statistical Abstract of the U.S., 1992, Bureau of the Census, U.S. Dept. of Commerce, 1992.

As discussed in Chapter 3, the Consumer Index provides a mechanism for stabilizing the value of the currency in order to determine what is happening to purchasing power. Thus, the calculation for correcting (or deflating) per capita disposable personal income for changes in the value of the currency would be:

$$\frac{\text{Nominal income}_i}{\text{CPI}_i} \times 100 = \text{Deflated income}_i \qquad (3A.3)$$

To correct the 1980 nominal per capita income ($8,421) for changes in the value of the dollar, the cursor should be placed in Cell D1 (Column D, Line 1). Enter the following:

$$(+B1/C1)*100 \qquad (3A.4)$$

Press "Enter." The result of this calculation ($10,219.666) will appear in Cell D1. It would be interpreted to mean that $10,219.67 would have been required in the 1982–84 period to purchase what might have been purchased for $8,421 in 1980.

To convert 1981 and subsequent year reported values for nominal per capita income figures into constant-value 1982–84 collars, use the following commands:

With the cursor in Cell D1: Press Slash (/) to get the menu. Select "Copy," press "Enter."

Move the cursor to Cell D2.

Lock the command to copy the formula in Cell D1 by pressing the period.

Move the cursor to Cell D11 (Cells D2 through D11 will be illuminated, indicating that the formula in Cell D1 will be used in all of these cells). Press "Enter."

The result of this procedure will be that Column D will contain the real values of Per Capita Disposable Personal Income, adjusted by the Consumer Price Income (1982–84 = 100). This real income will be expressed in terms of the level of 1982–84 dollars that would be required to purchase what the nominal income would purchase in that year.

CHAPTER **4**

Price Movements Over Time—Analysis of Trends

$\mathbf{I}$n Chapter 3, you were introduced to the use and interpretation of index numbers. We saw how the impact of inflation could be removed from a price series by simply dividing the raw prices by the index values of a deflator such as the Consumer Price Index.

When analyzing the prices for any commodity, one of the first things we ordinarily do is gain some at least intuitive estimates of the supply and demand for that product. We know that demand is defined as the schedule of quantities of a good that consumers are willing and able to purchase at a given series of prices in a given market at a given time, *ceteris paribus*. The *ceteris paribus* assumption is an important dimension of this definition since there are a number of factors, which affect the consumer's willingness and ability to buy. These factors will cause the demand function to shift if they should happen to change. Among these factors are:

1. The general level of prices, correction for which we have already discussed
2. Numbers of consumers
3. Consumer purchasing power
4. Price and availability of substitute and complement goods
5. Consumer tastes and preferences

The definition for supply is identical with that for demand, except that it deals with the willingness and ability of producers to offer products for sale. As in the case of demand, there are a set of *ceteris paribus* conditions for supply that will cause the supply function to shift if they should change. Among these are:

1. Cost of variable resources
2. Income potential from alternative uses for fixed resources
3. Technology

A first approximation in estimating a demand function can be made simply by charting the price–quantity combinations for a product for some time period. Figure 4.1 compares annual average prices for Barrows and Gilts in seven major markets for the 1975–1992 period. It is apparent that as production has increased, prices have generally declined. A line drawn through this scatter of points would be entirely consistent with our definition of demand.

It must be recognized that each of the 18 points in Figure 4.1 represents an intersection of the average supply and demand functions for a given year, as is suggested by the dotted lines intersecting at the price–

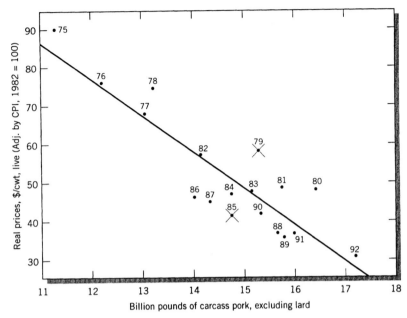

FIGURE 4.1. Price–Quantity Combinations for Commercial Pork Production and the Seven-Market Annual Average Real Price for Barrows and Gilts, United States, 1975–1992.

SOURCE: *Livestock and Meat Statistics, 1984-88*, USDA-ERS, Statistical Bulletin No. 784, and various issues of *Livestock and Poultry Situation and Outlook Report*, USDA-ERS, since 1988.

quantity relationships for 1979 and 1985 in Figure 4.1. If there had been no changes in demand and supply over this period, rather than 18 points, there would only be a single point. So it is obvious that the *ceteris paribus* conditions of both supply and demand have changed with some frequency over this 18-year period.

When we look at the hog price and pork production variables over the entire 18-year period of time (Figures 4.2 and 4.3), it becomes apparent that there is something going on. The raw price is very erratic, but with a general upward movement. When raw prices are corrected for changes in the general price level, we see that while the real prices are still very erratic, the steady inflation in the general price level has actually obscured a general *downward* drift in the real prices for hogs over this period. Like price, commercial pork production has been somewhat erratic, but there has still been a strong upward "drift." These drifts in the data over long periods of time are called *trends*. The down trend in real prices for hogs appears to be much stronger than the up trend in commercial pork production. Real prices trended downward by more

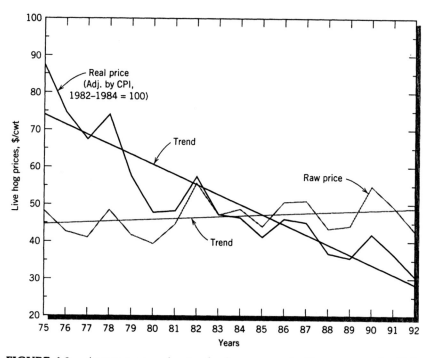

FIGURE 4.2. Average annual price for barrows and gilts, seven major U.S. markets, with trend estimates, 1975–82.

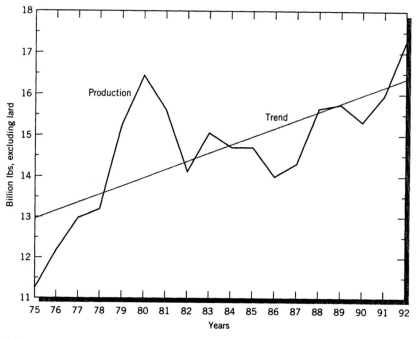

FIGURE 4.3. Commercial pork production (billion lb) with trend estimate, United States, 1975–92.

54

than half over this period whereas commercial pork production increased by only a third. Does this suggest that the average American ate all that much more pork?

When we talked about the ceteris paribus conditions of demand, we said that if the numbers of consumers changed, we could expect the demand function to shift. We know that the 1975–92 period is after the post-World War II Baby Boom. Nevertheless, population did continue to grow during the 1970s and 1980s—albeit at a reduced rate. United States population increased from 215 million in 1975 to about 255 million in 1992—an increase of 18 percent, a growth rate of a bit less than 1.0 percent each year. If we convert our total commercial pork production into the production *per person* (per capita), we can correct for population growth.

Correcting for population growth disperses the scatter of price–quantity combinations, relative to a downward sloping line through the data, but the apparent demand relationship is present nevertheless (Figure 4.4). The data over time are entirely consistent with the expectations that economic theory would give us (Figure 4.5). The peaks in price are closely associated with the lows in per capita production. There is a

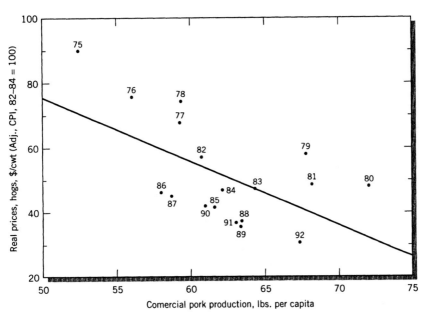

FIGURE 4.4. Price–Quantity Combinations, commercial pork production per capita with seven-market annual real price for barrows and gilts, United States, 1975–92.

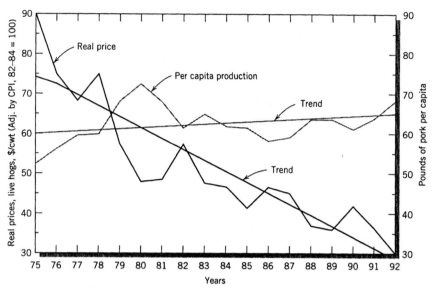

FIGURE 4.5. Commercial pork production per capita and average annual real prices for barrows and gilts, seven major markets, United States, 1975–92.

slight upward trend in per capita production—about 28 percent over the 18 years compared with the 52 percent increase in *total* commercial production—associated with the 67 percent real price decline. This obviously suggests that there has been a decline in per capita demand for pork. A further examination of the data in Figure 4.4 confirms this. The data since 1984 are grouped well below the line describing the relationship for the entire range of data while those for the 1970s are grouped above that line.

Gradual changes in the conditions of supply and/or demand, which occur over a long period of time, can cause clear increases or decreases in price that may not be detected in year-to-year analyses. Development of new uses for a commodity and gradual adaptation of those new uses—corn sweeteners, for example—may result in a very slight annual change in the price of a product or in the quantity that can be sold at a given price. Changing customs such as those associated with the decline of ethnic neighborhoods in metropolitan centers may affect the long time trend in demand. The reduction in lamb and mutton consumption from about 5 pounds per capita in the early 1960s to less than 1.5 pounds per capita in the early 1990s is a case in point. Gradual adaptation of improved production technology may cause long-term trends in supply relationships.

Some of these developments may tend to increase prices whereas offsetting developments may tend to reduce them. Thus, prices over long periods of time may increase, decrease, or be unchanged. Meanwhile, the price is fluctuating from day to day, from season to season, and from cycle to cycle *around this long-term trend.* Basically, trend analysis uses a time variable as a surrogate for capturing the effect of changes in other variables that either cannot be measured or in groups of variables that change so gradually that collecting the information isn't worth the effort.

SELECTING A PERIOD FOR TREND ANALYSIS ————————————————————

There are several ways in which a trend can be "fitted," but regardless of the fitting method, the starting point should be to **chart the data.** One can stare at numbers by the hour, but very few people (if any) can look at numbers and determine very much about the "pattern" of the data. In Figure 4.6, we have expanded the period over which we are examining the real price for barrows and gilts to include the period since 1950. Aside from the cyclical patterns, there are at least three longer-term trends in these data. The most obvious trend is the overall downward trend in real hog prices for the entire 43-year period. But when the information is examined more closely, it becomes apparent that something happened in the early 1970s that broke the pattern that had previously prevailed.

The decade of the 1970s was enormously turbulent and notoriously unstable. Virtually the entire inventory of U.S. grains was sold to Russia in 1972–73, triggering rapid escalation in grain prices, and very shortly thereafter rapid meat price escalation. Consumers boycotted the meat counters, and retail meat prices were frozen in 1973. Also in 1973, the American dollar was devalued when the U.S. government announced that it would not longer settle international trade accounts in gold. A U.S. president resigned his office in the summer of 1974 following the introduction of a bill of impeachment, and his successor embargoed the export of both U.S. soybeans and wheat. The OPEC oil cartel and the multinational oil companies doubled the prices for energy beginning in the last quarter of 1973, completing the process in the winter of 1975. The energy price increase triggered a spiral of inflation that after a couple of years in double digits tapered off and receded to an annual rate of 3–5 percent.

These dramatic enonomic changes concentrated in a very short period of time created a completely new economic environment at least for

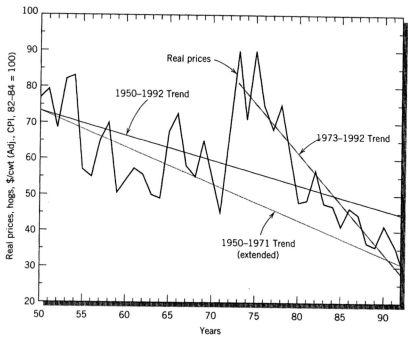

FIGURE 4.6. Average annual real price for barrows and gilts in seven major U.S. markets, 1950–92, with trend estimates (prices adjusted by CPI, 1982–84 = 100).

meats. Cost of production inputs (grains) had accelerated dramatically. The international exchange rate for the dollar had dropped precipitously, enlarging U.S. access to international grain markets (thereby enlarging the competition faced by U.S. meat producers bidding for feed resources). Rapid energy price escalation and the resulting general economic inflation had forced a restructuring of consumer buying habits. The impacts showed up in real prices for live hogs initially as a dramatic increase in the level of prices and subsequently in a much sharper downward trend in those prices.

If a 1950–71 trend is extended through 1992 in Figure 4.6, the resulting 1992 expected trend value is very near the value based on the 1973–92 trend. Whether the 1973–92 period will prove to be an aberration to a much longer term trend remains to be seen. But at this point, the trend that would most probably be the *relevant* trend for purposes of analysis is the one that describes the period since 1972 or perhaps since 1975. The basic point of this discussion is that periods over which trends are to be analyzed should be selected to reflect what is most likely to be relevant to the immediate future. If there are obvious breaks in the level or direction of the long-term trend, the earlier information should be eliminated.

FITTING TRENDS _____

Once the period the trend is to describe has been selected, the next step is to determine the actual line that is to represent the trend. That line may be either straight or curved. It may be drawn freehand or calculated mathematically. The advantage of the calculated trend line is that the same result is achieved whoever calculates the trend. This does not mean that a mathematically calculated trend is necessarily superior to one that is drawn freehand. Many experienced analysts can draw freehand trends that are amazingly close to a calculated trend. But a calculated trend does reduce the numbers of arguments.

A mathematically calculated trend may be either linear or curvalinear in form (Figure 4.7). A semilogarithmic or full-logarithmic trend is linear in logarithms, but is curvalinear in ordinary arithmetic numbers. Thus,

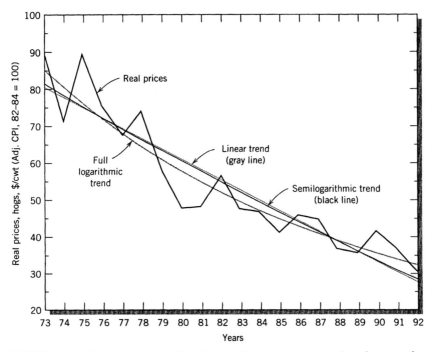

FIGURE 4.7. Alternative trend estimates for average annual real prices for barrows and gilts, seven major markets, United States, 1973–92.

if a curvalinear trend appears to be appropriate (as is the case in live hog prices for the period since 1972) the use of logarithms permits the analyst to define such a trend. However, if there are enough data, the most recent portion of the curvalinear trend could be approximated with a linear trend.

Simple linear regression may be used to mathematically calculate the single line that best describes the relationship between any two sets of paired values. These sets of paired values may be time and some other variable such as prices or production in a trend line. They may be two variables such as prices or quantities as we have already seen. Or they may be two variables such as weight and height of students in a college level class.

Let's illustrate this by considering the weights and heights of people in a class at some major state university. If the only information we had were the weights of the 13 students described in Table 4.1, the first approach to describing the class for most people would be to add up the total weight and divide that total by the numbers of people involved.

$$\Sigma \, Y_i/n = \bar{Y}^1 \tag{4.1}$$

$$2{,}013/13 = 154.8 \text{ pounds average weight} \tag{4.2}$$

Our calculated average weight suggests that the people who are enrolled in Agricultural Price Analysis at Silo Tech University on the average weigh 154.8 pounds. Similarly, if the only information we had were the heights of these students, we could approach a general description of the class by calculating an average height.

$$\Sigma \, X_i/n = \bar{X} \tag{4.3}$$

$$895/13 = 68.8 \text{ inches average height} \tag{4.4}$$

Once we have information on the heights of the various individuals in the class to "pair" with their weights, we can do more to describe the class than to simply calculate the average weight and/or average height. We can plot these paired values to determine if there is any further inference to be drawn (Figure 4.8).

We can tell from the "scatter" of points defining the paired weights and heights of the individuals in this class that there is a positive relationship between weight and height. That is, we would normally expect a taller person to weigh more than a shorter person. And while this is by no means absolutely true, the scatter of points suggests that it is generally true. We can draw a freehand line through the points to describe

---

[1] The Greek letter Σ (capital sigma) is used to denote summation. That is, when one sees Σ X_i the message is, "Add all of the X observations." The $\bar{X}$ (i.e., the bar above the X) implies an average value for the X variable and n refers to the number of observations.

TABLE 4.1. Weight and Height of Students Enrolled in Agricultural Price Analysis at Silo Tech University, Some Semester in the 1990s

Observation Number (i)	Name	Weight in lb. (Y_i)	Height in in. (X_i)
1	Barbara, Hannah	127	69
2	Barton, Clarence	195	74
3	Collins, Joseph	175	70
4	Coors, George	168	72
5	Dooley, Thomasina	118	64
6	Drake, Francis	175	76
7	Drummond, Fife	162	71
8	Skinnon, Bones	160	72
9	Smith, Jake	225	68
10	Hill, Billy	151	68
11	Nance, Bruce	132	65
12	Quincy, Joan	128	67
13	Petit, Lanie	97	59
$n = 13$		$\Sigma Y_i = 2013$	$\Sigma X_i = 895$
		$\overline{Y} = 154.8$	$\overline{X} = 68.8$

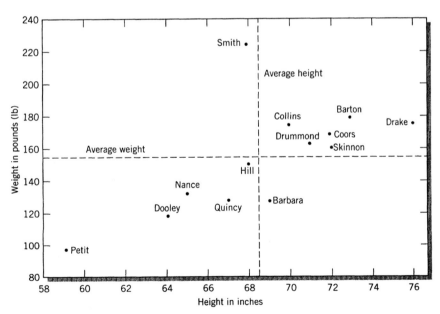

FIGURE 4.8. Weight and height, students in price analysis, Silo Tech University.

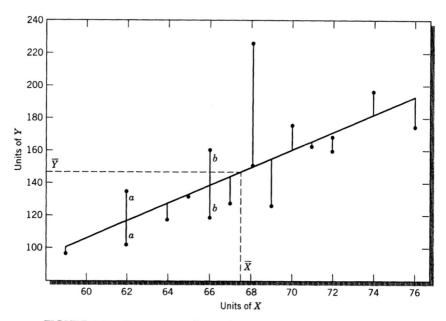

FIGURE 4.9. Regression relationship between paired observations.

this relationship, but each of us would probably draw the line a bit differently. The point describing Jake Smith in Figure 4.8 clearly lies outside the general relationship suggested by the scatter of points. It would probably be appropriate to eliminate this "outlier" from consideration in drawing a line to describe the relationship.

A calculated *regression* line describing this relationship would be the same regardless of who constructed it. Let's see just what is involved in calculating a regression line to describe the relationship between two variables. In fitting a trend line or a regression line of relationship between two variables, it is important to have as much deviation below the line as above the line. The sum of the vertical distances between the observation and the regression line for those observations that lie above the line and that for those below the line should be equal (Figure 4.9). That is, the line should be drawn such that an observation, which lies distance *a* above the line, is offset by another observation that lies distance *a below* the line. The problem is that *any* line that passes through the *average (or mean)* value of both the X variable and the Y variable ($\bar{Y}$ and $\bar{X}$ represent the averages or "means" of these two variables) will fulfill this criterion.

Chapter 5 will examine the detail of calculating a regression line for use in estimating trends or relationships between any two variables.

Simple Linear Regression and the Estimation of Trends*

---

* The author is indebted to a colleague, Dr. Bruce L. Dixon, for his review and constructive suggestions regarding materials in this chapter.

In Chapter 4, we saw how very slow changes in related variables could cause long-term upward or downward drifts (or trends) in various data series. We discussed the selection of the time period that would be relevant for purposes of trend analysis. We fitted a trend using a simple freehand approach and recognized that a freehand approach to fitting that trend invited disagreement among analysts. We recognized that a mathematically calculated trend eliminated these disagreements. We suggested that simple least-squares linear regression analysis could be used to calculate the relationship between two variables. If the independent variable were defined as time, the regression approach gave us a precise estimate of the trend line. But regression analysis can be and was used to analyze the relationship between any two variables.

One of the examples used in Chapter 4 was the relationship between the weights and heights of people in a college class. We will see a calculation of this relationship a bit later in this chapter, but first, let's define what we are attempting to describe. Would weight be more likely to be affected by height or would height more probably be dependent upon weight? Each of us in our personal observation knows that there is some positive relationship between weight and height, but each of us also knows that in an adult population weights of individuals—even the weights of *given* individuals at different times—may vary, but heights tend to be fixed. Thus, weight is far more likely to be dependent upon height than is the reverse circumstance. For convenience, let's designate our dependent variable of weight as Y and our independent height variable as X, conforming with standard algebraic procedure.

Our first approximation in describing the physical characteristics of this class in Chapter 4 was to calculate the simple arithmetic averages (or **means**) of height and weight. A close examination of Table 5.1 will reveal that another student has been added to the class. Jane Doe is a late registrant. At four feet eleven inches, Ms. Doe is very short, and at 618 pounds, she is—to say the least—voluptuous. It is obvious that Ms. Doe is something of an "outlier" as far as the rest of the data are concerned. She has added 33.1 pounds to the average weight of the class and has reduced the average height by 0.7 inches. Let's drop the names and use the observation numbers (i) to identify our paired observations. Thus, the first three columns of Table 5.2 represent a considerably condensed version of Table 5.1.

TABLE 5.1. Weight and Height of Students Enrolled in Agricultural Price Analysis at Silo Tech University, A Semester in the 1990s

Observation Number (i)	Name	Weight in Pounds (Y_i)	Height in Inches (X_i)
1	Barbara, Hannah	127	69
2	Barton, Clarence	195	74
3	Collins, Joseph	175	70
4	Coors, George	168	72
5	Dooley, Thomasina	118	64
6	Drake, Francis	175	76
7	Drummond, Fife	162	71
8	Skinnon, Bones	160	72
9	Smith, Jake	225	68
10	Hill, Billy	151	68
11	Nance, Bruce	132	65
12	Quincy, Joan	128	67
13	Petit, Lanie	97	59
	$n = 13$	$\Sigma Y_i = 2,013$	$\Sigma X_i = 895$
		$\bar{Y} = 154.8$	$\bar{X} = 68.8$
Late Registrants:			
14	Doe, Jane	618	59
Including Ms. Doe			
	$n = 14$	$\Sigma Y_i = 2,631$	$\Sigma X_i = 954$
		$\bar{Y} = 187.9$	$\bar{X} = 68.1$

THE CONCEPTS OF VARIANCE AND STANDARD DEVIATION _____

How dependable is the mean as an indicator of the expected weights of people in this class? We could get our first indication by getting some measure of how widely dispersed the various individual weights are around that mean. If we simply calculate the difference between the individual weights observed and the mean we calculated for all 14 students, we can see that there is considerable dispersion (Column 6 of Table 5.2). If we calculate the average (or the mean) of these deviations, we learn nothing since the sum of these deviations is zero and the average deviation therefore *must* be zero. But if we **square** those deviations, the products are all positive. The sum of those deviations divided by one less than the number of observations gives us an estimate of the

TABLE 5.2. Height and Weight of Students

(1)	(2)	(3)	(4)	(5)	(6)	(7)	(8)	(9)	(10)	(11)
	Height in Inches	Weight in Pounds	Including Ms. Doe ($n = 14$) Deviations from the Means				Excluding Ms. Doe ($n = 13$) Deviations from the Means			
Obs. No. i	X_i	Y_i	$(X_i - \bar{X})$	$(X_i - \bar{X})^2$	$(Y_i - \bar{Y})$	$(Y_i - \bar{Y})^2$	$(X_i - \bar{X})$	$(X_i - \bar{X})^2$	$(Y_i - \bar{Y})$	$(Y_i - \bar{Y})^2$
1	69	127	0.9	.81	-60.9	3,708.81	0.2	0.04	-27.8	772.84
2	74	195	5.9	34.81	7.1	50.41	5.2	27.04	40.2	1,616.04
3	70	175	1.9	3.61	-12.9	166.41	1.2	1.44	20.2	408.04
4	72	168	3.9	15.21	-19.9	396.01	3.2	10.24	13.2	174.24
5	64	118	-4.1	16.81	-69.9	4,886.01	-4.8	23.02	-36.8	1,354.24
6	76	175	7.9	62.41	-12.9	166.41	7.2	51.84	20.2	408.04
7	71	162	2.9	8.41	-25.9	670.81	2.2	4.84	7.2	51.84
8	72	160	3.9	15.21	-27.9	778.41	3.2	10.24	5.2	27.04
9	68	225	-0.1	.01	37.1	1,376.41	-0.8	.64	70.2	4,928.04
10	68	151	-0.1	.01	-36.9	1,361.61	-0.8	.64	-3.8	14.44
11	65	132	-3.1	9.61	-55.9	3,124.81	-3.8	14.44	-22.8	519.84
12	67	128	-1.1	1.21	-59.9	3,588.01	-1.8	3.24	-26.8	718.24
13	59	97	-9.1	82.81	-90.9	8,262.81	-9.8	96.04	-57.8	3,340.84
14	59	618	-9.1	82.81	430.1	184,986.01				
Σ	954	2,631	0.0[1]	333.74	0.0[1]	213,522.94	0.0[1]	243.72	0.0[1]	14,333.72

Average. $\bar{X} = 68.8$ $\bar{Y} = 154.8$, excluding Ms. Doe (observation 14)

$\bar{X} = 68.1$ $\bar{Y} = 187.9$, including Ms. Doe

[1] May not add precisely because of rounding errors.

variance of the weights of the population sample currently enrolled in the class. The square root of that variance gives us the *standard deviation*.

$$\frac{\Sigma(Y_i - Y)^2}{(n - 1)} = \hat{\sigma}^2 \quad \text{(Variance)}[1] \tag{5.1}$$

$$\hat{\sigma}^2 = 184{,}980/13 = 14{,}229 \tag{5.2}$$

$$\sqrt{\hat{\sigma}^2} = \hat{\sigma} \quad \text{(Standard deviation)} \tag{5.3}$$

$$\hat{\sigma} = \sqrt{14{,}229} = 119.2 \tag{5.4}$$

We would expect two-thirds of the observations to fall within one standard deviation (plus or minus) of the mean, 95 percent of them to fall within two standard deviations, and only a quarter of a percent to lie outside three standard deviations of the mean. Thus, the larger the variance and the larger the standard deviation, the greater is the degree of dispersion from the mean.

When we calculate our standard deviations excluding our fictional Ms. Doe (the last two columns of Table 5.2), we can see that relative to the two means, the standard deviation is only 29 percent of the mean if Ms. Doe is excluded from the data, whereas it is 64 percent of the mean with her inclusion.

$$\sigma^2 = 14{,}333.72/12 = 1{,}194.475, \text{ excluding Ms. Doe} \tag{5.5}$$

$$\sigma = \sqrt{1{,}194.475} = 34.6, \text{ excluding Ms. Doe} \tag{5.6}$$

Further, Ms. Doe is in that quarter of a percent that lies more than three standard deviations from the mean.

$$3\sigma \text{ (including Ms. Doe)} = 3(119.2) = 357.6, \text{ whereas}$$
$$(Y_{14} - \bar{Y}) = 430.1 \tag{5.7}$$

Thus, it is pretty clear that Ms. Doe should probably be eliminated from consideration if we expect the mean to be truly descriptive of the population from which the people came who might have enrolled in this class.

---

[1] The carat above the σ indicates that it is an estimate of the "true" value of σ. That is, the students actually enrolled in this course are only a *sample* of the population that *might* have enrolled, and the variance of the sample is only an estimate of the variance of the population

THE SIGNIFICANCE OF DEGREES OF FREEDOM _____

One further matter needs to be discussed before we look at our calculated line describing the relationships between the heights and weights of people in this class. In our calculation of the mean, we added the total weights of individuals in the class and divided by the number of observations. But when we calculated the variance, we divided by one *less* than the number of observations. Why would we reduce the number of observations by one?

If you are asked to provide any three numbers that will add to 100, the first of those numbers is absolutely free to be anything you want it to be. The same is true for the second. But the third is constrained by the limitation that the total can neither exceed nor be less than a hundred. Thus, since only two of these numbers are "free" within the context of our problem, there are only two "degrees of freedom" associated with these three numbers. The average or mean value of these three observations regardless of the value of the numbers can only be 33.333 if the total is constrained to equal 100. Thus, when the sample mean is used in subsequent calculations, one degree of freedom has been lost since that mean can exist if and only if one of the numbers that goes into summing to the total is predetermined by the values of the other two. We will hear more about degrees of freedom when we discuss the estimation of a regression line, but in general, there is a loss of one degree of freedom for each variable. The degree of freedom is lost because of estimating the intercept with the vertical axis. We lose the degree of freedom in order to get an unbiased estimate of the population variance.

THE REGRESSION RELATIONSHIP _____

Now, we can consider the regression equation that describes the relationship between the heights and weights of people in this class. The calculated regression equation if we include Ms. Doe is:

$$\text{Expected weight} = 792 - 8.88 \times \text{height in inches} \qquad (5.8)$$

This may be interpreted as meaning that the students who enroll in Agricultural Price Analysis at Silo Tech University may be expected to weigh 792 pounds, less 8.88 pounds per inch of height. This regression equation explains 12 percent of the variation from the sample mean of weights of students in this class—it is clearly nonsense. Our fictional student—Ms. Doe—at 59 inches tall and 618 pounds is such an obvious outlier that she has confused the entire calculation. The suggestion that weights would be expected to decline as heights increase is ludicrous.

If we eliminate Ms. Doe from the analysis, our calculated relationship becomes:

$$\text{Expected weight} = -204.705 + 5.22 \times \text{height in inches} \quad (5.9)$$

This estimate explains 46 percent of the variation in the weights of these 13 people and would be interpreted to mean that a person who is 5 feet 10 inches (70 inches) tall would be expected to weigh:

$$(5.22)(70) - 204.705 = 365.4 - 204.7 = 160.7 \text{ pounds} \quad (5.10)$$

If you will recall when this group of people was first introduced in Chapter 4, it was suggested that Jake Smith (Observation 9) was also something of an outlier. At 225 pounds, he is more than two standard deviations from the average weight of the original 13 people in the group, and at 68 inches tall he is of barely average height. If Mr. Smith is excluded from the analysis, the estimate becomes:

$$\text{Expected weight} = -230.1 + 5.5 \times \text{height in inches} \quad (5.11)$$

This estimate explains 82 percent of the variation in the weights of the 12 people remaining in the analysis.

ESTIMATING A REGRESSION LINE _____

When we considered our ability to describe the physical characteristics of a group of college students, we started with observations of a dependent variable of weight. In the absence of further information, about the most we could say was that the average or mean weight of the class of 13 people was 154.8 pounds. When we added information regarding an "independent" variable of height and paired that information with the observations of weight, we had information from which we could draw further inference.

To understand how and why a regression line works, let's start with only two paired observations (Table 5.3 and Figure 5.1). Assume the relationship between X_i and Y_i is of the nature:

$$Y_i = a + bX_i + e_i \quad (5.12)$$

where:

a is the intercept of the regression line on the vertical axis

b is the slope of that regression line, and

e_i is the "error" or the difference between the regression line and the individual observations of the dependent variable Y.

Then:

$$\hat{Y}_i = Y_i - e_i = a + bX_i \quad (5.13)$$

TABLE 5.3

Observation No. (i)	Value of X	Value of Y
1	3	2
2	6	4
$n = 2$	$\Sigma X_i = 9$	$\Sigma Y_i = 6$
	$\overline{X} = 4.5$	$\overline{Y} = 3$
Degrees of freedom $= 0$		

Our expected value (the caret above the Y denotes an expected value) of the dependent variable will be defined by a line that intersects the vertical axis at a and has a slope of b.

Our first attempt to describe the information in Table 5.3 would ordinarily be to calculate the means of the two variables. The mean value of Y is 3.0 and that for X is 4.5. These means are represented on Figure 5.1 by the horizontal line at $\overline{Y}$ and the vertical line at $\overline{X}$. The total of the vertical deviations above the $\overline{Y}$ line is exactly the same as the total of the

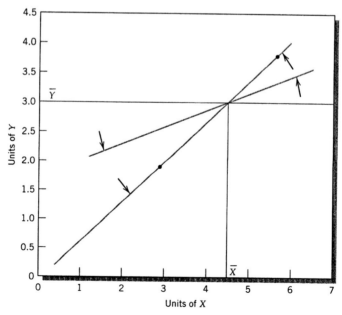

FIGURE 5.1

vertical deviations below that line. (The total of the horizontal deviations from the mean value of $\overline{X}$ is also exactly equal on the two sides of this value.)

If we rotate the line at the mean value of Y on a pivot point of the mean value of X, the vertical deviations above and below any one of these rotated lines is equal. But the rotated line is progressively more and more precise in describing the apparent relationship between these two variables up to the point where the line passes not only through the two mean values but also through the two observation points. With only two observations, however, one end of the line is predetermined by the first observation and the other end of the line is predetermined by the second observation. There would probably be no disagreement among analysts regarding the appropriate position for this line since there is only one place on the diagram where a line "best" fitting these two points could possibly lie. That is, *there is no degree of freedom* that could allow this line to lie in any other position. The degrees of freedom, then, are defined to be *the numbers of observations less the number of parameters to be estimated.* (The "parameters" being estimated are a and b—the intercept and the slope.) Our line intercepts the vertical axis at zero— thus $a = 0$—and the estimated slope is two Y for every three X that is, $\frac{4}{6} = \frac{2}{3} = 0.666667$). Thus, with only these two observations, our regression line would be:

$$\hat{Y}_i = 0 + 0.67\ X_i \qquad\qquad (5.14)$$

Now, let's expand our number of observations to six (Table 5.4 and Figure 5.2). We can calculate our two mean values at $\overline{Y} = 3.5$ and $\overline{X} = 4.83$. We can locate this point on the diagram and rotate a line on this pivot point. Any line through this point has the same total deviations of vertical distance above the line as exists from those points below the line. But with four degrees of freedom, it isn't nearly so evident as to what line best describes the apparent relationship between the two variables. We can see that the relationship is positive with Y generally increasing as X increases. But just *how* positive is it? That is, how great is the slope or the b value in our $\hat{Y} = a + bX_i$ equation?

It is very clear that the condition of the sum of vertical deviations equal to zero is not a sufficient condition for getting unique estimates of a and b. An alternative is to get estimates of a and b that minimize the sum of the squared deviations of the observations less the values as predicted by the regression line. This rids us of the negative algebraic signs that result from calculating the differences from the means.

When we calculate the deviation of each observation from its mean (Table 5.5), let's use lower case x and y to designate the $(X_i - \overline{X})$ and the $(Y_i - \overline{Y})$ values. Thus, Σx_i would be the sum of the deviations of the observations of the independent variable from its average value, and Σy_i

TABLE 5.4

Observation No. (i)	Value of X	Value of Y
1	3	2
2	6	4
3	4	4
4	5	3
5	4	2
6	7	6
$n = 6$	$\Sigma X_i = 29$	$\Sigma Y_i = 21$
	$\overline{X} = 4.83$	$\overline{Y} = 3.5$
Degrees of freedom $= 4$		

would be the sum of the deviations of the dependent variable from its average value. Except for rounding errors, these two sums must equal zero for reasons already discussed. When we square the deviations, the "weight" or emphasis placed on those observations farthest from the means is relatively increased—meaning that if we are rotating the line passing through the two means, there is more mathematical pull exerted by those observations farther from the mean.

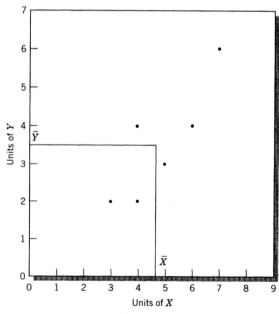

FIGURE 5.2

TABLE 5.5

Obs. No. (i)	Raw Data X_i	Raw Data Y_i	Deviations from the mean of X $(X_i - \bar{X})$ x_i	Deviations from the mean of X $(X_i - \bar{X})^2$ x_i^2	Deviations from the mean of Y $(Y_i - \bar{Y})$ y_i	Deviations from the mean of Y $(Y_i - \bar{Y})^2$ y_i^2	Cross Products $(X_i - \bar{X})(Y_i - \bar{Y})$ x_iy_i	Expected Values $\hat{Y}_i$	Expected Values $(Y_i - \hat{Y}_i)$	Expected Values $(Y_i - \hat{Y}_i)^2$
1	3	2	-1.83	3.36	-1.5	2.25	2.75	1.89	-0.11	0.01
2	6	4	1.17	1.36	0.5	0.25	0.58	4.52	0.52	0.27
3	4	4	-0.83	0.69	0.5	0.25	-0.42	2.77	-1.23	1.51
4	5	3	0.17	0.03	-0.5	0.25	-0.08	3.65	0.65	0.42
5	4	2	-0.83	0.69	1.5	2.25	1.25	2.77	0.77	0.59
6	7	6	2.17	4.69	2.5	6.25	5.42	5.40	-0.60	0.36
Σ	29	21	0.00	10.83	0.0	11.50	9.50	21.00	0.00	3.17
Mean	4.83	3.50								

73

In order to determine the slope of our line, we need an indication of the nature of the interaction between the two variables. This indication of interaction may be achieved by cross-multiplying the deviations from the two means. If an observation is either above or below both means (that is, an observation that falls in the upper-right or lower-left quadrant as defined by the two means), the product of the cross-multiplied calculation will be positive. If that observation is above the mean of one of the variables but below the mean of the other (that is, an observation that falls in the upper-left or lower-right quadrant), the product will be negative. If the *sum* of these cross-products ($\Sigma x_i y_i$) is negative, the estimate of the b value—or the slope of the line—will be negative (Figure 5.3). If that sum is positive, the estimate of the b value or slope will be positive (Figure 5.4).

The calculation of the estimated b value is a very simple matter. You will recall from your first course in junior high school algebra that the slope of a line is calculated by dividing the "rise" of that line by the "run." The rise of the relationship or interaction between our X and Y variables was measured by calculating the sum of the cross-products of the deviations from the two means ($\Sigma x_i y_i$). The run is measured by the total of the squared deviations of the observations of the X variable from

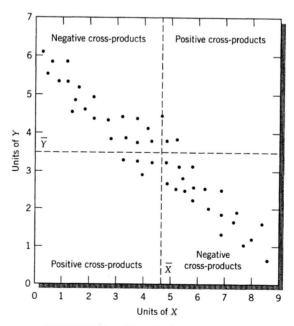

FIGURE 5.3.   Negatively sloped line.

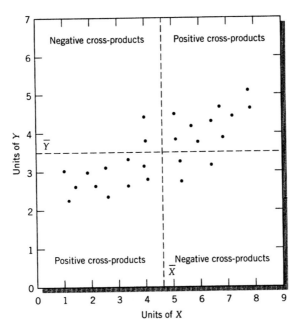

FIGURE 5.4. Positively sloped line.

the average value of that variable (Σx_i). Thus,

$$\hat{b} = \frac{\Sigma x_i y_i}{\Sigma x_i^2} \qquad (5.15)$$

In our example:

$$\hat{b} = 9.50/10.83 = 0.877 \qquad (5.16)$$

giving the slope of a line that minimizes the sum of the squared deviations from the mean of the dependent variable Y.

The position of the regression line (that is, the point at which the line intercepts the vertical axis—the a value in our equation) can be estimated very simply by the formula:

$$\hat{a} = \overline{Y} - b\overline{X} \qquad (5.17)$$

In our example:

$$a = 3.50 - 0.877(4.83) = -0.738 \qquad (5.18)$$

Thus, our regression line describing the relationship between X_i and Y_i would be:

$$\hat{Y}_i = -0.738 + 0.877\,X_i \qquad (5.19)$$

The position of the regression line in relation to the data in our example is shown in Figure 5.5.

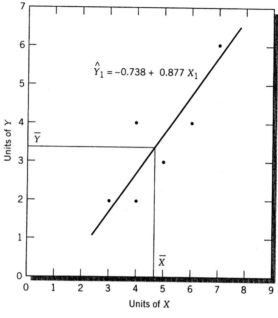

FIGURE 5.5

HOW GOOD IS THE FIT? _____

The R^2 Statistic

How much of the observed variation does our least-squares regression line explain? We can see that the sum of the Y observations in the raw data (ΣY_i) is exactly the same as the sum of the expected values for that variable $(\Sigma \hat{Y}_i)$. We can also see in Table 5.5 that the deviations of the raw data from the mean and the deviations of the raw values from the expected values are both equal to zero. The sum of the squares of the differences between the actual values and the expected values is 3.17 compared with a total sum of squares of the deviations from the mean of 11.5.

We can estimate the portion of the $\Sigma(Y_i - \hat{Y}_i)^2$ deviations that is accounted for by the regression line by:

$$b\Sigma x_i y_i \qquad (5.20)$$

If we divide this by the total sum of squares (Σy_i^2), we get the proportion of the total variation that is explained by our regression line. The number that results from the calculation:

$$R^2 = \frac{b\Sigma x_i y_i}{\Sigma y_i^2} \qquad (5.21)$$

is a purely statistical measure called the **coefficient of determination** identified as R^2. In the case of the information in our example shown in Table 5.5, the R^2 would be:

$$R^2 = 0.877(9.5)/11.5 = 0.72 \qquad (5.22)$$

The R^2 statistic is interpreted in exactly the same way as a percentage. An R^2 of 0.72 means that 72 percent of the total variation is explained by the factor(s) included in the regression analysis. Twenty-eight percent is associated with the errors—a portion of which might be explained by other factors such as gender, age, or ethnic heritage. This R^2 statistic may also be interpreted as the square of the simple correlation coefficient between the dependent variable Y and the independent variable X.

THE STANDARD ERROR OF THE ESTIMATE _____

In Equations 5.1 and 5.3, you were introduced to the concepts of variance (σ^2) and standard deviation (σ). The standard error of the estimated value of $Y(s_{\hat{y}})$ is very similar to the concept of the standard deviation. The primary difference is that the standard deviation is an indicator of the degree of dispersion around the mean value of Y, whereas the standard error is an indicator of the degree of dispersion around the *regression line.*

We have already recognized in Equations 5.11 and 5.12 that the difference in the observed and expected values of our dependent variable is in the error term (e_i). These differences or errors in the estimate of the dependent variable are measured vertically from our regression line, suggesting that the entire error is associated with the dependent variable Y.

Our total sum of squares of the deviations from the mean was measured by Σy_i^2. In our calculation of the R^2 statistic, we recognized that $b\Sigma x_i y_i$ measured the part of the deviations from the mean that was explained by the regression line. But

$$\hat{b} = \frac{\Sigma x_i y_i}{\Sigma x_i^2} \qquad (5.23)$$

Therefore:

$$\hat{b}\Sigma x_i y_i = \left(\frac{\Sigma x_i y_i}{\Sigma x_i^2}\right) \qquad (\Sigma x_i y_i) = \frac{(\Sigma x_i y_i)^2}{\Sigma x_i^2} \qquad (5.24)$$

Thus,

$$\Sigma e^2 = \Sigma y_i^2 - \frac{(\Sigma x_i y_i)^2}{\Sigma x_i^2} \qquad (5.25)$$

which provides a measure of the sum of the squared deviations from the mean, which have not been explained by the regression line.

When we calculated the variance and the standard deviation, our measures of dispersion from the mean were:

$$\sigma^2 = \frac{\Sigma(Y_i - \bar{Y})^2}{n - 1} \quad \text{and} \quad \sigma = \sqrt{\sigma^2} = \sqrt{\frac{\Sigma(Y_i - \bar{Y})^2}{n - 1}} \tag{5.26}$$

But our variance and standard deviations were measured from the mean. Our unexplained variation is measured from the regression line. That unexplained variation can be utilized in exactly the same way to get a measure of dispersion:

$$S_{\hat{Y}} = \sqrt{\frac{\Sigma y_i^2 - (\Sigma x_i y_i)^2/\Sigma x_i}{n - 2}} \tag{5.27}$$

$$= \sqrt{\frac{\Sigma(Y_i - \bar{Y})^2 - [\Sigma(X_i - \bar{X})(Y_i - \bar{Y})]^2/\Sigma(X_i - \bar{X})^2}{n - 2}} \tag{5.28}$$

You will note that the denominator of the fraction appearing under the radical was $(n - 1)$ in the cases of the variance and standard deviation and is $(n - 2)$ in the case of the standard error of the Y estimate. This is because the calculation of the variance was based on the deviations from the sample mean of Y. But since the mean of X also appears in the calculation of $s_{\hat{Y}}$, a second degree of freedom is lost. In the case of our example in Table 5.5, the standard deviation and the standard error calculations would be:

$$\sigma = \sqrt{\frac{11.5}{5}} = \sqrt{2.3} = 1.52 \tag{5.29}$$

$$S_{\hat{Y}} = \sqrt{\frac{11.5 - 9.5^2/10.83}{4}} = \sqrt{\frac{11.5 - 8.33}{4}} = \sqrt{0.798} = 0.89 \tag{5.30}$$

Thus, the dispersion around the regression line is only a little more than half that around the mean of Y. That is, two-thirds of the observations would be expected to fall within 0.89 of the regression line as compared with 1.52 of the average value of Y.

THE STANDARD ERROR OF THE b VALUE _____

A second statistical measure that is commonly calculated for purposes of gaining some insight into the relevance and dependability of a regression analysis is the standard error of the estimate of the b value, which measures the slope of the regression line. Since our regression analysis estimating the relationship between two variables is typically conducted using only a portion (or a sample) of all the possible observations, the estimated slope of the regression line is likely to vary from one sample to another. The potential for variation in the estimated slope of the regression line is measured by the standard error of the b value (s_b), which may be calculated:

$$S_b = \sqrt{S_Y^2 / \Sigma x_i^2} \qquad (5.31)$$

For samples with at least 30 degrees of freedom, if s_b is less than half the b value, the b value is considered to provide a significant degree of explanation of the relationship between the two variables (that is, the b value is considered to have been proven to be significantly different from zero).

SOME SHORTCUTS FOR COMPUTATIONS ————————————————

Now that you have seen the concepts of how regression analysis utilizes deviations from the mean in estimating the least-squares regression line, there are some shortcuts to calculating the sums of deviations squared that can reduce the time spent in calculating these numbers. Let's examine the proofs of these shortcuts:

SUM OF SQUARED DEVIATIONS FOR INDEPENDENT VARIABLE

$$\text{Let } x_i = (X_i - \bar{X}), \quad \text{and} \qquad (5.32)$$

$$x_i^2 = (X_i - \bar{X})^2 \qquad (5.33)$$

$$\Sigma x_i^2 = \Sigma (X_i - \bar{X})^2 \qquad (5.34)$$

$$= \Sigma (X_i^2 - 2X_i\bar{X} - \bar{X}^2) \qquad (5.35)$$

$$= \Sigma X_i^2 - 2\bar{X} \Sigma X_i + n\bar{X}^2 \qquad (5.36)$$

$$= \Sigma X_i^2 - 2\bar{X} \Sigma X_i + n\bar{X}\bar{X} \qquad (5.37)$$

$$\text{But } \bar{X} = \frac{\Sigma X_i}{n} \quad \text{and} \quad n\bar{X} = \Sigma X_i$$

Therefore:

$$\Sigma x_i^2 = \Sigma X_i^2 - 2\bar{X}n\bar{X} + n\bar{X}\bar{X} \qquad (5.38)$$

$$= \Sigma X_i^2 - 2n\bar{X}^2 + n\bar{X}^2 \qquad (5.39)$$

$$\Sigma (X_i - \bar{X})^2 = \Sigma X_i^2 - n\bar{X}^2 \qquad (5.40)$$

SUM OF SQUARED DEVIATIONS FOR DEPENDENT VARIABLE

Same Proof as for independent variable, such that

$$\Sigma(Y_i - \overline{Y})^2 = \Sigma Y_i^2 - n\overline{Y}^2 \tag{5.41}$$

SUM OF CROSS-PRODUCTS OF DEVIATIONS FROM MEANS

Let $x_i y_i = (X_i - \overline{X})(Y_i - \overline{Y})$ and $\Sigma x_i y_i = \Sigma(X_i - \overline{X})(Y_i - \overline{Y})$

$$\Sigma x_i y_i = \Sigma(X_i Y_i - X_i \overline{Y} - \overline{X} Y_i + \overline{X}\overline{Y}) \tag{5.42}$$

$$= \Sigma X_i Y_i - \overline{Y}\Sigma X_i - \overline{X}\Sigma Y_i + n\overline{X}\overline{Y} \tag{5.43}$$

$$= \Sigma X_i Y_i - \frac{(\Sigma Y_i)}{n}(\Sigma X_i) - \frac{(\Sigma X_i)}{n}(\Sigma Y_i) + n\overline{X}\overline{Y} \tag{5.44}$$

$$= \Sigma X_i Y_i - \frac{(\Sigma X_i)(\Sigma Y_i)}{n} - \frac{(\Sigma X_i)(\Sigma Y_i)}{n} + n\overline{X}\overline{Y} \tag{5.45}$$

$$= \Sigma X_i Y_i - \frac{2(\Sigma X_i)(\Sigma Y_i)}{n} + n\overline{X}\overline{Y} \tag{5.46}$$

$$= \Sigma X_i Y_i - \frac{2(\Sigma X_i)(\Sigma Y_i)}{n} + \frac{n(\Sigma Y_i)}{n}\frac{(\Sigma X_i)}{n} \tag{5.47}$$

$$= \Sigma X_i Y_i - \frac{2(\Sigma X_i)(\Sigma Y_i)}{n} + \frac{(\Sigma Y_i)(\Sigma X_i)}{n} \tag{5.48}$$

$$= \Sigma X_i Y_i - \frac{(\Sigma X_i)(\Sigma Y_i)}{n} \tag{5.49}$$

USING SIMPLE REGRESSION IN TREND ANALYSIS

The calculated trend line is simply a specific case of the regression line, which may be used to estimate the relationship between any two variables. The only difference in a calculated trend line and any other regression analysis is that *time* is designated as the independent variable. As previously recognized, time is simply a surrogate for other variables, which may change by the same amount each period, or for other variables such as technological change that may not be readily subject to measurement.

Table 5.6 presents information regarding the New York wholesale prices for young hen turkeys over the 1965–90 period. The same data are presented in Figure 5.6. When one is considering only the raw prices, it would appear that turkey prices have tended strongly upward over the 25-year period in question. But when the raw prices are adjusted by the Consumer Price Index to correct for inflation, it becomes apparent that the trend in *real* turkey prices has been downward over this period.

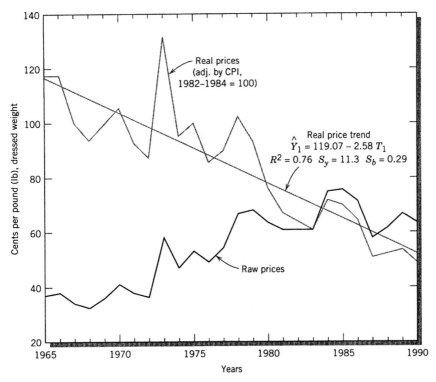

FIGURE 5.6. Raw prices and real prices, 8–16-lb young hen turkeys, whole-sale, New York, 1965–90, with real price trend.

Using our shortcut computations for the regression analysis shown in Equations 5.32 through 5.49 and the information in Table 5.6, the essential elements for computation of the regression equation would be as follows.

$$\Sigma y_i^2 = \Sigma Y_i^2 - n\overline{Y}^2 \tag{5.50}$$

$$= 197,187.26 - (266)(84.21)(84.21) \tag{5.51}$$

$$= 197,187.26 - 184,374.42 \tag{5.52}$$

$$\Sigma y_i^2 = 12,812.84 \tag{5.53}$$

$$\Sigma x_i^2 = \Sigma X_i^2 - n\overline{X}^2 \tag{5.54}$$

$$= 6,201 - (26)(13.5)(13.5) \tag{5.55}$$

$$= 6,201,4,738,5 \tag{5.56}$$

$$\Sigma x_i^2 = 1,462.5 \tag{5.57}$$

TABLE 5.6. Calculation of Trend in New York Wholesale Prices for 8–16-lb young hen turkeys, 1965–90.

Year	Trend Value (X_i)	New York Wholesale Price for 8–16 lb Hen Turkeys (cts/lb) (Y_i)	CPI (82–84 = 100)	Real Price Hen Turkey Whs NY (cts/lb)	Calculations for Regression (X_i^2)	(Y_i^2)	(X_i)(Y_i)
1965	1	37.0	31.5	117.44	1	13,791.41	117.44
1966	2	38.0	31.5	116.92	4	13,671.01	233.85
1967	3	33.5	33.4	100.30	9	10,059.97	300.90
1968	4	32.4	34.8	93.10	16	8,668.25	372.41
1969	5	36.3	36.7	98.91	25	9,783.20	494.55
1970	6	49.9	38.8	105.48	36	11,126.43	632.89
1971	7	37.5	40.4	92.82	49	8,615.88	649.75
1972	8	36.4	41.8	87.13	64	7,592.23	697.07
1973	9	58.8	44.4	132.51	81	17,557.69	1,192.55
1974	10	46.7	49.3	94.73	100	8,973.05	947.26

Year							
1975	11	53.2	53.7	99.07	121	9,814.65	1,089.76
1976	12	48.8	56.9	85.76	144	7,355.55	1,029.17
1977	13	54.0	60.6	89.11	169	7,940.40	1,158.42
1978	14	66.7	65.2	102.30	196	10,465.42	1,432.21
1979	15	68.1	72.6	63.80	225	8,798.75	1,407.02
1980	16	63.7	82.4	77.31	256	5,976.19	1,236.89
1981	17	60.7	90.9	66.78	289	4,459.12	1,135.20
1982	18	60.8	96.5	63.01	324	3,969.65	1,134.09
1983	19	60.5	99.6	60.74	361	3,689.71	1,154.12
1984	20	74.4	103.9	71.61	400	5,127.61	1,432.15
1985	21	75.5	107.6	70.17	441	4,923.45	1,473.51
1986	22	72.2	109.6	65.88	484	4,339.64	1,449.27
1987	23	57.8	113.6	50.88	529	2,588.80	1,170.25
1988	24	61.1	118.3	51.65	576	2,667.55	1,239.56
1989	25	66.7	124.0	53.79	625	2,893.40	1,344.76
1990	26	63.2	130.7	48.36	676	2,338.21	1,257.23
Σ	351	1,404.9	1,869.6	2,189.54	6,201	197,187.26	21,940.73
MEAN	13.5	54.0	84.21				

Source. *Poultry and Egg Statistics, 1960–65,* ERS-USDA Statistical Bulletin No. 747, December, 1986, and *Livestock and Poultry Situation and Outlook Report,* ERS-USDA, LPS-28, Various Issues since 1985. CPI from U.S. Bureau of Labor Statistics.

$$\Sigma x_i y_i = \Sigma X_i Y_i - \frac{(\Sigma X_i)(\Sigma Y_i)}{n} \tag{5.58}$$

$$= 25{,}782.28 - \frac{(351)(2{,}189.54)}{26} \tag{5.59}$$

$$= 25{,}782.28 - 29{,}558.79 \tag{5.60}$$

$$\Sigma x_i y_i = -3{,}776.51 \tag{5.61}$$

The slope of the regression line is:

$$\hat{b} = \frac{\Sigma x_i y_i}{\Sigma x_i^2} \tag{5.62}$$

$$= \frac{-3{,}776.5}{1{,}462.5} \tag{5.63}$$

$$\hat{b} = -2.582 \tag{5.64}$$

The point at which the **estimated** regression line intercepts the vertical axis (in this case, where $X_i = 0$, or in 1964) is calculated:

$$\hat{a} = \overline{Y} - b\overline{X} \tag{5.65}$$

$$= 84.21 - (-2.582)(13.5) \tag{5.66}$$

$$= 84.21 - 34.86 \tag{5.67}$$

$$\hat{a} = 119.07 \tag{5.68}$$

The regression line defining the trend in real wholesale prices for young hen turkeys in New York, then, would be:

$$\hat{Y}_i = 119.07 - 2.582 \, X_i \tag{5.69}$$

where X_i is 1 in 1965, and increases by 1 for each year.

For measuring how well this regression line fits the data:

$$R^2 = \frac{b(\Sigma x_i y_i)}{\Sigma y_i^2} \tag{5.70}$$

$$= \frac{(-2.582)(-3{,}776.51)}{12{,}812.84} \tag{5.71}$$

$$= 9{,}750.95/12{,}812.84 \tag{5.72}$$

$$R^2 = 0.76 \tag{5.73}$$

This R^2 statistic suggests that time alone explains two-thirds of the variation in real wholesale prices in New York for young hen turkeys. In general, if the trend analysis suggests that time alone explains as much as 15 percent of the variation in a price series, the trend is of enough significance that it probably should not be ignored.

The standard error of the estimate would be calculated:

$$S_{\hat{Y}} = \frac{Sy_i^2 - (Sx_iy)^2/Sx_i^2}{n-2} \tag{5.74}$$

$$= \sqrt{\frac{12,812.84 - (-3,776.51)(-3,776.51)/1,462.51}{24}} \tag{5.75}$$

$$= \sqrt{12,812.84 - 9,751.81/24} \tag{5.76}$$

$$= \sqrt{3,061.027/24} \tag{5.77}$$

$$= \sqrt{127.54} \tag{5.78}$$

$$S_{\hat{Y}} = 11.29 \tag{5.79}$$

The implication of Equations 5.74 through 5.79 is that in two-thirds of the 23 years, our observed real turkey prices would be expected to be within 11.3 cents of the calculated trend line and within 22.6 cents in 95 percent of the observations. This 11.3 standard error compares with a raw standard deviation (from the mean) of 22.6 cents.

The standard error of the estimated b value (or the slope of the regression line) would be calculated:

$$S_b = \frac{s_{\hat{Y}}^2}{\Sigma x_i^2} \tag{5.80}$$

$$= \sqrt{(11.29)(11.29)/1,462.5} \tag{5.81}$$

$$= \sqrt{127.54/1,462.5} \tag{5.82}$$

$$= \sqrt{0.0872} \tag{5.83}$$

$$S_b = 0.2953 \tag{5.84}$$

TESTS OF SIGNIFICANCE USING S_b ————————————

Earlier we suggested that for most data series, a s_b value less than half the value of the slope (b) would suggest a high degree of statistical significance in explaining the relationship between the variables if the numbers of observations were large enough to allow at least 30 degrees of freedom. In the case above, the s_b is less than one-eighth of the b value ($-2.6822/0.2953 = 8.74$), with 24 degrees of freedom.

The b/s_b ratio is a standard statistical measure called *"Student's t"*[2] which is utilized for calculating the significance of various types of statis-

---

[2] *"Student's t"* was discovered by W.S. Gosset in 1908. It was later perfected by R.A. Fisher in 1924, as reported by George W. Snedecor in *Statistical Methods Applied to Experiments in Agriculture and Biology,* 5th ed., Iowa State College Press, Ames Iowa, 1959.

TABLE 5.7   The entries in the table give the critical values of t for the specified number of degrees of freedom and areas in the right tail.

df	\.10	\.05	\.025	\.01	\.005	\.001
	Area in the Right Tail under the t Distribution Curve					
1	3.078	6.314	12.706	31.821	63.657	318.309
2	1.886	2.920	4.303	6.965	9.925	22.327
3	1.638	2.353	3.182	4.541	5.841	10.215
4	1.533	2.132	2.776	3.747	4.604	7.173
5	1.476	2.015	2.571	3.365	4.032	5.893
6	1.440	1.943	2.447	3.143	3.707	5.208
7	1.415	1.895	2.365	2.998	3.499	4.785
8	1.397	1.860	2.306	2.896	3.355	4.501
9	1.383	1.833	2.262	2.821	3.250	4.297
10	1.372	1.812	2.228	2.764	3.169	4.144
11	1.363	1.796	2.201	2.718	3.106	4.025
12	1.356	1.782	2.179	2.681	3.055	3.930
13	1.350	1.771	2.160	2.650	3.012	3.852
14	1.345	1.761	2.145	2.624	2.977	3.787
15	1.341	1.753	2.131	2.602	2.947	3.733
16	1.337	1.746	2.120	2.583	2.921	3.686
17	1.333	1.740	2.110	2.567	2.898	3.646
18	1.330	1.734	2.101	2.552	2.878	3.610
19	1.328	1.729	2.093	2.539	2.861	3.579
20	1.325	1.725	2.086	2.528	2.845	3.552
21	1.323	1.721	2.080	2.518	2.831	3.527
22	1.321	1.717	2.074	2.508	2.819	3.505
23	1.319	1.714	2.069	2.500	2.807	3.485
24	1.318	1.711	2.064	2.492	2.797	3.467
25	1.316	1.708	2.060	2.485	2.787	3.450
26	1.315	1.706	2.056	2.479	2.779	3.435
27	1.314	1.703	2.052	2.473	2.771	3.421
28	1.313	1.701	2.048	2.467	2.763	3.408
29	1.311	1.699	2.045	2.462	2.756	3.396
30	1.310	1.697	2.042	2.457	2.750	3.385
31	1.309	1.696	2.040	2.453	2.744	3.375
32	1.309	1.694	2.037	2.449	2.738	3.365
33	1.308	1.692	2.035	2.445	2.733	3.356
34	1.307	1.691	2.032	2.441	2.728	3.348
35	1.306	1.690	2.030	2.438	2.724	3.340
36	1.306	1.688	2.028	2.434	2.719	3.333
37	1.305	1.687	2.026	2.431	2.715	3.326
38	1.304	1.686	2.024	2.429	2.712	3.319
39	1.304	1.685	2.023	2.426	2.708	3.313
40	1.303	1.684	2.021	2.423	2.704	3.307
∞	1.282	1.645	1.960	2.326	2.576	3.090

tical measures. The *t* test is of particular use when the sample size is such that there are fewer than 30 degrees of freedom. The smaller the degrees of freedom, the larger the b/s_b ratio (or *t* value) required for a given level of significance associated with the parameter. The *t* test ignores the algebraic sign since the coefficient associated with the variable may be either positive or negative. In the example above, the *t* value is 8.74 with 24 degrees of freedom. The table of *t* values in Table 5.7 suggests that with 24 degrees of freedom, there is a 99.9 percent probability that the *b* value is different from zero if *t* has a value of at least 3.467. Thus, with a *t* value of 8.74, the slope associated with our regression line is statistically very significant indeed.

Another interpretation of the s_b might be that in two-thirds of all possible samples, the "true" value of the slope will fall within one standard error of the calculated *b*. In 95 percent of the cases, the true value would be expected to fall within two standard errors of the estimated *b*. Our calculated *b* of -2.68 ± 0.2953 gives a range of from -2.3857 to -2.9753. Thus, in repeated samples, if such intervals were similarly computed, two-thirds of those intervals would include the true value of *b*. That is, the smaller the value of the s_b, the more dependable the calculated *b* would be expected to be.

Appendix _____

This Appendix to Chapter 5 provides information regarding the manner in which standard spreadsheet computer software may be utilized in computing regression relationships in general and in computing trends in particular. The instructions provided are in terms of the commands either for LOTUS 1-2-3 or for the Lotus mode of QUATTROPRO software. However, virtually any spreadsheet software may be utilized in the manner shown.

Table 5A.1 will be recognized as an abbreviation and rearrangement of information included in Table 5.6, which was presented in the body of Chapter 5. The letters in parentheses at the head of the columns and the numbers in parentheses to the left of the rows in the table have been added for purposes of identifying rows and columns in the instructions. Since regression parameters are most easily estimated using deviations from the means of the dependent and independent variables, the first step must be to calculate the means.

> With the cursor in cell B43, type in @sum(B26.B41). This command instructs the computer to add all the numbers in column B between—and including—rows 26 and 41. The resulting sum will appear in cell B43.

TABLE 5A.1. Calculation of Trend in New York Wholesale Prices for 8–16-lb Young Hen Turkeys, 1975–90

			Column		
	A	B	C	D	E
R o w	Year	New York Wholesale Price for 8–16-lb Hen Turkeys (cts/lb)	CPI (82–84 = 100)	Real Price Hen Turkey Whs NY (cts/lb) (Y_i)	Trend Value (X_i)
(26)	1975	53.2	53.7	99.07	1
(27)	1976	48.8	56.9	85.76	2
(28)	1977	54.0	60.6	89.11	3
(29)	1978	66.7	65.2	102.30	4
(30)	1979	68.1	72.6	93.80	5
(31)	1980	63.7	82.4	77.31	6
(32)	1981	60.7	90.9	66.78	7
(33)	1982	60.8	96.5	63.01	8
(34)	1983	60.5	99.6	60.74	9
(35)	1984	74.4	103.9	71.61	10
(36)	1985	75.5	107.6	70.17	11
(37)	1986	72.2	109.6	65.88	12
(38)	1987	57.8	113.6	50.88	13
(39)	1988	61.1	118.3	51.65	14
(40)	1989	66.7	124.0	53.79	15
(41)	1990	63.2	130.7	48.36	16
(42)					
(43)	Σ			—	—
(44)					
(45)	MEAN			—	—

With the cursor in cell B45, type +B43/16. This instructs the computer to divide the sum previously calculated by the number of observations. The resulting mean will appear in cell B45.

Now return the cursor to cell B43 and use the following commands:

Press "Slash" (/) to activate the menu.

Select "Copy," and move the cursor to cell B45. Cells B43, B44, and B45 will all be illuminated.

Press "Enter" and move the cursor to cell D43.

Press the "period" key to lock in the formulae in cells B43 and B45 to be repeated in cells D43 through E45.

Move the cursor to E43. Cells D43 and E43 will be illuminated.

Press "Enter." The sums for X_i and Y_i will appear in Cells D43 and E43. The means will appear in D45 and E45.

Table 5A.2 expands the information in Table 5A.1 to include the calculations necessary for the raw variance, the regression trend line, and the statistical properties that test the validity of that trend line. To complete Table 5A.2, use the following commands:

With the cursor in cell D26, type +C26-8.5. This directs the computer to deduct the mean value for X from the first X observation.

With the cursor in cell E26, type D26*D26—directing the computer to square the deviation from the mean for the first X observation.

With the cursor in cell F26, type +B26-71.88. This directs the computer to deduct the mean value for Y from the first Y observation.

With the cursor in cell G26, type +F26*F26—directing the computer to square the deviation from the mean for the first Y observation.

With the cursor in cell H26, type +D26*F26. This directs the computer to multiply the deviation from the mean value of X by the mean value of Y.

With the cursor in cell D26, press "Slash" (/) to activate the menu.

Select "Copy" and move the cursor to cell H26. Cells D26 through H26 will be illuminated.

Press "Enter" to lock the formulae in cells D26 through H26 in the computer.

Move the cursor to cell D27, and press the period to anchor the range into which the formulae in cells D26 through H26 are to be copied.

Move the cursor to cell D41. Cells D27 through D41 will be illuminated.

Press "Enter." The correct calculations will appear in cells D27 through H41.

Place the cursor on cell C43—the cell for which you previously calculated the sum of the X_i.

Press "Slash" (/) to activate the menu.

Select "Copy" and press "Enter" to lock the formula in cell C23 into the computer.

Move the cursor to cell D43, and press the period to anchor the range within which the formula is to be utilized.

TABLE 5A.2. Calculations of Trend in New York Wholesale Prices for 8–16-lb Young Hen Turkeys, 1975–90

Row		A	B	C		Column				
		Year	Real Price Hen Turkey Whs. NY (cts/lb) (Y_i)	Trend Value (X_i)	D	E	F	G	H	I
							Deviations from the Means			
					$(X_i - \bar{X})$	$(X_i - \bar{X})^2$	$(Y_i - \bar{Y})$	$(Y_i - \bar{Y})^2$	Cross Products $(X_i - \bar{X})(Y_i - \bar{Y})$	Expected Value $(\hat{Y}_i)$
(26)	1975	99.07	1	—	—	—	—	—	—
(27)	1976	85.76	2	—	—	—	—	—	—
(28)	1977	89.11	3	—	—	—	—	—	—
(29)	1978	102.30	4	—	—	—	—	—	—
(30)	1979	93.80	5	—	—	—	—	—	—
(31)	1980	77.31	6	—	—	—	—	—	—
(32)	1981	66.78	7	—	—	—	—	—	—
(33)	1982	63.01	8	—	—	—	—	—	—
(34)	1983	60.74	9	—	—	—	—	—	—
(35)	1984	71.61	10	—	—	—	—	—	—
(36)	1985	70.17	11	—	—	—	—	—	—
(37)	1986	65.88	12	—	—	—	—	—	—
(38)	1987	50.88	13	—	—	—	—	—	—
(39)	1988	51.65	14	—	—	—	—	—	—
(40)	1989	53.79	15	—	—	—	—	—	—
(41)	1990	48.36	16	—	—	—	—	—	—
(42)									
(43)	Σ	1,150.22	136	0	—	0	—	—	1,150.22
(44)									
(45)	MEAN	71.88	8.5						

90

Move the cursor to cell H43. Cells D43 through H43 will be illuminated.

Press "Enter" to calcualte the sums of columns D through H.

If cells D43 or F43 show a total that is different from zero (except for rounding errors), you have an error. The sum of the deviations from a mean *must* be zero. The most probable error is in the typing or calculation of the mean.

The essential elements for calculating raw variance, the regression equation, the R^2 statistic, the standard error of the estimate and the standard error of the slope are all present in rows 43 and 45. These elements and location on the spread sheet at which they appear are as follows:

$$\text{Cell E43} = \Sigma x_i^2$$
$$\text{Cell G43} = \Sigma y_i^2$$
$$\text{Cell H43} = \Sigma x_i y_i$$
$$\text{Cell B45} = \overline{Y}$$
$$\text{Cell C45} = \overline{X}$$

A hand-held calculator may now be used with the formulae in Chapter 5 to complete the calculations for raw variance, the regression trend line, and so on. Once the calculations are made, the expected values for the regression trend equation may be computed simply by placing the cursor in cell I26 and typing the regression equation.

(+value computed for *a*) + (value computed for *b*)*C26

This formula may then be copied to cells I27 through I41 to give the expected values associated with each observation. The sum of these values *must* be equal to the sum of the Y_i.

A process similar to that above may be used to calculate regression relationships using the short form of the regression equation illustrated in Table 5.6.

Quick and Dirty Regression Calculations

It is important to go through the mechanics above in order to understand the way in which regression analysis works. However, once that understanding is achieved, there is a much quicker and easier method. Using the information in Table 5A.2, the regression analysis can be accomplished by using the following commands:

Press "Slash" to activate the menu

Select "Data" and "Regression"

The computer will call for the X and Y Ranges. Type C26.C41 for the X Range and B26.B41 for the Y Range.

The computer also calls for the Output Range. Type the location of the cell in which you wish the regression output to begin.

Select "Go" and press "Enter."

The regression output will appear, beginning in the cell you have previously designated. The appearance of the output for this particular problem will be:

Regression Output

Constant	100.26454413 (the a value)
Std Err of Y Est	7.8997303889
R-Squared	0.8126407118
No. of Observations	16
Degrees of Freedom	14
X-Coefficient	-3.338477878 (the b value)
Std Err of Co	0.42842303247 (the s_b

Figure 5A.1 shows the real price data with the regression trend line. The figure in parentheses below the b value is the standard error of the b. This is the normal notation for presenting regression equations. How good is the fit of this trend line?

With 81 percent of the variation in real prices for hen turkeys in New York ($R^2 = 0.81$) being explained by the trend, the fit is usually considered to be pretty good. With a standard error of the Y estimate being reduced to 7.9 from a raw standard deviation of 18.25, it is apparent that the deviations from the trend line are much less dispersed than were the deviations from the mean. The standard error of the b value is less than one-seventh of the b, which with 14 degrees of freedom, is highly significant. But could there be a trend than would be even more descriptive of the real price data for hen turkeys?

Alternatives to Linear Regression

Semilogarithmic Functions So far, we have limited ourselves to linear trend lines in the form $\hat{Y}_i = a + bX_i$. But time series data regarding prices or production of agricultural products frequently exhibit curvalinear forms. Functions that are linear in logarithms are curvalinear when ex-

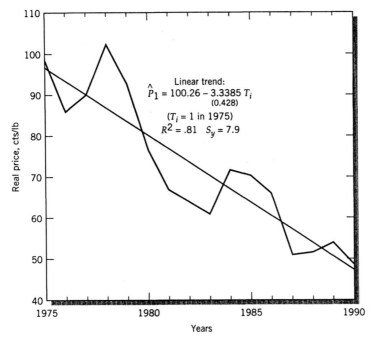

FIGURE 5A.1. Real prices, New York, hen turkeys, with linear trend.

pressed in ordinary numbers. Thus, by converting either the independent variable or the dependent variable to logarithmic form, we can calculate a trend line that exhibits a curve.

To convert the X_i and Y_i to logarithms as shown in Table 5A.3, use the following commands:

With the cursor in Cell D26, type @log(B26). This directs the computer to convert the 1975 real price for turkeys to logarithmic form.

With the cursor in Cell E26, type @log(C26), directing the computer to convert the trend value for 1975 into logarithmic form.

Return the cursor to cell D26. Press "Slash" (/) to activate the menu.

Select "Copy" and move the cursor to cell E26. Cells D26 and E26 will be illuminated. Press "Enter."

Move the cursor to cell D27 and press the period to anchor the formulae to be copied from cells D26 and E26 into the copy range.

Move the cursor to cell D41. Cells D27 through D41 will be illuminated.

TABLE 5A.3. Information for Calculating Semilogarithmic and Full Logarithmic Trends in Real Prices for Hen Turkeys at Wholesale in New York, 1975–90

	A	B	Column C	D	E
R o w	Year	Price Hen Turkey Whs. NY (cst/lb) (Y_i)	Trend Value (X_i)	$\log Y_i$	$\log X_i$
(26)	1975	99.07	1	1.995937	0.000000
(27)	1976	85.76	2	1.933308	0.301030
(28)	1977	89.11	3	1.949921	0.477121
(29)	1978	102.30	4	2.009878	0.602060
(30)	1979	93.80	5	1.972210	0.698970
(31)	1980	77.31	6	1.888212	0.778151
(32)	1981	66.78	7	1.823625	0.845098
(33)	1982	63.01	8	1.799376	0.903090
(34)	1983	60.74	9	1.783496	0.954243
(35)	1984	71.61	10	1.854957	1.000000
(36)	1985	70.17	11	1.846135	1.041393
(37)	1986	65.88	12	1.818727	1.079181
(38)	1987	50.88	13	1.706550	1.113943
(39)	1988	51.65	14	1.713056	1.146128
(40)	1989	53.79	15	1.730704	1.176091
(41)	1990	48.36	16	1.684441	1.204120
(42)					
(43)	Σ	1,150.22	136		
(44)					
(45)	MEAN	71.88	8.5		

Press "Enter." The logarithmic forms of the X_i and Y_i will appear in Columns D and E.

A semilogarithmic regression trend line is semilogarithmic because only one of the two variables is converted to logarithms. To construct a semilogarithmic trend with the dependent variable Y converted to logarithms, the commands would be exactly the same as for a linear trend except that D26.D41 would be substituted for the Y range. The results of this regression analysis are compared with those for the linear trend in Figure 5A.2.

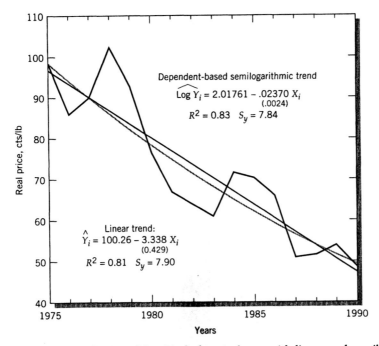

FIGURE 5A.2. Real prices, New York, **hen** turkeys, with linear and semilogarithmic trends.

It will be noted that the R^2 and $S_{\hat{Y}}$ statistics for the semilogarithmic trend are marginally better than was the case for the linear trend.[3] Also, the b/S_b ratio is a bit larger, indicating a greater degree of significance associated with the b value.

It should be recognized that the $S_{\hat{Y}}$ reported in logarithmic form in the regression output is meaningless. To get the standard error of $\hat{Y}$, it is necessary to manually calculate the squared deviations of the actual observations from the regression line [that is, the $\Sigma(Y - \hat{Y})^2$], and then to utilize the appropriate formulae in Chapter 5.

An alternative approach for the semilogarithmic trend would be to substitute the $\text{Log} X_i$ values in Column E of Table 5A.3 for the X range in the regression equation. The results of a trend based upon logarithmic values for the independent variable ($\text{Log} X_i$) may be quite different from

---

[3] Because of the change in units measuring of the dependent variable, both R^2 and the standard error of the estimate as normally computed are not comparable to the original model. It is necessary to convert the predicted observations back into their original form to then compute R^2 and standard error estimates that are comparable with the original equation.

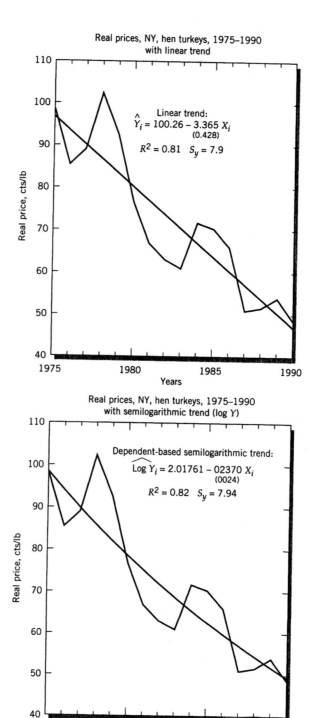

FIGURE 5A.3.

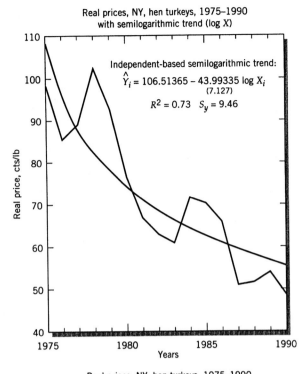

Real prices, NY, hen turkeys, 1975–1990
with semilogarithmic trend (log X)

Independent-based semilogarithmic trend:

$$\hat{Y}_i = 106.51365 - 43.99335 \log X_i$$
$$(7.127)$$
$$R^2 = 0.73 \quad S_y = 9.46$$

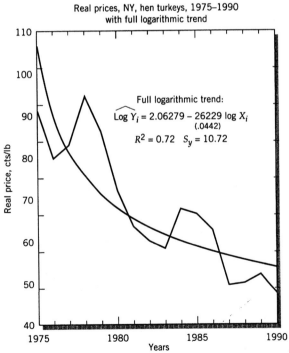

Real prices, NY, hen turkeys, 1975–1990
with full logarithmic trend

Full logarithmic trend:

$$\widehat{\text{Log } Y_i} = 2.06279 - 26229 \log X_i$$
$$(.0442)$$
$$R^2 = 0.72 \quad S_y = 10.72$$

FIGURE 5A.3. (*Continued*)

those based upon logarithmic values for the dependent variable (Log Y_i). The choice of which—if either—to use should be based upon which has the better fit to the observed data.

Full Logarithmic Trends The full logarithmic trend is calculated when both the dependent and independent variables are expressed in logarithms. Like the dependent variable-based semilogarithmic trend, the standard error of the Y estimate must be manually calculated. Figure 5A.3 compares the four alternative approaches to trend calculation. For these price data, the statistical properties show that the dependent variable based semilogarithmic and linear trends are clearly superior to the two alternatives. (In the two lower charts of Figure 5A.3, R^2 and S_y have been calculated from the expected values of the dependent variables after they have been converted to ordinary numbers.)

CHAPTER 6

Price Movements Over Time—Cycles

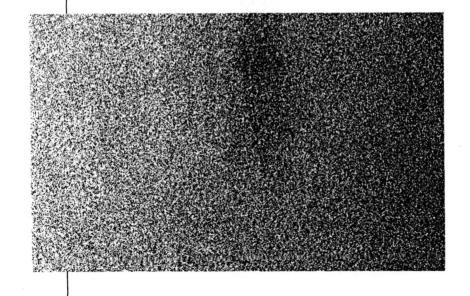

In Chapters 4 and 5, we discussed estimating the trend type of price movement over time, recognizing that real prices for some commodities tend to drift upward or downward over long periods. These upward or downward drifts in price can be traced to a number of factors, which may impact either the supply or the demand for the commodity in question. Continuing development and adaptation of new products may cause a slow upward drift in price. Continuing adaptation of improved production technology may cause a downward drift. The use of a time variable in trend analysis allows us to capture the effect of what are typically nonmeasurable variables that influence the prices of agricultural products.

Under the atomistically competitive conditions faced by much of the agricultural production sector, the price and production levels for a product are at least theoretically determined by the intersection of the market supply and demand curves. When an upward drift in prices occurs, the implication is that market demand for the product is shifting to the right more rapidly than is market supply (or conversely, that market demand is shifting to the left *less* rapidly than is market supply). If the trend in prices is downward, the implication is that the rate of growth in market supply exceeds that of market demand.

The price trend in our turkey example of Chapter 5, while very significant, by no means captured the entire variation in turkey prices (Figure 6.1). There is a fairly regular oscillation of prices *around* the calculated trend. When the data in this price trend are compared with data regarding turkey production, it becomes apparent that the downward trend in real turkey prices is related to a comparable upward trend in total turkey production. Further, the years in which real prices for turkey lie above the trend coincide generally with years in which production lies below the trend. Thus, the data and the trends regarding turkey prices and production are entirely compatible with the economic theory suggesting a negative relationship between prices and market quantities available.

Back in Chapter 4, we recognized that the paired price-quantity values for any given year represented the intersection of some sort of "annual average" supply and demand curves for that year. When we chart a scatter diagram of production-price points for turkeys over the time period shown in Figure 6.1, we can see that the scatter of points assumes a generally downward and to the right pattern (Figure 6.2). The downward and to the right nature of a line describing this pattern can be identified as a demand function of sorts.

We have recognized that each individual point in Figure 6.2 identifies the intersection of the average conditions of supply and demand for the

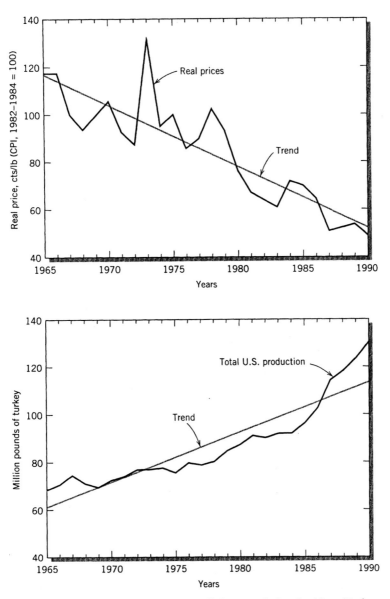

FIGURE 6.1. Turkeys: real prices, 8–16-lb hens, wholesale, New York, compared with total federally inspected U.S. turkey production, 1965–90.

SOURCE: *Poultry and Egg Statistics, 1960–89*, ERS-USDA, Statistical Bulletin No. 816, September 1990, and *Livestock and Poultry Situation and Outlook Report*, ERS-USDA, various issues since 1989.

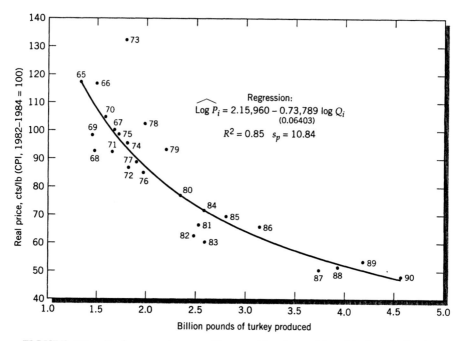

FIGURE 6.2.   Turkeys: price-quantity combinations, New York, wholesale, real prices, 8–16-lb hens and total U.S. turkey production, 1965–90.

SOURCE: *Poultry and Egg Statistics, 1960–89*, ERS-USDA, Statistical Bulletin No. 816, September 1990, and *Livestock and Poultry Situation and Outlook Report*, ERS-USDA, various issues since 1989.

years in question. The *line* through these points represents some sort of average or central tendency of those conditions over this 26-year period.[1] To the extent that the prices consumers are willing and able to pay for specified quantities of turkey (an inverted definition of demand) are reflected by this central tendency, it is some sort of average demand function over this period. The scatter of points around the demand function, presumably, is the result of variations in the *ceteris paribus* conditions—such as the availability of competing meats—that are not in fact constant. When a closer look is taken at this demand function, there is a very curious phenomenon that may be observed (Figure 6.3). If one begins with the 1965–66 period, there appears to be a pattern of about 2 years of relatively high prices, followed by about 2 years of relatively lower prices, followed in turn by 2 years of improved prices and a

---

[1] In this case, the full logarithmic relationship provides the best fit for the data. The R^2 statistic and both standard errors ($s_{\hat{y}}$ and s_b) are all superior to the linear relationship or either of the semilogarithmic relationships.

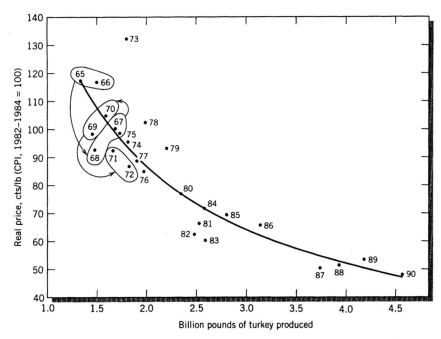

FIGURE 6.3. Turkey: price-quantity combinations, New York, wholesale, real prices, 8–16-lb hens versus total U.S. turkey production, 1965–90 with cyclical movements indicated.

subsequent 2 years of lower prices, and so on. This pattern persists until the early 1980s when the very rapid growth in turkey production begins to obscure this cyclical phenomenon. The growth in turkey production was, of course, generated by the consumer acceptance of large numbers of new turkey products such as luncheon meats, turkey "hams," and microwavable dinners. It remains to be seen whether the pattern will reestablish itself once the rate of growth in turkey production subsides and the industry becomes more stable.

We know from previous study of economics that various sorts of disturbances may occasionally cause the price and/or production to fall at some point other than the equilibrium position, which occurs at the intersection of the market supply and demand functions. This situation is expected to unleash a set of forces that will tend to restore that equilibrium. But where there is a considerable time lag in the response of production to a change in price, the time required for price and production to return to an equilibrium may be so long that other disturbances will typically prevent an equilibrium from being achieved. As a result, the price-quantity points oscillate *around* the underlying equilibrium position rather than ever actually achieving it.

The classic example of cyclical oscillation in production and price is the beef cattle sector. We have been aware of economic cycles in animal agriculture for at least three quarters of a century. These economic cycles spring from the time physiologically necessary for responding to economic incentives. A fair rule of thumb is that the *minimum* length of a cycle in livestock inventories (from peak to peak or from trough to trough) is about quadruple the time required from birth to first reproduction. In the case of cattle this cycle is likely to be no less than 8 years in length. The hog cycle is likely to be no less than 40 months, the broiler cycle no less than 27–28 months. Any of these biologically based cycles can be disrupted by cataclysmic economic events, but once the adjustments to the economic disruption are complete, the biological cycles will typically reassert themselves.

The U.S. Department of Agriculture began annual reporting of beginning cattle inventories in 1867 (Figure 6.4). In the 125 years of information since this reporting began, there have been at least nine complete cycles, but in no case has a cycle been shorter than 8 years. Also, during the first 109 years of this 125-year period, there was a strong upward trend through the cycle in inventories, with each subsequent peak and

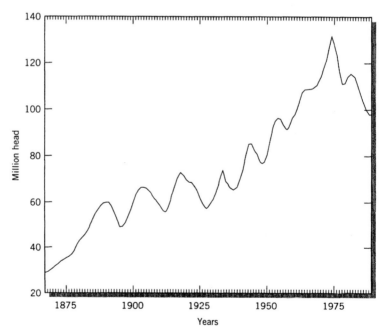

FIGURE 6.4. January 1 inventory, all cattle and calves United States, 1867–1991.

SOURCE: Economic Research Service, U.S. Department of Agriculture.

trough being at a higher level than were the previous ones. At some time in the very late 1970s or very early 1980s, this trend reversed direction.

Between 1928 and 1979, there were five complete cycles in cattle numbers. These cycles, in order, were 10, 11, 9, 9, and 12 years long. The expansion phases of these cycles were 6–8 years and the liquidation phases were 2–4 years. There has been one complete cycle since 1979, beginning about the time at which the trend in cattle numbers changed directions. The expansion phase of that cycle was only 3 years in length, and the liquidation phase was 7 years—clearly an anomaly when compared with previous cycles. But this anomaly was not limited to cattle. During the very early 1980s, the cycles for hogs, broilers, turkeys, and eggs were *all* disrupted. A primary player in the disruptions of these cycles was a change in the focus of monetary policy.[2]

Throughout the period from 1933 to 1979, the focus of monetary policy had been to maintain the rate of interest within a certain "acceptable" band. The rapid inflation during and after the first energy crisis in 1974–75 quite predictably made U.S. monetary policy makers extremely apprehensive regarding the potential impact of the second energy crisis in 1979–81. As a result, the focus of monetary policy shifted from managing *interest* rates by balancing the supply of money with the demand for funds toward a focus of managing *inflation* through Draconian limitations on the supply of money with little regard for the demand for funds and the consequent impacts upon interest rates.

The profligacy of U.S. fiscal policy throughout the 1980s and into the 1990s—with annual budget deficits in the range of $200–400 billions—was highly inflationary. The only monetary policy option available for offsetting the enormously inflationary pressure of the irresponsible fiscal policy was for monetary authorities to continue the very restrictive policies adopted during the second energy crisis. Real interest rates (the rate of interest less the rate of inflation) during the 1980s averaged about triple the average real interest rate for the previous 50 years. The beef industry has since World War II been as heavily leveraged financially as has any portion of American agriculture—one of the more heavily leveraged U.S. economic sectors.

The impacts of the change in monetary policy are very clear in Figure 6.4. The increased real interest rates in the early 1980s introduced a little item called *external capital rationing* into the cattle business. External capital rationing when freely translated into cowboy vernacular becomes "that gimlet-eyed bastard at the bank." Bankers, who are by nature

---

[2] John W. Goodwin and Danny R. Pippin, *The Cycle in U.S. Cattle Numbers as Related to Selected Supply Variables*, Arkansas Agricultural Experiment Station, Division of Agriculture, University of Arkansas, Report Series 314, February 1990.

gimlet eyed, were forced by restrictive national credit policies to become even more demanding in the 1980s, thus forcing an abortion of the increasing numbers phase of the cattle cycle that began in 1979. Those same policies forced a prolonged liquidation phase of that cycle and retarded the rate of herd rebuilding in the cycle that began in 1989.

The biological limitations imposed upon adjustments to economic forces can be clearly illustrated by the cycle in beef cattle inventories. The decision to produce a calf for market is not reflected in the meat counter for a minimum of 2½ years (Figure 6.5). Once the decision to produce is made, about 10 months is required for breeding and gestation. Another 9 months is required for growing the calf to weaning weight. Four to 8 months on pasture are required to get the calf to feeding weight, and another 4 to 5 months on feed is required prior to slaughter. Finally, 2 to 4 weeks are required for slaughter, processing, and distributing the beef produced. Obviously, a great many disturbances in the beef market can occur between the time the producer made his production decision and the time that decision is reflected as a chuck roast in the meat case.

The decision to *expand* the capacity for beef production is even more complicated. Let's suppose that a major drought has forced the liquidation of large numbers of mother cows throughout the Plains and the intermountain West. The resulting increase in the prices for the available calves encourages ranchers to raise more calves. The only way more calves can be produced is to withhold more heifers from market than would ordinarily be required to replace the spent cows culled from the brood cow herd. Thus, a total of about 4½ years is required for an initial decision to expand beef production to actually show up in the market place. Further, that initial decision to withhold heifers in order to make mothers rather than chuck roasts the following spring generates a *reduction* in beef production.

The initial reduction in the availability of beef generates further improvement in prices. Before the first decision to expand is ultimately reflected in the market place, cow–calf producers have had three consecutive calf crops from which improving market prices may encourage them to respond by a further withholding of heifers for purposes of expanding the breeding herd. This means that beef production will continue to expand for a full 3 years beyond the time that increased output resulting from the initial decision gets to market!

The cycles in beef production and prices that have arisen from the circumstances described above is repeated to greater or lesser extent in almost every product of animal agriculture and in a number of crops. Many fruit crops, for example, require several years for the trees to come into full production. And once the initial investment in establishing an orchard or a vineyard has been made, the penalties for reversing that

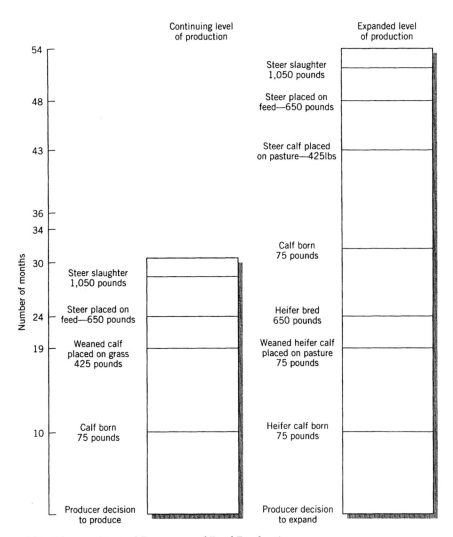

FIGURE 6.5. Typical Programs of Beef Production.

SOURCE: Henry C. Gilliam, Jr., *U.S. Beef Cow-Calf Industry*, NED, ERS, USDA, Agricultural Economics Report No. 515, September 1984.

decision can be enormous. Thus, the expanded production capacity may remain long past the time that the prices which generated the expansion are in effect. Also, many fruits and tree nuts—apples or pecans, for example—tend to have alternate years of heavy and light production. This will show up as a 2-year price cycle, perhaps oscillating around a much longer cycle. The longer cycle reflects the time required for the trees to begin producing.

The economic theory that has been developed to explain cycles in agricultural prices and production is the Cobweb theorem originally advanced by Mordecai Ezekiel in the 1930s. The Cobweb theorem has more recently fallen into some disrepute, but it is useful in understanding just how cycles come into being.

There are several assumptions associated with the cobweb model, at least some of which will be at odds with the facts for almost any agricultural product for almost any time period that an analysis is made. The probability that some of the fundamental assumptions may be inconsistent with reality, however, does not negate the usefulness of the model in understanding the reasons for the existence of cycles. Rather, it simply points to the need to be prepared to *modify* the model in order to make adjustments for the unreality assumed.

The essential assumptions of the cobweb model include:

1. Price is determined in an atomistically competitive market environment in which no seller has a market share large enough to enable him to influence the price.
2. Current prices are determined largely by currently available supplies, which are subject to little or no modification in the immediate period.
3. Producers *plan* production for the next period primarily on the basis of recently observed prices.
4. There is a lag of at least one production period between the time of a decision to produce and the actual availability of that production. That is, current production is a function of previously observed prices, and, under the constraint of the second assumption, current prices are largely a function of current supplies.
5. *Planned* production is ultimately realized as *actual* production—an heroic assumption in and of itself, given Mama Nature's propensity to sabotage even the best of biological plans.
6. Demand and supply relationships remain constant. That is, the *ceteris paribus* conditions do in fact remain constant long enough for the full adjustment process to occur—another heroic assumption.

Suppose some force such as an increase in the price of a substitute good has caused the market demand to shift from D to D'. As a result, the equilibrium market price rises from P_b to P_e (Figure 6.6). Producers who produced Q_{sb} in anticipation of price P_b now find that consumers are willing to pay the much higher price for P_a. The P_a price encourages producers to expand output to Q_{sa}, which in turn causes prices to fall to P_b. Producers reduce output in response to this lower price and a continuous oscillation of both price and output is established. That is, the new equilibrium position is never reached.

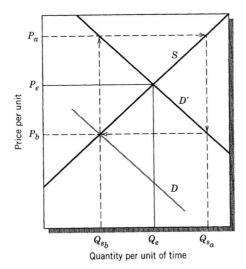

Price per unit

Quantity per unit of time

FIGURE 6.6.

The case of the continuous fluctuation in price and output—or the "stable cobweb"—occurs when market supply and market demand are equally elastic in the neighborhood of the market equilibrium. But suppose that market demand is relatively *less* elastic than is market supply (Figure 6.7). In this case, the price and output oscillate around the market equilibrium position, but are continually diverging farther and farther from that equilibrium. The resulting divergent pattern gives an enormously unstable pattern to both prices and output.

In the case in which the market demand is relatively more elastic at equilibrium than is market supply (Figure 6.8), the adjustment process allows price and output to oscillate around the market equilibrium, but always converging on that equilibrium. The rate of convergence upon the equilibrium is primarily related to the degree of difference in the relative price elasticities of supply and demand at the equilibrium position.

There are several immediately apparent inconsistencies among these three cobweb models, economic theory and reality. In the first place, the only one of these models that is consistent with the equilibrium theory advanced in most principles of economics courses is the third one in which market supply is less price elastic than is market demand. But except for the very short run, empirical research has shown the market supply of almost any agricultural product to be relatively more price elastic than is the market demand. Empirical research has further shown that the typical cycle in agricultural production is of the continuous type

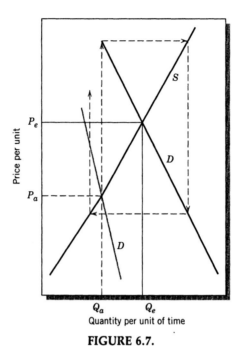

FIGURE 6.7.

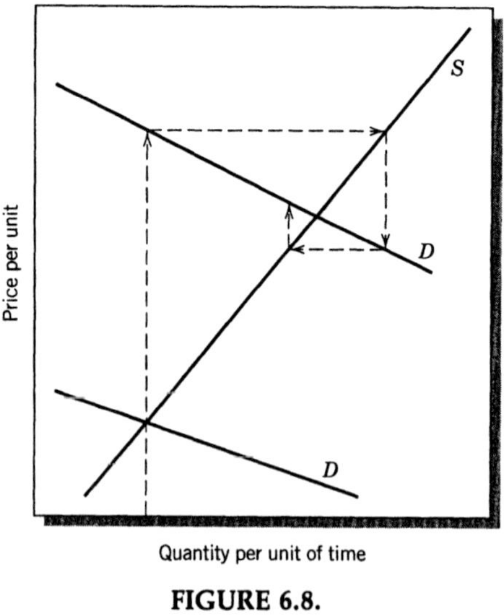

FIGURE 6.8.

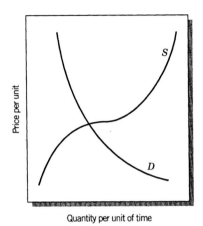

Quantity per unit of time

FIGURE 6.9.

rather than the divergent sort that would be suggested by the relatively greater price elasticity of the supply relationship. Thus, it is abundantly clear that there needs to be some modification of these models.

It is probable that the straight line relationships postulated for supply and demand in the cobweb models are inappropriate at least for most agricultural goods. It is far more likely that agricultural supply functions are of an "inverted S" type than a straight line (Figure 6.9). This type of supply function—quite inelastic on both ends and much less inelastic in the middle—suggests that at very low prices, only those resources, which are exceedingly well adapted, perhaps even exclusively adapted, to the production of the good in question, will be employed. As prices rise, those resources, which are somewhat less well adapted to this product, will be drawn into production. As prices continue to rise, more and more of the less and less well suited resources are attracted, up to the point at which *all* resources that can be used for this commodity are so employed.[3]

Agricultural demand functions may be straight line relationships as far as a single use for a product is concerned. Many of them can be at least approximated by a straight line for that portion of the demand function that is in the immediate neighborhood of the market equilibrium position. But when multiple uses for a commodity are considered, there is most probably some curve in the demand function. The demand

[3] Agricultural supply functions of this type were reported in the early 1960s in John W. Goodwin, James S. Plaxico, and W.F. Lagrone, *Aggregation of Normative Microsupply Relationships for Dryland Crop Farms in the Rolling Plains of Oklahoma and Texas*, Oklahoma Agricultural Experiment Station, Technical Bulletin T-103, Stillwater, Oklahoma, 1963.

for wheat, for example, is highly inelastic so long as prices are high enough to limit wheat to use as a food grain. A certain minimum quantity of wheat for human food products will command a very high price. Quantities larger than this minimum are not particularly desirable, and prices decline very rapidly as wheat availability is increased.

Once wheat prices decline sufficiently for wheat to compete with corn as an animal feed, the consumption response becomes much more price elastic. The wheat consumption increases associated with each five- or ten-cent decline in price are enlarged enormously once wheat prices are competitive with corn.

The configuration of the market supply–demand model that results from the modifications we have postulated allows for the continuously oscillating cobweb pattern in a situation where market supply is more price elastic than is demand at the equilibrium. Numerous other modifications in the cobweb model similar to the one we have already postulated can be used to bring the model closer to reality. But the point is, cycles in production and price are generally consistent with both economic theory and with what we see in the real world.

At least in a theoretical sense, the cycles in price and production are inversely related and have exactly the same phase (i.e., 2 years of increased production should be accompanied by 2 years of reduced prices as was shown in Figure 6.1). High prices not only encourage existing producers to expand output, but new producers are also encouraged to begin production of the good. As we have already seen, the length of time required for expansion of production to occur depends upon the physiology of the commodity, and (as Geoffery Sheperd states it) the psychology of the producer.

As we saw in Figure 6.1, these cycles of price and production are in fact inversely related. When per capita production increases, prices generally decline. When production is reduced, prices increase. The pattern is generally—but not absolutely—2 years of increased production followed by 2 years of reduced production.

If one were trying to anticipate the cycle in turkey prices and production, he would normally expect an up-turn in production 2 years following a down-turn and would expect prices to move in the opposite fashion. Chapter 7 will examine methods for measuring and anticipating cycles in price and production.

CHAPTER 7

Measuring
Cycles

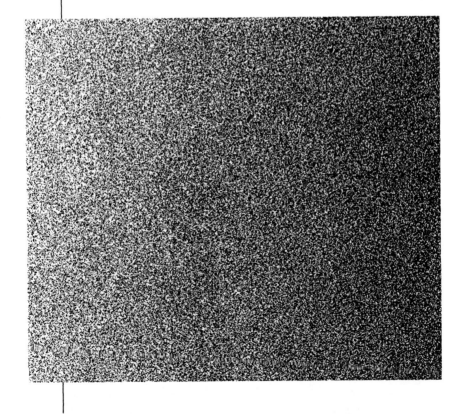

In Chapter 6, we discussed cycles in agricultural prices and the economic theory that analyzes the reasons for those cycles. We saw how the basis for cycles in the prices of agricultural commodities was fundamentally grounded in the biology of the production process for these products. We said that in a general way one could anticipate the impact of cycles by calculating trends through the production and price data, and then measuring the deviations from those trends. These deviations, averaged for sequential years of the cycle, can provide us with general estimates of the price differences we might expect in different phases of the cycle.

Let's return to our hog example of Chapter 4 and examine just how this might be done (Figure 7.1). You will recall that when we discussed trends in agricultural prices, we said that the selection of the time period for measuring the trend was important. In our example of hog prices, we said that there were at least three observable trends since 1950—one for the whole period, one for the 1950 to mid-1970s period, and one for the period since the mid-1970s. These trends are shown by the lighter lines in the upper part of Figure 7.1.

When you were introduced to the analysis of cycles in Chapter 6, we recognized that price cycles were rooted in the production cycles, which result from the biology of the commodity in question. Pork production is shown in the lower part of Figure 7.1. While there are no obvious breaks in the *trends* of per capita pork production, the variations in production *did* become much more erratic during the mid-1970s period when there was an obvious break in the price trend. This, of course, was related to the enormously destabilizing factors such as the Russian Grain Deal of 1972–73 and the first energy crisis of 1974–75, which dramatically rearranged the cost structure throughout all of animal agriculture.

The cycles in the pork sector may be identified simply by inspecting the data charted in Figure 7.1. Since the cycle in price tends to be driven by the cycle in production, it is appropriate that both production and price be considered in defining the cycle. If one begins with a cyclical peak in production, such as 1952 in the case of our example, that peak would be expected to coincide with a cyclical "trough" or "valley" in price.[1] There are four years before the next cyclical peak in production, which coincides with the next cyclical price trough. The simple process

---

[1] One could argue that the cyclical peak in production occurred in 1951, but since the trough in price is clearly 1952, that year is defined as the peak in the production cycle. Similar circumstance—circumstances considerably more difficult to resolve—occur in 1963–64, in 1984–85 and in 1988–89.

114

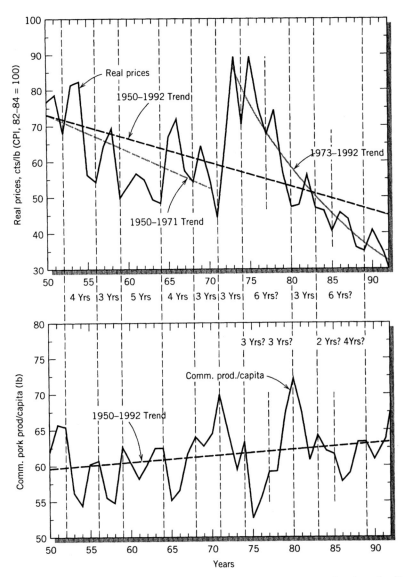

FIGURE 7.1. Commercial pork production per capita and real prices for live hogs, seven major U.S. markets, with trends, 1950–92.

SOURCE: *Livestock and Meat Statistics, 1973, 1983, and 1984-88,* Statistical Bulletins Nos. 522, 715, and 784, ERS, USDA, July 1973, December 1984, and September 1989, and *Livestock and Poultry Situation and Outlook Report,* ERS, USDA, various issues since 1989.

of counting the numbers of data periods (in our example, the years) between peaks in production and troughs in price will give a reasonable estimate of the length of the cycle. In the case of hogs—over the full 43 years of information—the cycle ranges from three to six years and appears to average just about four years in length.

One could argue for a hog cycle of a bit less than four years in length on the basis of the six-year cycle from 1974 through 1980. This period could be defined as two three-year cycles on the basis of the price trough in 1977 and the very limited magnitude of the 1977–78 increase in per capita pork production. Such an argument is entirely supportable. If it is accepted, the average length of the cycle would be about three and one-half years—very near the biological rule of thumb discussed in Chapter 6. The handling of cases such as this one and those mentioned in the footnote on the previous page are simply judgment calls for the analyst. There are no hard and fast rules.

A second judgment call situation occurs in the case of the period from 1983 through 1989. Commercial pork production per capita was at a peak in 1983. It declined substantially in 1984 and then moved "sideways" in 1985. Should this lateral move to 1985 be defined as a production peak? The 1985 trough in prices would support such a definition, but a two-year hog cycle is difficult to defend. You will recall the discussion in Chapter 6 regarding the reality that cataclysmic economic events can upon occasion disrupt cycles, and how all the cycles in U.S. animal agriculture were disrupted by the altered focus of monetary policy in the early 1980s. If this explanation is accepted, the data for 1983 and 1984 should probably be eliminated from the effort to estimate the amplitude of the price cycle for hogs.

Once the length of the cycle has been defined, one can go about the business of analyzing the cycle for amplitude (*amplitude* refers to the vertical distance the cycle can be expected to move from trough to peak and from peak to trough). We have already discussed a simple method for estimating the length of the cycle. Amplitude is a more complicated matter.

THE USE OF TRENDS IN MEASURING CYCLES _____

Under ordinary circumstances, we could calculate the deviations from a trend line to define the amplitude of a cycle in pork production and/or prices. The average value of the deviations from the trend for the first years of all the cycles previously observed would be an estimate of the expected cyclical difference during the first year of any cycle that is yet to come. Likewise, the average values of the deviations in the second years of previous cycles would be an estimate expected during the second year and so on.

We have already seen how there are several trends in the prices shown in Figure 7.1. The question becomes *which* of these trend lines should we use in estimating the amplitude of the cycle? If we use the trend for the full 41 years of data that includes the very disruptive events of the 1971–74 period, which changed the world as far as animal agriculture is concerned, we will have blended two clearly incompatible periods. A second option would be to use the entire period, but to eliminate the 1971–76 period from our consideration. However, if these years are eliminated, the emphasis placed on the 1950s and 1960s is increased relative to the more recent information.

If we use the full logarithmic trend in hog prices only since the mid-1970s, we have only three full cycles with which to work. One of these three (1974–80) is clearly peculiar in that it just may be two cycles rather than one. Therefore, we could treat the 1974–80 period as two cycles—giving us four cycles with which to work—emphasizing the period since the disruptive events of the early 1970s.

The full logarithmic trend for the 18-year period since 1973 is:

$$\hat{Log\,P_i} = 9.6977 - 4.16783\,Log\,T_i \qquad (7.1)$$
$$(0.33)$$

where T_i is the trend value and $T_1 = 73$ in 1973

$$R^2 = 0.89 \qquad S_p = 6.2$$

The deviations from that trend are shown in Figure 7.2. You will note that the information in Figure 7.2 is exactly the same as that in the upper portion of Figure 7.1 except that the long-term trend has been stripped from the data. These deviations also appear in Table 7.1, which is an example of what has been called a *periodogram* analysis of the cycle. In a periodogram, the data are grouped in the periods of the various cycles. The groupings in Table 7.1 are identical with those in Figure 7.1 from which we first defined the cycles in hog production and prices and with the groupings in Figure 7.2. The deviations between the observed prices and the expected values are calculated in the fifth column of the table. Then those deviations are distributed in the sixth through tenth columns on the basis of the year of the cycle with which they are associated. The average deviations associated with the various years of the cycle are then calculated.

In the case of our cyclical hog prices, our periodogram analysis would lead us to expect real prices during the first year following a cyclical peak in price to average about $5.02 below the price trend. The average impact for the second year of the cycle is about $5.02 *above* the trend. The

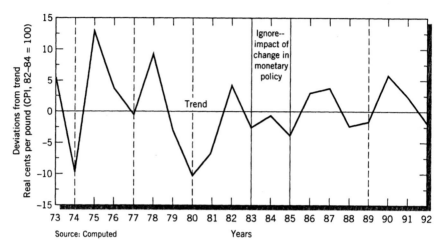

FIGURE 7.2. Deviations from trend in real live hog prices, seven markets, United States, 1973–92.

SOURCE: Computed.

average cyclical impact in the third year following a peak in price would be $2.13 above the trend value. In the fourth year following a price peak—when there *is* a fourth year—prices would be expected to average about $2.22 below the trend.

THE USE OF MOVING AVERAGES IN MEASURING CYCLES _____

In order to get our cyclical hog price pattern using a trend, we were confronted with an unhappy choice. We could limit ourselves to the period since 1973—as we did when we selected a time period for the trend. But that choice allowed us only four complete cycles from which to make estimates of the impact of the cycle upon prices. Two of those four cycles could be argued to be a single cycle, leaving us with only three complete cycles with which to work. Our second option was to use the entire 43-year period, with the possibility of eliminating the very unstable 1971–76 period from consideration.

The use of the entire 43-year period with the elimination of the 1971–76 period involves placing much greater emphasis on the period prior to the birth of most of today's college students than upon more recent history. As a result, it is difficult to place much confidence in the estimates we might derive from this procedure for estimating cyclical price impacts. A third difficulty in using the longer-term trend for analysis of

Year	Trend Value	Real Price Barrows & Gilts, 7 Major Mkts. (cts/lb)	Expected Price[a] (cts/lb)	Actual Less Expected Price	Cyclical Deviations				
					1st Yr	2nd Yr	3rd Yr	4th Yr	5th Yr
1973	73	$90.58	$85.44	+5.13					
1974	74	71.19	80.73	−9.54	−9.54				
1975	75	89.81	76.34	+13.47		+13.47			
1976	76	75.76	72.24	+3.52			+3.52		
1977	77	67.77	68.41	−0.64	−0.64				
1978	78	74.37	64.83	+9.54		+9.54			
1979	79	57.93	61.47	−3.54			−3.54		
1980	80	47.91	58.33	−10.42	−10.42				
1981	81	48.46	55.39	−6.93		−6.93			
1982	82	57.07	52.63	+4.44			+4.44		
1983	83	47.52	50.04	−2.52 }	Eliminate from Consideration—				
1984	84	46.86	47.60	−0.74 }	Impact of Altered Monetary Policy Focus				
1985	85	41.36	45.31	−3.95	−3.95				
1986	86	46.16	43.15	+3.00		+3.00			
1987	87	44.93	41.13	+3.80			+3.80		
1988	88	36.68	39.21	−2.53				−2.53	
1989	89	35.51	37.41	−1.90	−1.90				
1990	90	41.66	35.71	+5.95		+5.95			
1991	91	36.48	34.10	+2.38			+2.38		
1992	92	30.66	32.58	−1.92				−1.92	
Average Values (Five Cycles)[b]					−5.02	+5.02	+2.13	−2.22	

[a] Assumes that 1993 will be the beginning of a new price cycle.

[b] Expected price is calculated from $\log P_i = 9.6977 - 4.16783 \log T_i$, when $T_i = 73$ in 1973, 74 in 1974, and so on.

Source. Computed.

the hog cycle is that some entire price cycles are either above or below the trend. Further, the very sharp downward movement in prices since the mid-1970s creates a situation in which the last two cycles lie completely below the trend while the previous two (or three) are completely above the trend.

There is an alternative method for calculating trends for use in cyclical analyses that does provide some relief from the difficulties previously noted. That method is the use of "centered" moving averages. A moving average trend—used for purposes of trend analysis as such—has major limitations in that it is virtually impossible to anticipate when the moving average trend is apt to change directions. Further, because of the "centering" requirement, one is always some years in arrears in the calculation of such a trend, compounding the problem of anticipating directional changes. However, for purposes of cyclical analysis, the moving average trend does have some advantages over the regression based trends that we have generally used in our analyses. A major advantage is that a moving average trend takes into account the impact of events such as the Russian Grain Deal and the onset of the energy crisis, "spreading" the impacts of these events over longer periods of time.

In constructing a moving average trend for use in the analysis of cycles, the data periods used in the moving average should be uneven in number and as near the normal length of the cycle (or multiples of that period) as possible. The use of an uneven number of data periods accommodates the centering of the moving average. The moving average is "centered" on the basis of the concept that today's events are not independent of the events of previous periods, and that future events will be affected by the current situation.

For our analysis of the hog cycle, the normal length of the cycle appears to be three–five years. The average over the entire 43-year period is three and one-half years. When annual data are used, there are some cases of a three-year cycle and some of a five-year cycle. It is possible that at least some of these three- or five-year cycles arise from a cycle of 42 to 54 months rather than a cycle that is in precise multiples of 12-month periods. If we were using quarterly or monthly data—which we could do—we could look at 47- and 49- or 45- and 51-month moving averages and refine our cycle down to a quarterly or monthly basis. In the case of a commodity such as broilers, with a very short reproductive span, a monthly analysis of the cycle is essential.

The construction of a moving average is a simple—albeit a tedious— matter. Since we have identified three and one-half–four years as the normal cycle in hog production and prices, and since an uneven number of data periods is required for centering the calculations, we could use either a three-year and/or a five-year moving average trend for our cyclical analysis. The problem of centering a moving average with an even number of data periods in that moving average can be dealt with, although the adjustment does add to the complexity of the computations.

The conceptual framework for the moving average and for centering the moving average trend is that the circumstances in the current year are to some extent affected by circumstances in an earlier period. The current year's circumstances also have some implications for a future period. A good case in point is the very disruptive circumstances of the early 1970s. The impact of the Russian Grain Deal and of the onset of the Energy Crisis were to some extent moderated by the expectations that came from the earlier period. But the impacts of these disruptions lingered well beyond the time that they became apparent in the data. These temporal linkages are captured by the moving average.

A three-year moving average would be calculated first by constructing a three-year moving total (see Table 7.2). Simply sum the total of the values for the first three years of information, posting the results of that calculation at the middle (or second) year. Subtract the value for the first year from that total and add the value for the fourth year, posting the result at the middle of *that* three-year interval or at the third year of the data. Continue this procedure until the moving total has been calculated for the entire range of the data.

You will note that in the case of a three-year moving total, one year is lost at each end of the data. Two years would be lost at each end of a five-year moving total and four years at each end of a nine-year moving total. This loss of data at the ends of the series is the reason that one is always in arrears by some period in anticipating directional changes in a moving average trend.

Once the moving total is completely calculated, the calculation of the moving average is simply a matter of dividing each value in the moving

TABLE 7.2. Computational Procedure for Calculating a Three-Year Moving Total

Year	Real Hog Price	Three-Yr Moving Total	Elements of the Computation
1950	$76.91		
1951	79.13	$224.33	($76.91 + 79.13 + 68.29 = $224.33)
1952	68.29	229.60	($224.33 − 76.91 + 82.18 = $229.60)
1953	82.18	233.22	($229.60 − 79.13 + 82.75 = $233.22)
1954	82.75		

total by the number of data periods (in this case, the number of years) going into the make-up of that total.

The mechanics of calculating a moving total for an even number of data periods are complicated by the need to center the result of the calculation. The conceptual basis, however, is exactly the same as for the uneven number of data period moving total. A four-year moving total, using the same information that was used in the three-year moving total example is presented in Table 7.3. All that is involved in the four-year moving average is to add the values for the three center years to half the value for the year immediately preceding the three center years and half the value for the year following those three years, posting the resulting calculation on the middle year of the original three-year interval. That is, the four-year moving total price for 1952 would be calculated:

$$\begin{matrix}\text{four-year moving} \\ \text{total for 1952}\end{matrix} = 1950/2 + 1951 + 1952 + 1953 + 1954/2 \quad (7.2)$$

The result of this calculation is that one "loses" two years of information at the beginning of the period for which the moving total and moving average are calculated and another two years at the end of the period. Once the moving total has been calculated for the entire range of the data, the calculation of a four-year moving average is simply a matter of dividing all the moving totals by four.

When the moving average calculation is completed, the deviations between the moving average trend and the observed raw values of the data can be calculated. From this point forward, the estimation of cyclical values is identical to the procedure we discussed for the linear trend.

Tables 7.4 and 7.5 show the calculations for the periodograms measuring the price cycle based on the four-year and eight-year moving averages for real live hog prices. When the moving average prices are compared with the actual prices observed (Figure 7.3 and 7.4), it is apparent that the four-year moving average follows the gross movements in the price series that were ignored by the calculated trends. The eight-year moving average (which represents a multiple of a four-year cycle postulated for hog prices) likewise follows these gross movements, albeit at a somewhat "dampened" rate. In no case does a cycle fall completely above or completely below either of these moving average trends.

Either the four-year or eight-year moving average of hog prices is a defensible basis for a periodogram analysis measuring the cycle in hog prices. Because of the historical relationship between beef and pork prices and because the eight-year moving average very closely approximates the phasing of the cycle in cattle prices, the eight-year moving average might provide the most dependable measure.

A periodogram analysis of the cycle, based on the four-year and eight-year moving averages gives estimates of cyclical price expectations that

TABLE 7.3. Computational Procedure for Calculating a Four-Year Moving Total

Year	Real Hog Price	Four-Yr Moving Total	Elements of the Computation
1950	$76.91		
1951	79.13		
1952	68.29	$309.44	($76.91/2 + 79.13 + 68.29 + 82.18 + 82.75/2 = $309.44)
1953	82.18	$301.17	($79.13/2 + 68.29 + 82.18 + 82.75 + 56.71/2 = $301.17)
1954	82.75	$283.05	($68.29/2 + 82.18 + 82.75 + 56.71 + 54.52/2 = $283.05)
1955	56.71		
1956	54.52		

TABLE 7.4. Periodogram Calculations for Measuring the Cycle in Real Prices for Live Hogs, Four-Year Moving Average Basis

Year	Real Price	Four-Yr Mvg Avg Price	Real Pr Less Four-Yr Mvg Avg	Year of Cycle				
				1st Yr	2nd Yr	3rd Yr	4th Yr	5th Yr
1950	76.91							
1951	79.08							
1952	68.29	77.35	-9.06	-9.06				
1953	82.20	75.28	6.92		6.92			
1954	82.74	70.76	11.98			11.98		
1955	56.70	66.88	-10.18				10.18	
1956	54.51	63.13	-8.62	-8.62				
1957	64.95	60.73	4.22		4.22			
1958	70.00	59.83	10.17			10.17		
1959	50.20	58.80	-8.60	-8.60				
1960	53.86	56.04	-2.19		-2.19			
1961	57.33	54.24	3.09			3.09		
1962	55.58	53.68	1.90				1.90	
1963	50.21	54.38	-4.18					-4.18
1964	49.34	57.75	-8.41	-8.41				
1965	67.49	60.82	6.67		6.67			
1966	72.37	62.52	9.85			9.85		
1967	57.99	62.89	-4.90				-4.90	
1968	55.14	60.56	-5.42	-5.42				
1969	64.66	57.02	7.64		7.64			
1970	56.51	56.54	-0.03			-0.03		

Year							
1971	45.54	60.85	-15.31	-15.31			
1972	63.72	65.92	-2.20		-2.20		
1973	90.58	73.29	17.29			17.29	
1974	71.19	80.33	-9.14	-9.14			
1975	89.81	78.99	10.83		10.83		
1976	75.76	76.53	-0.77			-0.77	
1977	67.77	72.95	-5.17	-5.17			
1978	74.37	65.48	8.89		8.89		
1979	57.93	59.58	-1.65			-1.65	
1980	47.91	55.01	-7.09	-7.09			
1981	48.46	51.54	-3.08		-3.08		
1982	57.07	50.11	6.96			6.96	
1983	47.52	49.09	-1.57				-1.57
1984	46.86	46.84	0.02				0.02
1985	41.36	45.15	-3.79	-3.79			
1986	46.16	43.55	2.60		2.60		
1987	44.93	41.55	3.38			3.38	
1988	36.68	40.26	-3.58				-3.58
1989	35.51	39.05	-3.54				
1990	41.66	38.63	-3.03				
1991	36.48						
1992	30.66						
Average Cyclical Variation				-8.06	4.03	6.03	-3.69 / -2.08

Source. Computed.

TABLE 7.5. Periodogram Calculations for Measuring the Cycle in Real Prices for Live Hogs, Eight-Year Moving Average Basis

Year	Real Price	Mvg. Avg. Price	Less 8-Yr Mvg Avg	Year of Cycle				
				1st Yr	2nd Yr	3rd Yr	4th Yr	5th Yr
1950	76.91							
1951	79.08							
1952	68.29							
1953	82.20							
1954	82.74	70.24	12.50					
1955	56.70	68.00	-11.30					
1956	54.51	65.30	-10.79	-10.79				
1957	64.95	62.84	2.11		2.11			
1958	70.00	59.59	10.41			10.41		
1959	50.20	57.49	-7.29	-7.29				
1960	53.86	56.76	-2.90		-2.90			
1961	57.33	56.59	0.74			0.74		
1962	55.58	56.90	-1.32				-1.32	
1963	50.21	57.53	-7.32					-7.32
1964	49.34	58.10	-8.76	-8.76				
1965	67.49	58.64	8.85		8.85			
1966	72.37	59.16	13.21			13.21		
1967	57.99	58.92	-0.93				-0.93	
1968	55.14	59.53	-4.39	-4.39				
1969	64.66	61.87	2.79		2.79			
1970	56.51	63.24	-6.73			-6.73		

Year								
1971	45.54	65.16	−19.62	−19.62				
1972	63.72	68.43	−4.71		−4.71			
1973	90.58	69.92	20.66			20.66		
1974	71.19	71.23	−0.04	−0.04				
1975	89.81	73.12	16.70		16.70			
1976	75.76	72.91	2.86			2.86		
1977	67.77	69.28	−1.51	−1.51				
1978	74.37	65.77	8.60		8.60			
1979	57.93	62.24	−4.31			−4.31		
1980	47.91	57.79	−9.88	−9.88				
1981	48.46	54.34	−5.88		−5.88			
1982	57.07	50.92	6.15			6.15		
1983	47.52	48.35	−0.83				−0.83	
1984	46.86	46.83	0.03					0.03
1985	41.36	45.32	−3.96	−3.96				
1986	46.16	43.55	2.61		2.61			
1987	44.93	41.89	3.04			3.04		
1988	36.68	40.19	−3.51				−3.51	
1989	35.51							
1990	41.66							
1991	36.48							
1992	30.66							
Average Cyclical Variation				−6.91	4.46	4.34	−1.92	−3.68

Source. Computed.

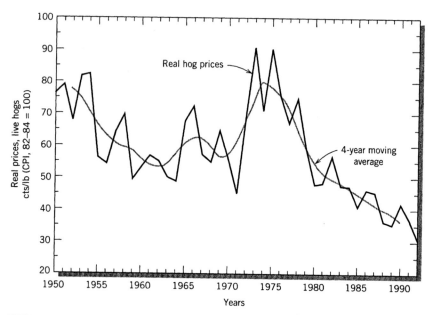

FIGURE 7.3. Real prices for barrows and gilts, seven major U.S. markets, 1950–92, with the four-year moving average price.

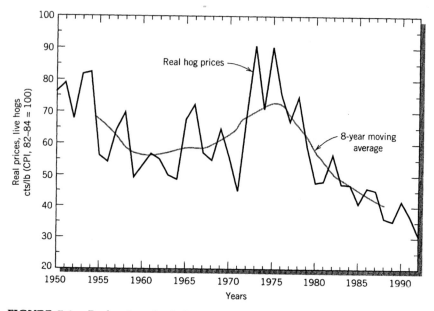

FIGURE 7.4. Real prices for barrows and gilts, seven major U.S. markets, 1950–92, with the eight-year moving average price.
SOURCE: Computed.

are a bit different in magnitude when compared with the estimates based on the 1973–90 full-logarithmic trend. This is precisely what one would expect, since the moving averages follow the gross movements in price. The relationship among the various years of the cycle is generally comparable for all three approaches. But with the shorter-term trend-based estimate, the expected positive cyclical price deviation during the third year of the cycle is less than that expected during the second year.

When we compare the results of our moving average estimates, we see nine (or ten, if we define the 1974–80 period to be two cycles) full hog production cycles between 1950 and 1990, with a loss of information at the beginning of the period and at the end. But in the case of the eight-year moving average, there were an additional two years at the beginning of the period that were lost because there was not a full cycle for inclusion in the periodogram analysis. Thus, with the eight-year moving average, there were eight (or nine) full cycles in a 30-year period, with an average length of three and one-half to four years. There are three cycles between 1959 and 1968 in which, based on the raw real prices, there could be some argument about either the beginning year or the ending year. The cycle, which began in 1959, could be argued to have ended in either 1963 or 1964. And the cycle, which began either in 1963 or 1964, could be argued to have ended in either 1967 or 1968.

In both cases, there are substantial differences in the deviation from the eight-year moving average trend for the two years in question. The fact that the price deviations continued to move away from the moving average in 1964 and in 1968 argues for these years as the designated ends of these cycles.

A third issue that was alluded to early in this chapter was whether the 1974–80 period comprised one or two cycles in hog prices. The trend analysis does not really give much help in clarifying this question. But both moving average analyses suggest very clearly that this period most probably comprises two cycles. The very substantial decline in the value of the moving average from 1977 to 1978 and the resulting positive deviation of the observed price from the moving average price in 1978 suggest that there are indeed two cycles during this period.

Appendix _____

The purpose of this appendix to Chapter 7 is to provide information regarding the manner in which standard spreadsheet computer software may be utilized in measuring cyclical variation, computing moving averages, and so on. The instructions provided are in terms of either LOTUS 1-2-3 or for the Lotus mode of QUATTROPRO software. However, virtually any spreadsheet software may be utilized in the manner shown.

Measuring Cyclical Variations

Deviation from a Trend   The alternative approaches for the calculation of trends were discussed in the Appendix to Chapter 5. Once the trend is calculated, the trend equation may be used to calculate the "expected" values of the dependent variable (i.e., $\hat{Y}$). Table 7A.1 shows the figures upon which Table 7.1 and Figure 7.2 in the body of Chapter 7 were based. The letters at the head of the columns and the numbers in the first column provide the basis for the Column–Row designation of the cells in the computer spreadsheet.

   To calculate the expected prices for the full Logarithmic trend in real hog prices, use the following commands:

   With the cursor in Cell E1, type the following:

   +9.699678-4.16894*C1, Press "Enter." The Logarithm of the expected price (1.93161) will appear in Cell E1.

   Move the cursor to Cell F1 and type the following:

   +10^E1. Common logarithms are by definition the power to which the number 10 must be raised to achieve the number associated with the logarithm. (Since $10^2 = 100$, the logarithm of 100 would be 2.00000) The command +10^E1 directs the computer to raise 10 to the power of the logarithm in Cell E1. Press "Enter." The price ($85.43) associated with the logarithm in Cell E1 will appear in Cell F1.

   Move the cursor to Cell G1. Type the following:

   +D1-F1. The difference (+5.15) between the actually observed price for 1973 ($90.58) and the expected price for 1973 (85.43) will appear in Cell G1.

   Return the cursor to cell E1 and execute the following commands:

   Press (/) to activate the menu. Select "Copy."

   Move the cursor to Cell G1. Cells E1, F1, and G1 will be illuminated, indicating that the formulae in these cells will be copied to the range to be selected. Press "Enter."

   Cell E1 will be illuminated. Move the cursor to Cell E2 and press the period to anchor the formulae to be copied.

   Move the cursor to cell E18. Cells E2 through E18 will be illuminated,

TABLE 7A.1. Measuring Cyclical Deviations from a Calculated Trend

Row	(A) Year	(B) T_i	(C) Trend Value $\text{Log}\,T_i$	(D) Real Prices Barrows and Gilts Seven Major Mkts (cts/lb)	(E) Expected Prices $\text{Log}\,P_i^a$	(F) Expected Prices P_i (cts/lb)	(G) Difference in Actual and Expected (cts/lb)
1	1973	73	1.86332	$90.58	1.93166	$85.44	+5.14
2	1974	74	1.86923	71.19	—	—	—
3	1975	75	1.87506	89.81	—	—	—
4	1976	76	1.88081	75.76	—	—	—
5	1977	77	1.88649	67.77	—	—	—
6	1978	78	1.89209	74.37	—	—	—
.	.	.	.	.	.	.	.
.	.	.	.	.	.	.	.
.	.	.	.	.	.	.	.
18	1990	90	1.95424	41.66	—	—	—

[a] The equation from which $\text{log}\,P_i$ is calculated is $\text{Log}\,P_i = 9.6977 - 4.1678\,\text{Log}\,T_i$, where $T_i = 73$ in 1973.

131

indicating that the formulae in Cells E1, F1, and G1 will all be copied through Row 18. Press "Enter."

The results of the calculations will appear in Columns E, F, and G, in Rows 2 through 18. The differences in Column G may then be used to estimate the cyclical variations by years of the cycle.

Constructing Moving Averages:

Table 7A.2 at the left below shows the information needed for constructing the moving average prices in Chapter 7. To calculate the three-year moving average, use the following commands:

Remember, the first and last year of data are lost when calculating a three-year moving average. Thus, Cell C21 will be left blank. With the cursor in Cell C22, type

(+ B21 + B22 + B23)/3 and press "Enter."

Press slash (/) to activate the menu and select "Copy." Press "Return."

TABLE 7A.2. Construction of Three-Year, Four-Year and Nine-Year Moving Average Real Prices for Live Hogs

R o w	(A) Year	(B) Real Price	Columns (C) Three-Yr Mvg Av Price	(D) Four-Yr Mvg Av Price	(E) Nine-Yr Mvg Av Price
21	1950	76.91			
22	1951	79.08	74.65		
23	1952	68.29	—	77.35	
24	1953	82.20	—	—	
25	1954	82.74	—	—	70.24
26	1955	56.70	—	—	—
.	.	.	.	.	.
.	.	.	.	.	.
.	.	.	.	.	.
36	1985	41.36	—	—	—
37	1986	46.16	—	—	—
38	1987	44.93	—	—	
39	1988	36.68	—	—	
40	1989	35.51	—		
41	1990	41.66			

Move the cursor to Cell C23 and press the period to lock the formula in Cell C22 into the range to be copied.

Move the cursor to Cell C40 (remember, Cell C41 will be lost because of the three-year moving average). Cells C23 through C40 will be illuminated.

Press "Enter." The three-year moving average values will appear in Column C.

In calculating the four-year moving average, it must be remembered that two years of information will be lost at the beginning and end of the period. To calculate the four-year moving average, place the cursor in Cell D23 and use the following commands:

Type (+ 0.5*B21 + B22 + B23 + B24 + 0.5*B25)/4. This formula instructs the computer to use half the first-year price, the full price for the following three years and half the fifth year price in calculating the four-year moving average. Press "Enter." The four-year moving average price for 1952 (77.35) will appear in Cell D23.

Press "slash" (/) to activate the menu and select "Copy." Press "Return."

Move the cursor to Cell D24 and press the period to anchor the range within which the formula in Cell D23 is to be copied.

Move the cursor to Cell D39 (the numbers in D40 and D41 are lost because of the four-year moving average). Cells D24 through D39 will be illuminated. Press "Enter" and the values for the four-year moving average price will appear in Column D.

The nine-year moving average price may be calculated in precisely the same manner as were the three-year and four-year moving averages. The only difference will be that four data periods will be lost on each end of the period during which the moving average is calculated. Thus, the nine-year moving average price calculations would begin in Cell E25 and end in Cell E37.

The differences between the observed real price and the moving average prices may be calculated in precisely the same manner as was shown in Table 7A.1 for use in estimating the average seasonal pattern for the sequential years of the price cycle.

CHAPTER **8**

Price
Movements
Over Time—
Seasonality

In Chapters 6 and 7, we discussed the cyclical price phenomena in agriculture, recognizing that cycles in prices for agricultural products are rooted in the biologically induced production cycles. What we normally think of as a cyclical movement occurs over a span of several production periods. We recognized that a fair rule of thumb, at least in animal agriculture, was to expect a cycle to be at least quadruple the period of time required from birth to first reproduction.

There is a special case of cyclical price movement that is of a nature different from the sorts of cycles previously discussed. This special case is the regular movement that is observed *within* a production period, which is related to the normal patterns of temperature and precipitation that occur throughout a year. This special case of cyclical price movement is, of course, the phenomenon of price seasonality.

Virtually all agricultural commodities are characterized by at least some degree of seasonality in the availability of products, and a consequent seasonality in the prices those products command. This seasonality, like cycles, frequently originates in the biological realities that regulate production. Most annual crops such as coarse grains and oil seeds are planted in the spring for harvest in the fall. Some—such as many of the small grains—are planted in the fall for harvest during the summer. But regardless of the crop, most have a fairly tightly time-constrained period of harvest, following which there is no additional product until the next harvest. We have already identified one of the functions of the price system to be the rationing of such products over the time between harvests to insure that the goods are available between harvests.

Even the agricultural commodities—the biology of which man has been able to direct to exhibit the characteristic of a continuous flow of production—exhibit seasonality in their degree of availability. Milk, for example, is produced throughout the year. But there is a spring "flush" associated with the rapid growth of green pastures in the spring and the natural biological tendency of cows to calve in the spring. By careful management, farm managers can regulate at least to some extent the timing with which their livestock get romantic, thus assuring some flow of production throughout the year. But left to her own devices, Mamma Nature will insure that the bulk of animal reproduction occurs in the spring.

Even though humankind has been able through genetic and nutritional technology to insure that eggs are produced the year round, Nature still encourages laying hens to increase egg production in the spring in order that the chicks can be mature by the time cold weather arrives. The annual horticultural crops such as lettuce, and tomatoes, that can be produced throughout the year in Florida, California, and the Rio Grande Valley, have seasonal increases in availability as other areas enter production during the spring and summer months. Beef and pork can be produced throughout the year, but these products are also subject to the seasonal patterns induced by seasonality in reproductive periods and feed supplies. Those influences are ultimately reflected in seasonal production patterns and consequent seasonal patterns in price.

Some agricultural products are also subject to seasonality in demand. Steaks and chops, for example, seem to be in greater demand during the summer cook-out season. Many livestock and meat price analysts routinely anticipate price strength with the advent of warm weather. Turkeys exhibit a dramatic seasonal peak in demand at Thanksgiving, with a secondary peak at Christmas, and a tertiary peak at Easter. Ice cream exhibits a classic period of seasonal demand increases in the summer. Perishable products, such as fresh fruits, must be moved to market almost without regard to prices when they are in season. (If you don't sell it, you smell it.) If the price is sufficient to cover the cost of harvest and marketing, the product will typically be harvested and offered for sale. The nature of consumer demand is such that consumers will utilize an increased volume of almost any product, but if and only if the price for that product is reduced. Thus, early in the season, when a commodity such as peaches or strawberries begins to become available, the early-season product commands very high prices. In the early part of the season, only those people with intense desire for the product and adequate levels of purchasing power will purchase the very limited quantities that are available. But as the availability of the product increases seasonally, the price will decline and people with less intense desires will begin to purchase. As the season's full production becomes available, the prices typically erode substantially.

The producers of perishable agricultural products are well aware of the patterns of price seasonality and will attempt to seek "windows" of seasonal price opportunity. Tomato producers in southeast Arkansas, for example, will attempt to set tomato plants so that the first market-ready tomatoes are harvested the first week in June. This coincides with the normal decline in the availability of the late spring Florida tomato crop, but leads by about a month the normal early summer crop from California. If Florida should happen to get a freeze in late January, Florida tomato producers will be forced to replant and the late spring Florida tomato crop will be at its peak about the time the Arkansas tomatoes become available. Delayed plantings in Arkansas are not an answer since delayed Arkansas plantings would get to market on top of the early summer California crop. The result is the loss of the Arkansas producer's expectation of a "window" of seasonal price opportunity.

The storable crops such as grains, oil seeds, and cotton have seasonal price patterns that at least theoretically cover the cost of storage and handling over the period until the next harvest. The actual price pattern during any single year may vary widely from the "normal" seasonal pattern as the marketing agencies that are normally involved in the processes of price discovery evaluate developments and revise expectations of future conditions. "Weather" markets in response to very favorable reports of crop conditions or to reports of drought in key production areas may overshadow the normal seasonal patterns. In recent years, rumors, and occasionally the actuality, of major grain or oil seed purchases by Russia or the People's Republic of China have caused episodic variations from normal seasonal price patterns. For these reasons, it is important that an extended period of years be utilized in seasonal price analyses in order to isolate the true seasonal price period.

During the early part of the 1970s, when the United States became a major participant in the world market for wheat, the seasonal price pattern for wheat was that prices were typically lowest at the beginning of harvest in June (Figure 8.1). Those prices would increase seasonally through mid-October when export commitments were generally completed. Wheat prices would taper off through November when the corn harvest increased the availability of all grains. In December, as wheat

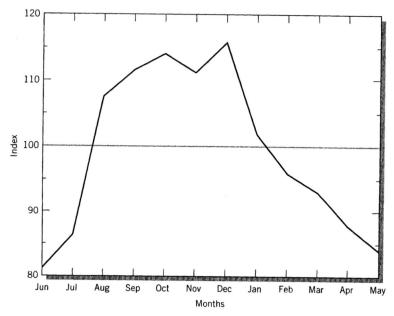

FIGURE 8.1. Wheat—Seasonal index of prices received by farmers, United States, 1971–75 crops.

SOURCE: *Agricultural Statistics, USDA, 1977.*

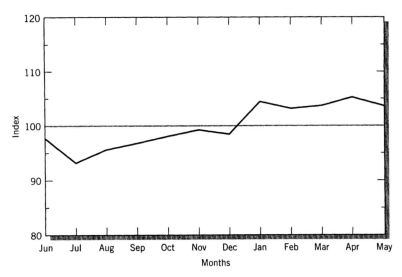

FIGURE 8.2. Wheat—Seasonal index of prices received by farmers, United States, 1981–1985 crops.

SOURCE: Computed from information in *Agricultural Statistics*, USDA, 1986.

producers began to make plans to hold a part of their wheat inventories until after January 1 in order to spread their incomes into two tax years, the volume of wheat going to market would be reduced. The reduction in wheat marketings would cause prices to rise to a December seasonal peak. Then after the first of the year, wheat prices would decline fairly rapidly as producers released wheat to generate the cash needed for spring farming operations.

In the first half of the 1980s, the seasonal price pattern for wheat changed dramatically (Figure 8.2). Several consecutive years of federal budget deficits in the neighborhood of $200 billion had created a rapid escalation in real interest rates in order to attract the overseas funds needed to finance the deficit. These overseas funds were necessary to avoid aggravating an already serious problem of inflation. The consequent bidding for dollars on the part of foreign investors drove the value of the dollar higher against the other major currencies, causing U.S. products to be dramatically more expensive in terms of those currencies.

Wheat exports—and domestic wheat prices—declined precipitously. The outcome of the effort to finance the deficit with overseas funds was that the domestic availability of U.S. wheat became so abundant that wheat was priced as a *feed* grain rather than a *food* grain, competing with corn for domestic markets. The result was that the seasonal price low at harvest time persisted, but the seasonal price pattern for wheat emulated that of corn, rising seasonally throughout the marketing year until grain from the next harvest became available. Also, the *amplitude* of the seasonal pattern was substantially reduced, again reflecting the feed-grain status of wheat.

MEASURING SEASONALITY _____

The Simple Average Approach

How does one go about defining a seasonal price pattern? There are a variety of methods for estimating price seasonality. Probably the easiest and quickest—and also the least accurate—method is the use of a simple average. If we continue with our wheat example, we can chart the monthly average wheat prices received by farmers over the marketing periods for the 1984–1991 wheat crops (Figure 8.3). We can see that there is a substantial downward movement in these prices for the 1984–86 crops and another general down move for the 1988–1990 crops. The first of these downward price moves reflects changes in the currency exchange value of the dollar circumstance that we discussed earlier,[1] and the second most probably results from changes in the 1990 Farm Bill. We can also see the general pattern of low prices early in the season, with prices rising through the marketing year until the approach of a new harvest. But we know that along with the changing value of the dollar in the currency exchanges, there was a total of more than 30 percent in domestic economic inflation over this seven-year period. Thus, before we go any further, we need to adjust these prices for inflation.

Table 8.1 shows the "raw" monthly wheat prices over the 1984–1991 period and Table 8.2 shows the Consumer Price Index for this period.[2] Dividing the raw price for any month by the corresponding value for CPI gives a "real" wheat price for that month. The results of this calculation are shown in Table 8.3 and Figure 8.4. We can see that the two down price moves are even stronger in the real wheat prices than was

---

[1] The upward price movement in 1986–1988 was most probably largely the result of the conference of the seven industrialized nations (Japan, the United Kingdom, France, the United States, West Germany, Canada, and Italy) during which it was agreed that these nations would take the action necessary to reduce the value of the U.S. dollar as compared with other currencies.

[2] It will be noted that each of these "years" in Tables 8.1 and 8.3 begin with the month of June, reflecting the reality that the wheat crop, which is harvested beginning in June of any given year, is marketed over the period through May of the following year when the next harvest begins. Thus, the "crop year" reflects the period over which any crop is marketed.

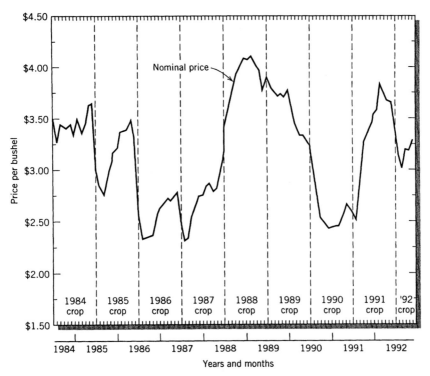

FIGURE 8.3. WHEAT—prices received by farmers, by months, by crop marketing year, United States, 1984–1992.

SOURCE: *Agricultural Prices, 1990 Summary*, NASS-ASB, USDA, June 1991.

the case in terms of nominal (or raw) wheat prices. But the general pattern of low prices early in the season rising through the marketing year persists.

If we chart the monthly real prices for each individual year in Table 8.3, "stacking" the years on top of one another, we see the same general pattern in all years except for 1989–1990 and 1990–1991—a period of dramatic price declines associated with changes in price supports included in the 1990 farm bill (Figure 8.5). These price declines most probably mask the normal seasonal pattern, since the latter part of the 1990–1991 marketing year demonstrates a resumption of the normal pattern.

To calculate a seasonal price indexed based on a simple average calculation, we would simply array the prices by months for each of the crop years, calculating a eight-year average price for each month and for the entire period (Table 8.4). Then using the eight-year annual average price as a base, we could construct our index by dividing each eight-year average monthly price by the overall eight-year average. The resulting

TABLE 8.1. Wheat—Monthly Average Prices Received by Farmers, by Marketing Year, United States, 1984–1992 Crops

Mktg Year	Jun	Jul	Aug	Sep	Oct	Nov	Dec	Jan	Feb	Mar	Apr	May	Annual Average
						(Dollars per Bushel)							
1984–85	3.46	3.29	3.43	3.43	3.43	3.45	3.38	3.50	3.40	3.49	3.63	3.66	3.46
1985–86	3.09	2.93	2.89	3.01	3.10	3.22	3.25	3.38	3.38	3.38	3.43	3.30	3.20
1986–87	2.47	2.25	2.26	2.28	2.30	2.43	2.49	2.53	2.58	2.57	2.63	2.66	2.45
1987–88	2.44	2.32	2.36	2.53	2.62	2.69	2.70	2.75	2.79	2.74	2.79	2.97	2.64
1988–89	3.37	3.50	3.61	3.74	3.88	3.94	4.02	4.03	4.07	4.03	4.01	3.72	3.83
1989–90	3.85	3.78	3.74	3.72	3.75	3.72	3.79	3.71	3.56	3.49	3.49	3.40	3.61
1990–91	3.08	2.79	2.58	2.46	2.43	2.39	2.40	2.42	2.43	2.53	2.63	2.61	2.56
1991–92	2.55	2.50	2.63	2.80	3.07	3.25	3.44	3.54	3.78	3.72	3.65	3.64	3.21
1992–93	3.43	3.15	3.01	3.20	3.21	3.29	3.31						

Source. Agricultural Prices, 1990 Annual Summary and Monthly Issues for 1991, NASS-ASB-USDA, June 1991.

TABLE 8.2. Consumer Price Index (1982–84 = 100), by Months, United States 1984–92

Year	Jan	Feb	Mar	Apr	May	Jun	Jul	Aug	Sep	Oct	Nov	Dec	Average
1984						103.8	104.1	104.5	105.0	105.3	105.3	105.4	103.9
1985	105.6	106.0	106.5	106.9	107.3	107.6	107.8	108.0	108.4	108.7	109.1	109.4	107.6
1986	109.7	109.4	108.9	108.7	109.0	109.5	109.6	109.8	110.3	110.4	110.5	110.6	109.7
1987	111.2	111.6	112.1	112.7	113.1	113.5	113.8	114.4	115.0	115.3	115.4	115.4	113.6
1988	115.7	116.0	116.5	117.1	117.5	118.0	118.5	119.0	119.8	120.2	120.3	120.5	118.3
1989	121.1	121.6	122.3	123.1	123.8	124.1	124.4	124.6	125.0	125.6	125.9	126.1	124.0
1990	127.4	128.0	128.7	128.9	129.2	129.9	130.4	131.6	132.7	133.5	133.8	133.8	130.7
1991	134.6	134.8	135.0	135.2	135.6	136.0	136.2	136.6	137.2	137.4	137.7	137.9	136.2
1992	138.1	138.6	139.3	139.5	139.7	140.2	140.5	140.9	141.3	141.8	142.0	142.3	140.4

Source. Basic Statistics-Price Indexes, Commodities, Producer, Cost of Living, Standard and Poor's Statistical Service, Standard and Poor's Corporation, August 1974 and subsequent issues.

TABLE 8.3. Wheat—Real Monthly Prices Received by Farmers, United States, 1984–1985 Through 1992–93 Crop Year

Mktg Year	Jun	Jul	Aug	Sep	Oct	Nov	Dec	Jan	Feb	Mar	Apr	May	Annual Average
						(1982–84 Dollars per Bushel)							
1984–85	3.33	3.16	3.28	3.27	3.26	3.28	3.21	3.31	3.21	3.28	3.40	3.41	3.28
1985–86	2.87	2.72	2.67	2.78	2.85	2.65	2.97	3.08	3.09	3.10	3.16	3.03	2.94
1986–87	2.26	2.05	2.06	2.07	2.08	2.20	2.25	2.28	2.31	2.29	2.33	2.35	2.21
1987–88	2.15	2.04	2.06	2.20	2.27	2.33	2.34	2.38	2.41	2.35	2.38	2.53	2.29
1988–89	2.86	2.95	3.03	3.12	3.23	3.28	3.34	3.33	3.35	3.30	3.26	3.00	3.17
1989–90	3.10	3.04	3.00	2.98	2.99	2.95	3.01	2.91	2.78	2.71	2.71	2.63	2.90
1990–91	2.39	2.14	1.96	1.85	1.82	1.79	1.79	1.80	1.80	1.87	1.95	1.92	1.92
1991–92	1.88	1.84	1.93	2.04	2.23	2.36	2.51	2.56	2.73	2.67	2.62	2.61	1.92
1992–93	2.45	2.24	2.14	2.26	2.26	2.32	2.33	2.56	2.73	2.67	2.62	2.61	2.33

Source. Computed from Tables 8.1 and 8.2.

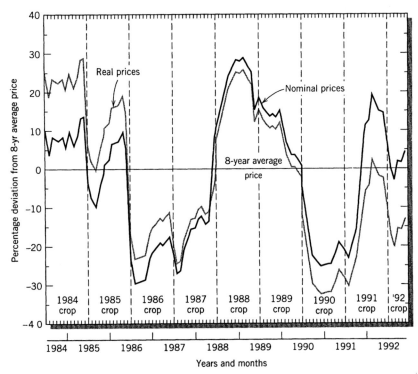

FIGURE 8.4. WHEAT—Raw and Real prices received by farmers, expressed as a percentage deviation from the seven-year average price, by month and crop marketing year, United States, 1984–1992.

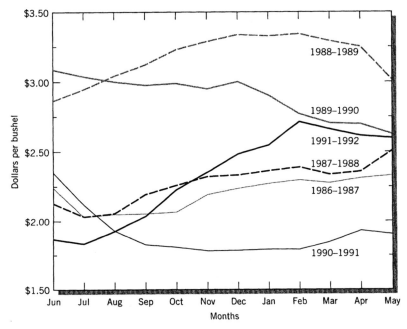

FIGURE 8.5. WHEAT—prices received by United States farmers, by months, by crop marketing years, 1986–1992.

TABLE 8.4. Wheat—Calculation of the Seasonal Index in Real Monthly Prices Received by Farmers, United States, 1984–1991 Crops

Crop Year	Jun	Jul	Aug	Sep	Oct	Nov	Dec	Jan	Feb	Mar	Apr	May	Annual Average
						(1982–1984 Dollars per Bushel)							
1984–85	3.33	3.16	3.28	3.27	3.26	3.28	3.21	3.31	3.21	3.28	3.40	3.41	3.28
1985–86	2.87	2.72	2.67	2.78	2.85	2.95	2.97	3.08	3.09	3.10	3.16	3.03	2.94
1986–87	2.26	2.05	2.06	2.07	2.08	2.20	2.25	2.28	2.31	2.29	2.33	2.35	2.21
1987–88	2.15	2.04	2.06	2.20	2.27	2.33	2.34	2.38	2.41	2.35	2.38	2.53	2.29
1988–89	2.86	2.95	3.03	3.12	3.23	3.28	3.34	3.33	3.35	3.30	3.26	3.00	3.17
1989–90	3.10	3.04	3.00	2.98	2.99	2.95	3.01	2.91	2.78	2.71	2.71	2.63	2.90
1990–91	2.37	2.14	1.96	1.85	1.82	1.79	1.79	1.80	1.80	1.87	1.95	1.92	1.92
1991–92	1.88	1.84	1.93	2.04	2.23	2.36	2.51	2.56	2.73	2.67	2.62	2.61	2.33
8-yr av.	2.60	2.49	2.50	2.54	2.59	2.64	2.68	2.71	2.71	2.70	2.72	2.69	2.63
Seasonal Index	98.9	94.8	95.1	96.5	98.5	100.4	101.7	102.9	103.0	102.6	103.6	102.1	
					Calculation of Range of Instability								
1984–85	101.7	96.3	100.0	99.6	99.3	99.9	97.8	101.0	97.8	99.9	103.5	104.0	
1985–86	97.6	92.4	91.0	94.5	97.0	100.4	100.1	104.8	105.1	105.6	107.4	103.0	
1986–87	102.1	92.9	93.2	93.5	94.3	99.5	101.9	102.9	104.6	103.7	105.6	106.4	
1987–88	93.9	89.0	90.1	96.1	99.2	101.8	102.2	103.8	105.0	102.7	104.0	110.4	
1988–89	90.1	93.2	95.7	98.5	101.8	103.3	105.2	105.0	105.6	103.9	102.8	94.8	
1989–90	107.0	104.8	103.5	102.6	103.0	101.9	103.6	100.4	95.9	93.5	93.4	90.7	
1990–91	123.5	111.4	102.1	96.6	94.8	93.0	93.4	93.6	93.9	97.6	101.3	100.2	
1991–92	80.5	78.8	82.6	87.6	95.7	101.3	107.1	110.2	117.1	114.6	112.3	111.8	
High	123.5	111.4	103.5	102.6	103.0	103.3	107.1	110.2	117.1	114.6	112.3	111.8	
Low	80.5	78.8	82.6	87.6	94.3	93.0	93.4	93.6	93.9	93.5	93.4	90.7	

index would be interpreted as the expected monthly percentage deviation that might be expected from the season average price. Thus, an index value of 102.9 for January would suggest that we would normally expect January prices in any wheat marketing year to be about 3 percent higher than the season average price.

In order to glean some estimate of how dependable our seasonal index might be, we could construct a range or "zone" of seasonal instability (the lower part of Table 8.4). This range of instability is calculated in the case of the simple average index by dividing the price for each month of a marketing year by the annual average price for that year, and then selecting the high and low values for each month as the limits of the range of seasonal instability. Our January seasonal index value of 102.9 is bounded by a range of seasonal instability of 93.6 to 110.2. That is, the lowest the January price has been within the years of our investigation is 93.6 percent of the season average price. The highest is 10.2 percent above the season average price. Thus, if we market wheat in January, we might expect the price we receive to be no worse than 93.6 percent of the season average, but perhaps as much as 10.2 percent above the season average.

When we chart the 1984–1992 simple average seasonal price index for wheat and its range of instability (Figure 8.6), the seasonal price pattern emerges. It is apparent that the index is fairly instable in the May–June–July period—just preceding and during the harvest season. However, the direction of seasonal price movement indicated by the limits of the range of instability is generally compatible with the central tendency of movement. During the remainder of the year, the pattern is generally fairly stable, with a greater apparent potential for prices to be below rather than above the season average.

A part of the instability immediately around the harvest season arises from the impact of adjustment to changes in the price support operations mandated by the 1990 Farm Bill. But a greater part probably arises from the sharp downward moves in real wheat prices that resulted from changing currency values during the period. The simple average approach to measuring price seasonality is based on monthly deviations from a longer term average price. But as Figure 8.4 illustrates, real prices during the first. second, fifth, and sixth years of the period lie totally above this average. The prices of the third, fourth, and seventh years lie totally below the eight-year average.

While the simple average-based seasonal index is quick and easy to construct, it is most appropriate during periods in which there is general stability in virtually all dimensions of the market for the commodity in question.

The simple average approach to measuring price seasonality can be modified to at least partially compensate for the limitations observed

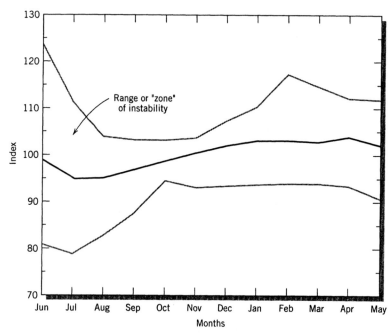

FIGURE 8.6.   WHEAT—seasonal Price Index, by months, United States, 1984–
1985 through 1991–1992 crop marketing years.

simply by calculating the real price for any given month during a crop
year as a percentage of the season average price *for that year* (Table
8.5).[3] Once the individual monthly percentages have been calculated,
the simple average percentage for each month can be calculated as an
index of price seasonality. The high and low percentage observations for
each month measure the range of instability.

A quick comparison between the simple average estimate of the seasonal price index for wheat and the modification of that index reveals
that the modified estimate is only very marginally different from the
basic calculation, whereas the range of seasonal instability is identical.

---

[3] This modification suggests an assumption that each crop year is independent from all
other crop years, and that the relevant basis for examining price seasonality is therefore
each separate season average price rather than a longer-term average price. That assumption might be valid if there were no carry-over of products from one year to the next (as in
the case of some fresh fruits and vegetables), but its validity is suspect in the case of
storable commodities such as grains. It will be noted that the body of Table 8.5 is identical
with the portion of Table 8.4 in which the range of instability was calculated.

TABLE 8.5. Modified Simple Average Calculation of Simple Average Seasonal Price Index for Wheat, 1984–85 Through 1990–91 Crop Years

Crop Year	Jun	Jul	Aug	Sep	Oct	Nov	Dec	Jan	Feb	Mar	Apr	May
1984–85	101.7	96.3	100.0	99.6	99.3	99.9	97.8	101.0	97.8	99.9	103.5	104.0
1985–86	97.6	92.4	91.0	94.5	97.0	101.4	100.1	104.8	105.1	105.6	107.4	103.0
1986–87	102.1	92.9	93.2	93.5	94.3	99.5	101.9	102.9	104.6	103.7	105.6	106.4
1987–88	93.9	89.0	90.1	96.1	99.2	101.8	102.2	103.8	105.0	102.7	104.0	110.4
1988–89	90.1	93.2	95.7	98.5	101.8	103.3	105.0	105.6	103.9	102.8	94.8	94.8
1989–90	107.0	104.8	103.5	102.6	103.0	101.9	103.6	100.4	95.9	93.5	93.4	90.7
1990–91	123.5	111.4	102.1	96.6	94.8	93.0	93.4	93.6	93.9	97.6	101.3	100.2
1991–92	80.7	78.8	82.6	87.6	95.7	101.3	107.1	110.2	117.1	114.6	112.3	111.8
Average (Index)	99.5	94.9	94.8	96.1	98.2	100.1	101.5	102.7	103.1	102.7	103.8	102.7
High	123.5	111.4	103.5	102.6	103.0	103.3	107.1	110.2	117.1	114.6	112.3	111.8
Low	80.5	78.8	82.6	87.6	94.3	93.0	93.4	93.6	93.9	93.5	93.4	90.7

149

The Moving Average Approach

We have seen the simple average approach to measuring price seasonality in which the average price for each particular month over a period of years was "indexed" to the overall average price for the entire period. We recognized that whereas this approach was quick and easy, the use of an overall average price as a base for the seasonal price index ignores the presence of any trend in the price data. The simple average approach for the seasonal price index ignores the presence of any trend in the price data. Thus, the simple average approach is appropriate only in cases in which there is general stability in the markets for the commodity of interest throughout the period for which the seasonal index is constructed.

We saw how we could modify this simple average approach by calculating the percentage that a given monthly price in a given year represented of the annual average price for that year. Once the calculations were completed, we could calculate the average for the monthly percentage over the multiyear period, giving a seasonal price index with each annual average price serving as the base for the index in each year. This modification ameliorates the problem of prices for entire crop years falling above or below the index base as was the case for the simple average calculation of the seasonal index, but it does not eliminate it. Indeed, this modification introduces a new problem of abrupt breaks in the base for the seasonal price index.

These limitations may be addressed in precisely the same fashion as we addressed similar problems in our analysis of the cycles in hog prices—through the use of a centered moving average. There are several ways that a centered moving average can be constructed for purposes of defining seasonal price patterns. Since it is necessary to use an uneven number of periods for purposes of centering the moving average, the normal approach to a seasonal index is to use 13 months of information. That is, one-half of the prices for January of one year and for January of the following year would be added to the prices of February through December, divided by 12 for an average and posted (and also charted) at July.[4]

The construction of the 12-month moving average based seasonal price index is conducted in precisely the same fashion as was demonstrated in the case of the cycle (Table 8.6). The construction begins with

---

[4] If one is using a hand calculator rather than a computer, the computations can be simplified by constructing a 13-month moving average rather than a 12-month average. This procedure does conceptually place undue weight on the end months (two January's, for example, would appear in the July calculation). But as a practical matter, the resulting difference in the calculation is typically so small that the additional computational effort is rarely justified.

TABLE 8.6. WHEAT—Moving Average Calculation of Seasonal Index

Year and Month	Real Price Received by U.S. Farmers	12-Mo Mvg Total	12-Mo Mvg Av	Real Price as a Percent of 12-Mo Mvg Av
1984 –jun	3.33			
–jul	3.16			
–aug	3.28			
–sep	3.27			
–oct	3.26			
–nov	3.28			
–dec	3.21	39.15	3.26	98.3
1985 –jan	3.31	38.70	3.23	102.8
–feb	3.21	38.18	3.18	100.8
–mar	3.28	37.63	3.14	104.5
–apr	3.40	37.18	3.10	109.6
–may	3.41	36.82	3.07	111.2
–jun	2.87	36.54	3.04	94.3
–jul	2.72	36.30	3.03	89.8
–aug	2.67	36.13	3.01	88.8
–sep	2.78	35.98	3.00	92.6
–oct	2.85	35.78	2.98	95.6
–nov	2.95	35.47	2.96	99.9
–dec	2.97	34.97	2.91	102.0
1986 –jan	3.08	34.33	2.86	107.7
–feb	3.09	33.69	2.81	110.1
–mar	3.10	33.03	2.75	112.8
–apr	3.16	32.29	2.69	117.3
–may	3.03	31.53	2.63	115.3
–jun	2.26	30.79	2.57	87.9
–jul	2.05	30.03	2.50	82.1
–aug	2.06	29.24	2.44	84.5
–sep	2.07	28.44	2.37	87.2
–oct	2.08	27.62	2.30	90.5
–nov	2.20	26.87	2.24	98.2
–dec	2.25	26.48	2.21	102.0
1987 –jan	2.28	26.42	2.20	103.3
–feb	2.31	26.42	2.20	105.0
–mar	2.29	26.48	2.21	103.9
–apr	2.33	26.65	2.22	105.1
–may	2.35	26.81	2.23	105.3
–jun	2.15	26.92	2.24	95.8
–jul	2.04	27.01	2.25	90.6
–aug	2.06	27.11	2.26	91.3
–sep	2.20	27.18	2.27	97.1
–oct	2.27	27.24	2.27	100.1
–nov	2.33	27.35	2.28	102.3
–dec	2.34	27.79	2.32	101.0

TABLE 8.6. (*Continued*)

Year and Month	Real Price Received by U.S. Farmers	12-Mo Mvg Total	12-Mo Mvg Av	Real Price as a Percent of 12-Mo Mvg Av
1988 –jan	2.38	28.60	2.38	99.7
–feb	2.41	29.55	2.46	97.7
–mar	2.35	30.49	2.54	92.6
–apr	2.38	31.43	2.62	91.0
–may	2.53	32.38	2.70	93.7
–jun	2.86	33.35	2.78	102.8
–jul	2.95	34.32	2.86	103.3
–aug	3.03	35.27	2.94	103.2
–sep	3.12	36.21	3.02	103.5
–oct	3.23	37.12	3.09	104.3
–nov	3.28	37.80	3.15	104.0
–dec	3.34	38.16	3.18	104.9
1989 –jan	3.33	38.33	3.19	104.2
–feb	3.35	38.35	3.20	104.7
–mar	3.30	38.26	3.19	103.3
–apr	3.26	38.07	3.17	102.7
–may	3.00	37.79	3.15	95.4
–jun	3.10	37.46	3.12	99.4
–jul	3.04	37.09	3.09	98.3
–aug	3.00	36.60	3.05	98.4
–sep	2.98	36.02	3.00	99.1
–oct	2.99	35.46	2.95	101.0
–nov	2.95	35.00	2.92	101.3
–dec	3.01	34.44	2.87	104.7
1990 –jan	2.91	33.63	2.80	103.9
–feb	2.78	32.66	2.72	102.2
–mar	2.71	31.58	2.63	103.1
–apr	2.71	30.43	2.54	106.8
–may	2.63	29.27	2.44	107.9
–jun	2.37	28.08	2.34	101.3
–jul	2.14	26.91	2.24	95.4
–aug	1.96	25.87	2.16	91.0
–sep	1.85	24.96	2.08	89.1
–oct	1.82	24.16	2.01	90.4
–nov	1.79	23.42	1.95	91.5
–dec	1.79	22.82	1.90	94.3
1991 –jan	1.80	22.43	1.87	96.2
–feb	1.80	22.26	1.86	97.2
–mar	1.87	22.34	1.86	100.7
–apr	1.95	22.64	1.89	103.1
–may	1.92	23.13	1.93	99.9
–jun	1.88	23.78	1.98	94.9

TABLE 8.6. (*Continued*)

Year and Month	Real Price Received by U.S. Farmers	12-Mo Mvg Total	12-Mo Mvg Av	Real Price as a Percent of 12-Mo Mvg Av
–jul	1.84	24.52	2.04	90.1
–aug	1.93	25.36	2.11	91.3
–sep	2.04	26.22	2.19	93.4
–oct	2.23	26.96	2.25	99.3
–nov	2.36	27.64	2.30	102.5
–dec	2.51	28.27	2.36	106.6
1992 –jan	2.56	28.75	2.40	106.9
–feb	2.73	29.06	2.42	112.8
–mar	2.67	29.27	2.44	109.5
–apr	2.62	29.40	2.45	107.0
–may	2.61	29.39	2.45	106.6
–jun	2.45	29.28	2.44	100.4
–jul	2.24			
–aug	2.14			
–sep	2.26			
–oct	2.26			
–nov	2.32			
–dec	2.33			

Source. Agricultural Prices, 1988 and 1990 Summaries, NASS-ASB, U.S. Department of Agriculture, June 1989 and June 1991.

the calculation of a 12-month moving total. The first 13 months of price data are used, summing the middle 11 months and adding to this half of the first and thirteenth months, with the resulting total posted at the midpoint of that 13-month interval (or at the seventh month of the data). Then half of each of the first and second months of the data are deducted from the total and half the thirteenth and fourteenth months are added, with the resulting sum being posted at the midpoint of the new 13-month interval or at the eighth month of the data. This process is continued until a 12-month total has been calculated for each month in the period for which the seasonal price index is to be constructed. It will be noted that there is a "loss" of six months of data on each end of the 12-month moving total price. This is characteristic of any moving total or moving average calculation. Thus, the moving average is always in arrears to the extent of just less than half of the interval for which the moving average is constructed.

Once the calculation of the 12-month moving total has been accomplished, each figure in that column can be divided by 12 to get the 12-

month moving average that will serve as the base for the seasonal price index. If we compare the 12-month moving average seasonal price index base with the bases for the other two indexes we examined, we can see that we have a base that does indeed pass through each year of the price data (Figure 8.7). Further, the abrupt breaks in the base that are associated with the modification of the simple average approach to seasonal price indexes are eliminated.

After the 12-month moving average real price has been calculated, the real prices observed for the individual months can be divided by the corresponding value of the 12-month moving average to get the individual monthly elements of the seasonal price index. The index values for the individual months can be rearranged into specific monthly categories (Table 8.7). From these monthly categories, the seasonal price index can be constructed simply by averaging the index values for each month. Since the monthly values are already in index form, the high and low values for each month provide the range of seasonal instability.

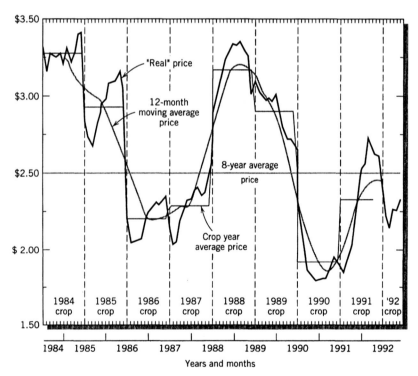

FIGURE 8.7.   WHEAT—Real prices received by farmers, by months, by marketing years, with annual and 12-month moving average, United States, 1984–1992.

TABLE 8.7. WHEAT—Seasonal Price Index, 12-Month Moving Average Calculation

Crop Year	Jun	Jul	Aug	Sep	Oct	Nov	Dec	Jan	Feb	Mar	Apr	May
1985–86	94.3	89.8	88.8	92.6	95.6	99.9	102.0	107.7	110.1	112.8	117.3	115.3
1986–87	87.9	82.1	84.5	87.2	90.5	98.2	102.0	103.3	105.0	103.9	105.1	105.3
1987–88	95.8	90.6	91.3	97.1	100.1	102.3	101.0	99.7	97.7	92.6	91.0	93.7
1988–89	102.8	103.3	103.2	103.5	104.3	104.0	104.9	104.2	104.7	103.3	102.7	95.4
1989–90	99.4	98.3	98.4	99.1	101.0	101.3	104.7	103.9	102.2	103.1	106.8	107.9
1990–91	101.3	95.4	91.0	89.1	90.4	91.5	94.3	96.2	97.2	100.7	103.1	99.9
1991–92	94.9	90.1	91.3	93.4	99.3	102.5	106.6	106.9	112.8	109.5	107.0	106.6
Seasonal index	96.6	92.8	92.7	94.6	97.3	99.9	102.2	103.1	104.2	103.7	104.7	103.4
Range of seasonal instability:												
High	102.8	103.3	103.2	103.5	104.3	104.0	106.8	107.7	112.8	112.8	117.3	115.3
Low	87.9	82.1	84.5	87.2	90.4	91.5	94.3	99.7	97.7	92.6	91.0	93.7

Note. The last six months of data for the 1984–85 crop year have been eliminated from this seasonal calculation since there is a full year of information for the 1991–92 crop year. One should endeavor to work with the same numbers of observations for all months in the calculation of seasonality.

When the values for the 12-month moving average based seasonal price index and the corresponding range of instability are charted (Figure 8.8), we see that some of the seasonality in real wheat prices was masked by the sharp year-to-year changes in prices. Also, the range of instability is much less in the early part of the marketing year. The moving average based index emphasizes the reality that the greatest instability in seasonal wheat prices occurs immediately preceding and during harvest. This is precisely what one would expect. There is a proverb in Kansas—the largest wheat producing state—that every wheat crop is "lost" at least six times between January 1 and harvest. This, of course, refers to the "weather" markets in which prices rise when rainfall is short and fall when moisture is abundant. Since the most critical weather period for wheat is the April–July period, the greatest range of seasonal price instability occurs during those months.

When we compare the results of the three approaches to the construction of a seasonal price index, we see that the simple average calculation and its modification yield very similar results, underscoring the reality that these two approaches are of rather limited applicability in a volatile market situation that exhibits a strong downward (or upward) price trend (Figure 8.9). The seasonal peaks and troughs in wheat prices occur in the same months with all three approaches. A secondary peak in the early part of the calendar year is defined by all three approaches. But the

Twelve-month moving average seasonal calculation

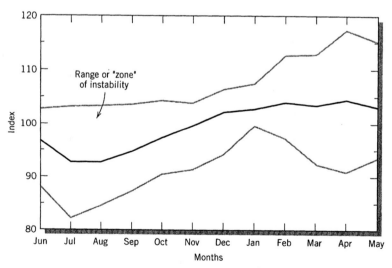

FIGURE 8.8.   WHEAT—Seasonal price index by months, United States, 1984–85 through 1991–92 crop marketing year.

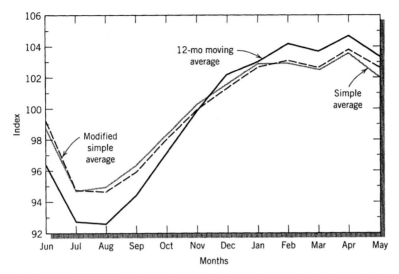

FIGURE 8.9. WHEAT—Comparison of alternative methods for calculating seasonal indices of prices received by farmers, United States, 1984–85 through 1991–92 crop marketing years.

moving average calculation that takes the trends into account is more reflective of the actual degree of price seasonality.

In constructing seasonal price indices, it is desirable to include at least one full cycle in the analysis—and at least five years of prices in any case. If a commodity has a cycle of less than five years, a more dependable seasonal price index can be gleaned if multiples of cycles are used in the seasonal index. If, for example, a commodity has a three-year cycle, then either six or nine years of data in the seasonal price analysis will probably yield more dependable results than would a single cycle.

Under economic conditions less volatile than we have experienced since the early 1970s, much longer periods of time would ordinarily be recommended for estimating seasonality. However, with the enormous volatility we have observed since the United States abandoned its long-standing policy of settling international accounts in gold (1973) and since the OPEC countries began to do their thing in the energy markets (1974–75), very significant disruptions in almost all economic variables may be identified. Using relatively short periods of time in the estimation of seasonality may unquestionably give rise to some error in the construction of seasonal price indices. But attempting to bridge the disruptive influences of factors such as the 1974–75 and 1979–81 Energy Crises, the 1972–73 Russian Grain Deal, the deregulation of financial institutions, massive federal budget deficits beginning the 1980s, and the consequent impacts upon real interest rates most probably create the potential for even greater error.

Our study of price movements over time is just about complete. Let's review that study and integrate what we have learned about the various price movements. First of all, we recognized that the general price inflation in the U.S. economy over the past 20 years required that we "deflate" all variables that were quoted in dollar terms in order to correct for the eroding value of the dollar. We used the Consumer Price Index with a 1982–84 base period for this purpose. We saw how a CPI value of 130.7 for 1990 suggests that the dollar in 1990 would purchase only 76.5 percent of the goods and services that a 1982–84 dollar would buy. Thus, it is essential that we stabilize the value of the dollar in order to examine what has happened and is happening to the *value* (i.e., the ability of a good to command other goods and services) of any commodity.

Once we had corrected our price series for inflation, converting current (or nominal) prices into real prices, we saw how we could calculate a trend in order to define any long-term upward or downward drift in value that might spring from factors such as the continuing adaptation of new technology or the continuing growth in the usage of new products that might be developed. We recognized that it was important to be judicious in the selection of a time period for trend analysis, identifying periods during which there were obvious changes in the direction and/ or level at which the trend occurred.

Once we had defined the trend, we examined a different sort of trend—the centered moving average trend. We recognized that the linear trend was useful for defining long-term drifts in the levels of prices for a commodity, but that linear trend did not identify any regular changes in direction of price movement. A centered moving average trend—particularly a moving average trend in which the numbers of years in the moving average is of about the same length as that of any suspected cycle—will follow the gross sorts of disruptions that may obscure the cycle. It is important that the number of years used in calculating in the moving average be uneven in number in order to allow for the "centering" of the resulting calculation. However, an adjustment for even numbers of years may be made by using half-years in the calculation.

We recognized that cyclical analysis could also be conducted on the base of a linear trend, but the centered moving average approach does have the advantage at least for defining the "phasing" ("phase" referring to the "growth" or "decline" in the cyclical pattern) of the cycle. Thus, for any product, we may have a cyclical price movement over time that moves around any price trend that might exist. In our discussion of cycles, we recognized that they were driven by the biological realities of the production process. Therefore, in defining *price* cycles, our starting point was the *production* cycle.

We moved from our analysis of price cycles to an analysis of the seasonal price variations that are normally observed over the course of each marketing year. We recognized that as a special type of cycle, price seasonality could be most effectively and dependably estimated through the use of a second type of centered moving average—a 12-month (or a 13-month) moving average, the center month of which would follow the cyclical pattern. Like the more general and longer-term general cycle, the seasonal price cycle is typically driven by the seasonally based biological realities of the production process. The seasonal price pattern would move around the cyclical pattern which in turn moves around any trend that might exist. Thus, the seasonal pattern, which moves around a cyclical pattern, which, in turn, moves around a trend, might appear as in Figure 8.10.

Our analyses of price movements over time have been purely mechanical analyses with time as the driving force. We have shown how these mechanical analyses are entirely compatible with economic theory in that seasonally high prices are typically associated with seasonally reduced production. Cyclically high prices are associated with cyclically based reductions in product availability. Increasing or decreasing long-term price trends are associated with gradual and continuing shifts in the supply and/or demand relationships that may occur so slowly that identifying these shifts from year to year is impossible.

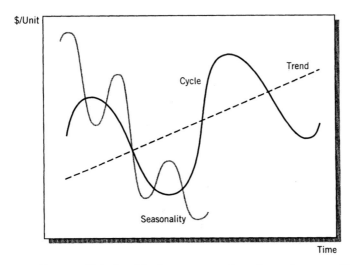

FIGURE 8.10.   Relationship between trend, cycle, and seasonality.

We know that there are a great many factors that influence the conditions of supply and/or demand that are *not* time driven. Our time-based mechanical analysis of price movements is useful—even necessary—as a starting point for the analysis and forecasting of the price of a commodity at some future point. But that mechanical analysis is in no way sufficient for producing a dependable forecast.

Time had nothing to do with the decision of the multinational oil companies and the OPEC cartel decision to create the energy crises of 1974–75 and 1979–81. We have seen how these episodic events disrupted the expected trend and cyclical price patterns for many agricultural products. The decision of the Soviet Politburo in 1972 to upgrade the diets of the Russian people by massive grain imports was largely independent of time. Yet the impact of that decision upon price was substantial and counter to the expected time-based price movements. The decision of the Reagan administration to implement the $30 billion Payment In Kind program in 1983 was in no way time based, but the seasonal price pattern for the 1983 wheat crop was very different as a result. The disintegration of the Soviet Empire in the early 1990s was largely independent of time. The trend, cyclical, and seasonal impacts of this event remain to be seen, but it is a pretty good bet that there will *be* some impacts, particularly upon the grain and oil seed markets.

The regular, mechanically derived estimates of movements in price over time are useful as a starting point. But as we have already seen, we used moving averages to "smooth" the data for both our cyclical and seasonal analyses. It is the aberrations from that smoothed data that must be explained and predicted. If there were no aberrations from our trend, cyclical, and seasonal patterns, there would be no need for price analysis or forecasting. Computers could grind out the expected prices for the next hundred years at the touch of a button. The problem with this approach is that computers cannot take into account the innate cussedness of man. If managers had access to such a predictive process and if that predictive process were in fact accurate, man would take the sorts of actions that destroyed that accuracy.

Our mechanical analysis has to this point been limited to analyzing the relationships between price and production over time, all other things being equal, that is, *ceteris paribus*. Explaining and predicting the *aberrations* from the expected price movements over time is where the economic analyst becomes important. This process involves a return to our economic theory and to defining the sorts of *ceteris* that may not in fact be *paribus*, and then estimating the expected aberrant impact of these differences. These are the issues with which subsequent chapters will deal.

Appendix _____

The purpose of this appendix is to provide information regarding the use of the computer in constructing seasonal price indices. The computer commands are provided in terms of LOTUS 1-2-3 or the Lotus mode of QUATTROPRO software, but any standard spreadsheet software may be utilized in this manner.

Simple Average Seasonal Calculations

Table 8A.1 is an abbreviated version of Table 8.4 in Chapter 8. To construct the simple average seasonal index, take the following steps:

With the cursor in Cell N7, type the following:

@sum(B7.M7)/12

This directs the computer to add the values for each month in the 1984–85 crop year and to divide them by 12 in order to get an annual average price. The annual average price (3.28) will appear in Cell N7.

With the cursor remaining in Cell N7, press "Slash" (/) to activate the menu. Select "Copy" and press "Enter."

Move the cursor to Cell N8 and press the period to anchor the range to which the formula in Cell N7 is to be copied. Move the cursor to Cell N14. Cells N8 through N14 will be illuminated.

Press "Enter." Annual average prices for all Crop Years will appear in Cells N8 through N14.

Move the cursor to Cell B16 and type:

@sum(B7.B14)/8

This instructs the computer to add the eight values for the month of June and to divide the resulting total by eight to get an average price for the month of June. When "Enter" is pressed, the average price for June (2.60) will appear in Cell B16.

With the cursor in Cell B16, press "Slash" (/) to activate the menu. Select "Copy" and press "Enter." This instructs the computer to copy the formula in B16 to other locations on the spreadsheet.

Move the cursor to C16 and press period to anchor the range to which the formula in B16 is to be copied. Move the cursor to N16. Cells C16 through N16 will be illuminated. Press "Enter." The eight-year

TABLE 8A.1. Wheat—Simple Average Calculation of Seasonal Index of Real Prices (CPI, 1982–84 = 100)

R o w	Crop Year	B Jun	C Jul	D Aug	....	L Apr	M May	N Ann Avg
7	1984–85	3.33	3.16	3.28	....	3.40	3.41	3.28
8	1985–86	2.87	2.72	2.67	....	3.16	3.03	2.94
9	1986–87	2.26	2.05	2.06	....	2.33	2.35	2.21
10	1987–88	2.15	2.04	2.06	....	2.38	2.53	2.29
11	1988–89	2.86	2.95	3.03	....	3.26	3.00	3.17
12	1989–90	3.10	3.04	3.00	....	2.71	2.63	2.90
13	1990–91	2.37	2.14	1.96	....	1.95	1.92	1.92
14	1991–92	1.88	1.84	1.93	....	2.62	2.61	2.33
15								
16	8-Yr Av.	—	—	—	....	—	—	—
17								
18	Seas Index	—	—	—	....	—	—	—
19								
20			Calculation of Range of Instability					
21								
22	1984–85	—	—	—	....	—	—	—
23	1985–86	—	—	—	....	—	—	—
24	1986–87	—	—	—	....	—	—	—
25	1987–88	—	—	—	....	—	—	—
26	1988–89	—	—	—	....	—	—	—
27	1989–90	—	—	—	....	—	—	—
28	1990–91	—	—	—	....	—	—	—
29	1991–92	—	—	—	....	—	—	—
30								
31	High	—	—	—	....	—	—	—
32								
33	Low	—	—	—	....	—	—	—

average prices for the individual months and the overall eight-year annual average price ($2.63) will appear in Row 16.

Move the cursor to Cell B18 and type:

$$(+B16/2.63)*100$$

This instructs the computer to calculate the eight-year average price for the month of June as a ratio with the overall eight-year average annual price. When that ratio is multiplied by 100, it is converted to an "index" (or percentage) value.

With the cursor in Cell B18, press "Slash" (/) to activate the menu. Select "Copy." This instructs the computer to copy the formula in Cell B18 to other locations in the spreadsheet.

Move the cursor to Cell C18 and press the period to anchor the range to which the formula in B18 is to be copied. Move the cursor to Cell M18. Cells C18 through M18 will be illuminated. Press "Enter." The monthly price index values will appear in Row 17.

You are now ready to calculate the Range of Instability. Move the cursor to Cell B22 and type:

(+B7/the VALUE you calculated in Cell N7)*100

That is, type (+B7/3.28)*100

This instructs the computer to calculate the June 1984, price as a percentage of the average price for the entire marketing year.

Repeat this procedure for Cells B23 through B29. Be sure to use the VALUES you calculated in Cells N8 through N13 that correspond with the Crop Years with which you are working. The end result will be a series of percentages in Column B.

With the cursor in B22, press "Slash" to activate the menu. Select "Copy" and move the cursor to B29. This instructs the computer to copy the formulae in Cells B22 through B29 to other locations. Cells B22 through B29 will be illuminated. Press "Enter."

Move the cursor to Cell C22 and press the period to anchor the range to which the formulae in B22.B29 are to be copied. Move the cursor to Cell N22. Cells C22 through N22 will be illuminated. Press "Enter." The monthly percentages of annual average prices will appear in the cells in Columns B through N and Rows 22 through 29.

The High and Low index (or percentage) values can be entered (or copied) into the cells in Rows 31 and 33.

Modified Simple Average Seasonal Price Calculations

The modified simple average seasonal price calculation utilizes the lower part of Table 8A.1 in which the Range of Instability was calculated. In order to accomplish this calculation, there needs to be additional space between Rows 29 and 31 of Table 8A.1.

To add Rows, move the cursor to any cell in Row 30. Press "Slash" to activate the menu. Select "Worksheet," "Add," and "Row." Move the cursor down as many rows as you wish to add. The illuminated cells will indicate the numbers of rows you have instructed the computer to add. If only one row is added, Row 30 will become Row 31, and so on.

With the cursor in Cell B31 (i.e., in the B column of the new Row), type the following:

@Sum(B22.B29)/8

This instructs the computer to calculate the average index (or percentage for the month of June.

Copy the formula in Cell B31 to Cells C31 through M31. The Modified Simple Average Seasonal Index will appear in Row 31.

Calculation of the 12-Month Moving Average Seasonal Index

Table 8A.2 is an abbreviated version of Table 8.6 in Chapter 8. To construct the 12-month moving average seasonal index, take the following steps:

With the cursor in Cell C15, type:

(+.5*B9 + @Sum(B10.B20) +.5*B21)

This instructs the computer to add half the value for June, 1984, plus the full values for the next 11 months, plus half the value for June 1985, to get a 12-month total for this period.

With the cursor remaining in Cell C15, press "Slash" to activate the menu and select "Copy." Move the cursor to Cell C16 and press the period to anchor one end of the range to which the formula in Cell C15 is to be copied. Move the cursor to Cell C114. Cells C16 through C114 will be illuminated. Press "Enter." The 12-month moving total for the entire period (less the loss of six months on either end) will appear in Column C.

With the cursor in Cell D15, type:

+C15/12

This instructs the computer to calculate the 12-month centered average for the 12-month centered total that appears in Cell C15. The 12-month centered average for December 1984 (3.26) will appear in Cell D15.

TABLE 8A.2. Wheat—Moving Average Calculation of Seasonal Index of Prices Received by Farmers

			Columns		
		B	C	D	E
R	Year	Real Price	12-Mo	12-Mo	Real Price as
o	and	Received by	Mvg	Mvg	a Percent of
w	Month	U.S. Farmers	Total	Total	12-Mo Mvg Avg
s					
9	1984–				
	jun	3.33			
10	–jul	3.16			
11	–aug	3.28			
12	–sep	3.27			
13	–oct	3.26			
14	–nov	3.28			
15	–dec	3.21	39.15	3.26	98.3
16	1985–jan	3.31	38.70	3.23	102.8
17	–feb	3.21	—	—	—
18	–mar	3.28	—	—	—
19	–apr	3.40	—	—	—
20	–may	3.41	—	—	—
21	–jun	2.87	—	—	—
22	–jul	2.72	—	—	—
23	–aug	2.67	—	—	—
24	–sep	2.78	—	—	—
25	–oct	2.85	—	—	—
.	.	.	.	.	.
.	.	.	.	.	.
.	.	.	.	.	.
109	1992–jan	2.56	—	—	—
110	–feb	2.73	—	—	—
111	–mar	2.67	—	—	—
112	–apr	2.62	—	—	—
113	–may	2.61	—	—	—
114	–jun	2.45	—	—	—
115	–jul	2.24			
116	–aug	2.14			
117	–sep	2.26			
118	–oct	2.26			
119	–nov	2.32			
120	–dec	2.33			
121					

With the cursor remaining in Cell D15, press "Slash" to activate the menu. Select "Copy" and press "Enter." This instructs the computer to copy the formula in Cell D15 to another location(s) in the spreadsheet.

Move the cursor to Cell D16 and press the period to anchor the range to which the formula in Cell D15 is to be copied. Move the cursor to D114. Cells D16 through D114 will be illuminated. Press "Enter." The 12-month centered moving average real price for wheat will appear in Cells D15 through 114.

Move the cursor to Cell E15 and type:

$$(+B15/D15)*100$$

This instructs the computer to calculate the real price for December of 1984 as a percentage of the 12-month centered moving average price for that month.

With the cursor remaining in Cell E15, press "Slash" (/) to activate the menu. Select "Copy" and press "Enter." This instructs the computer to copy the formula in Cell E15 to another location(s) in the spreadsheet.

Move the cursor to Cell E16 and press the period to anchor the range. Move the cursor to E114. Cells E16 through E114 will be illuminated. Press "Enter." The percentage elements from which the seasonal index is to be constructed will appear in Cells E15 through E114.

You now have the elements for constructing the moving-average based seasonal price index. In order to compute the index, the information you calculated in Column E of Table 8A.2 must be rearranged in the format shown in the blank Table 8A.3. Since the moving-average calculation requires a loss of data, the first moving-average data you have for the 1984–85 crop year is for December 1984. After Table 8A.3 has been set up, the data may be rearranged by using the following commands:

With the cursor in Cell E15, press "Slash" (/) to activate the menu. Select "Range," "Value." The computer will ask for the range from which values are to be copied. Move the cursor to Cell E114. Cells E15 through E114 will be illuminated. The computer will ask for the range to which values are to be copied. Press "Enter." The information in Cells E15 through E114 is now expressed in values rather than formulas. These values can now be transposed into a horizontal table. (Failure to complete this step will result in an error signal.)

TABLE 8A.3. Wheat: Seasonal Price Index 13-Month Moving Average Calculation

Row		Crop Year	B Jun	C Jul	D Aug	E Sep	F Oct	G Nov	H Dec	I Jan	J Feb	K Mar	L Apr	M May
									Columns					
101		1984–85							—	—	—	—	—	—
102		1985–86	—	—	—	—	—	—	—	—	—	—	—	—
103		1986–87	—	—	—	—	—	—	—	—	—	—	—	—
104		1987–88	—	—	—	—	—	—	—	—	—	—	—	—
105		1988–89	—	—	—	—	—	—	—	—	—	—	—	—
106		1989–90	—	—	—	—	—	—	—	—	—	—	—	—
107		1990–91	—	—	—	—	—	—	—	—	—	—	—	—
108		1991–92	—	—	—	—	—	—	—	—	—	—	—	—
109														
110		Seasonal												
111		Index	—	—	—	—	—	—	—	—	—	—	—	—
112														
113		Range of Seasonal Instability:												
114														
115		High	—	—	—	—	—	—	—	—	—	—	—	—
116														
117		Low	—	—	—	—	—	—	—	—	—	—	—	—
118														

167

With the cursor in Cell H101, press "Slash" (/) to activate the menu. Select "Range," "Transpose." The computer will ask for the range to be transposed. Type:

E15.E20

This instructs the computer to select the data for December 1984, through May 1985, to be transposed from a vertical array to a horizontal array.

Press "Enter." The computer will now ask for the location to which the specified information is to be transposed. Since your cursor is already in that location, if you press "Enter" again, the transposition will be completed. The numbers in Range E15.E20 will appear in Cells H through M of Row 101.

Since there is a full crop year of information for 1985–86, move the cursor to Cell B102. Repeat the process of calling for "Range," "Transpose." When the computer asks for the range to be transposed, type:

E21.E32

This instructs the computer to select the information in Cells E21 through E32 for transposition to a horizontal format.

Press "Enter." Since your cursor is again in the location at which you want the transposition to begin, Press "Enter" again. The numbers in Range E21.E32 will appear in Row 102.

Continue this process until all of the numbers which appear in Column E of Table 8A.2 have been entered into the appropriate locations in Table 8A.3. The appearance of the table should be as shown in Table 8A.4.

You can immediately identify the Range of Instability by entering the high and low values in each column in the appropriate spaces in Lines 115 and 117.

To calculate the Moving-Average based Seasonal Index, place the cursor in Cell B111. Type

@Sum(B102.B108)/7

This instructs the computer to calculate an average index value for the month of June.

Note: The December–May period in the 1984–85 crop year is eliminated from the seasonal calculation since there is a full year of information for the 1991–92 crop year. That is, the same numbers of observations should be used for all months in calculating a seasonal index.

TABLE 8A.4. Wheat: Seasonal Price Index 13-Month Moving Average Calculation

Row		Crop Year	B Jun	C Jul	D Aug	E Sep	F Oct	G Nov	H Dec	I Jan	J Feb	K Mar	L Apr	M May
101		1984–85							98.3	102.8	100.8	104.5	109.6	111.2
102		1985–86	94.3	89.8	88.8	92.6	95.6	99.9	102.0	107.7	110.1	112.8	117.3	115.3
103		1986–87	87.9	82.1	84.5	87.2	90.5	98.2	102.0	103.3	105.0	103.9	105.1	105.3
104		1987–88	95.8	90.6	91.3	97.1	100.1	102.3	101.0	99.7	97.7	92.6	91.0	93.7
105		1988–89	102.8	103.3	103.2	103.5	104.3	104.0	104.9	104.2	104.7	103.3	102.7	95.4
106		1989–90	99.4	98.3	98.4	99.1	101.0	101.3	104.7	103.9	102.2	103.1	106.8	107.9
107		1990–91	101.3	95.4	91.0	89.1	90.4	91.5	94.3	96.2	97.2	100.7	103.1	99.9
108		1991–92	94.9	90.1	91.3	93.4	99.3	102.5	106.6	106.9	112.8	109.5	107.0	106.6
109														
110		Seasonal												
111		Index	—	—	—	—	—	—	—	—	—	—	—	—
112														
113		Range of Seasonal Instability:												
114														
115		High	102.8	—	—	—	—	—	—	—	—	—	—	—
116														
117		Low	87.9	—	—	—	—	—	—	—	—	—	—	—
118														

169

With the cursor remaining in Cell B111, press "Slash" to activate the menu. Select "Copy" and press "Enter."

Move the cursor to Cell C111 and press the period to anchor the range to which the formula in Cell B111 is to be copied. Move the cursor to Cell M111. Cells in range C111.M111 will be illuminated.

Press "Enter." The 12-month moving-average based Seasonal Index for real wheat prices during the 1984–85 through 1990–91 crop years will appear in Row 111.

CHAPTER **9**

Supply–Demand Relationships— Supply

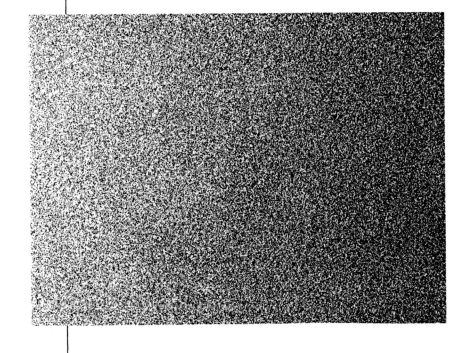

When each of us studied principles of economics, we learned about the conceptual relationships of supply and demand. We saw how demand sloped downward and to the right as a result of the realities that most consumers were willing to utilize more of almost any good if the price were reduced. We saw how producers would respond to increased prices by expanding output in order to fully realize the benefits associated with the higher price. We saw how the equilibrium position occurred when the supply and demand functions intersected, defining the quantity of product that would be produced and consumed and the market price at which this occurred. And while these concepts made sense in the context of the world with which we were all acquainted, most of us never understood just exactly how one would go about defining and quantifying the supply and demand relationships in a real world setting.

Back in Chapter 4 when we discussed the analysis of trends, you were introduced to the price–quantity scatter diagram (Figure 9.1). At that time, we recognized that each point in the scatter diagram represented the intersection of some sort of average supply and demand curves for the year or period in question. Thus, the information in the scatter diagram is in actuality a series of equilibria, observed at different points in time. If the product in question is a "storable" annual crop harvested once and only once a year, then stored for use throughout the year (and perhaps beyond), the "supply" curve for that period would be essentially vertical. That is, the annual supply of corn or wheat or soybeans for any given marketing year—once the harvest is completed—is for all intents and purposes fixed until the next crop is ready for harvest. That fixed supply would be made up of the current year's production, plus any carry-over from previous years, less exports, plus imports. The only opportunity for any deviation from a vertical short-run supply function in the case of such products occurs in the export–import category, which allows domestic users of the good to "bid" some of the product away from other countries or would allow foreign users to bid some of the U.S. product away from Americans.

The equilibria at points *a, b,* and *c* in Figure 9.1 are clearly outside the main body of the scatter of equilibrium points. It is probable that these points are associated with highly unusual circumstances that are outside the range of conditions that might normally be expected. Most analysts will eliminate such points from consideration in their analysis, explaining the conditions with which they are associated.

The export–import activity is obviously an enormously sensitive issue in a free society, since excessive exports of a good drive domestic prices

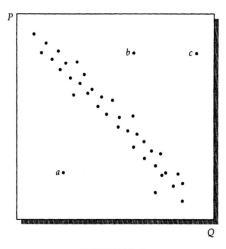

FIGURE 9.1

to levels that consumers resent. The events of 1973–74, when in the aftermath of the so-called Russian Grain Deal U.S. food prices began to rise very rapidly, illustrates one dimension of just how sensitive this issue can be. The Nixon–Ford Administration responded to public resentment of increasing food costs by placing an embargo on the exports of both soybeans and wheat. These actions resulted in precipitous reductions in the domestic prices for these commodities and generated an even more bitter resentment on the part of producers who felt betrayed, robbed, disenfranchised—and plain mad.

The buyers of U.S. wheat and soybeans weren't terribly thrilled by these embargoes, either. Japan, a major buyer of U.S. grains and soybeans, made substantial investments in Brazil and Argentina to establish a soybean industry in those countries. The objective, of course, was to provide an alternative to the United States as a supplier of this critically important item in Japanese diets. These embargoes undoubtedly played some role in the defeat of Gerald Ford for the presidency in 1976. The 1980 embargo of wheat exports to the Soviet Union in retaliation for the Soviet invasion of Afghanistan likewise played a role in the failure of President Carter's re-election effort.

The import area is equally fraught with peril. The U.S. beef industry effort to limit U.S. imports of Australian, New Zealand, and Argentine beef throughout the 1965–75 period is a case in point. The Reagan administration's effort to "jaw-bone" the Japanese into limiting automobile and electronics exports to the United States in an effort to avoid very punitive Congressional action in the trade area is another. In any case, since the United States represents the world's largest food surplus area, the import of large volumes of food stuffs other than items such as coffee, bananas, and certain specialty items such as some cheeses and fruit juice concentrates into the United States in most years is fairly minor.

Since adjustments in the available supplies of the annual crops can occur only at discrete time intervals—with supply being essentially fixed for the interim time periods—the scatter diagram of the equilibria implies that prices during these interim periods are determined exclusively by the position of the demand function. The short-run supply(s) in Figure 9.2 is fixed at exactly the same quantity for the equilibria at both points *a* and *b*. The difference in P_a and P_b is clearly exclusively associated with the difference in D_a and D_b. The apparent inverse relationship between prices and quantities in Figure 9.2 further suggests that supply has been much more volatile than has demand. That is, the fixed, vertical supply functions have occurred across the entire range of the horizontal axis, whereas demand has been constrained within the area between D_a and D_b.

If supply has in fact been significantly more volatile than demand, a regression line through the matched pairs of price–quantity combinations would provide an estimate of a demand function over the entire time period included in the scatter diagram. The vertical deviations from this longer-term demand function would most probably be associated

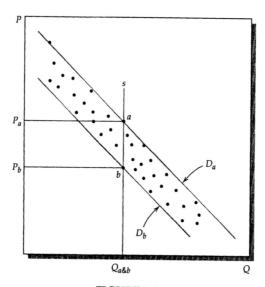

FIGURE 9.2

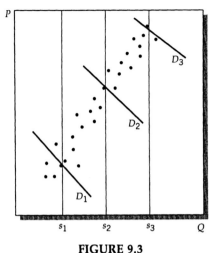

FIGURE 9.3

with year-to-year changes in one or more of the *ceteris paribus* conditions of demand—changes in variables such as income, price of substitute goods, and so on.

Occasionally, one may encounter a scatter of price–quantity points that appears to suggest a positive relationship between price of the product and the quantity available (Figure 9.3). The normal first reaction to this circumstance would be that the scatter defines a supply function rather than demand. But there is typically some elapse of time (or lag) between the time decisions are made to adjust production in response to changes in price and the time the adjusted level of product actually becomes available. Thus, the apparent positive relationship between price and quantity that is suggested by the configuration of the scatter chart of the various years' equilibria is most likely the result of demand being far more volatile than supply. The very rapid growth in the demand for soybeans during the 1940s and 1950s, for example, gives this sort of scatter chart. The excessive growth in demand relative to supply obscures the demand relationship.

When we are dealing with the continuously produced agricultural commodities such as livestock and livestock products, the supply for any given period in time (other than the immediate market period) has something other than a vertical slope. That is, the continuously produced products exhibit the more "normal" positively sloped supply function that suggests that producers will respond to higher prices with increased volumes of product available. The lags between the time of basic production decisions and the actual realization of production give the same general sorts of implications to a price–quantity scatter chart for these products as is observed in the case of the once-a-year types of crops. But a female beef animal that becomes a chuck roast today cannot become a mother next spring. Thus, in the case of the continuously produced farm products, a decision to make more product available in response to a current price may well place limits upon future supplies.

In general, agricultural supply relationships tend to be more volatile (and more elastic with respect to price) than do demand relationships. There are several reasons for this. First of all—to the undying chagrin of the Animal Rights Activists—most decision makers are far more willing to allow quick judgments and decisions regarding plants and animals (the basis for agricultural supply functions) than they are regarding people (the basis for demand functions). Second, the capacity of the human stomach is limited, unless one happens to be feeding adolescents. Since most agricultural products are produced and sold in the inelastic portion of the market demand curve, price changes do not make a great deal of difference in the levels of product consumed. Third, people are creatures of habit, and those habits change only very, very slowly.

There are numerous examples of the manner in which habit retards the rates of demand change in response to new knowledge. It was pretty clearly established that there was a link between cigarette smoking and lung cancer in the early 1960s. But it was well into the 1970s before the tobacco consumption statistics demonstrated that U.S. consumers had reduced their demand for cigarettes. The cholesterol controversy regarding the validity of a postulated link between red meat consumption and heart disease started in the late 1970s. But as late as 1993 the available evidence suggested that the public at large remained unconvinced of the validity of this link.

Consumers will readily substitute superior goods for inferior goods (e.g., animal proteins for vegetable proteins), but an increase in income is typically required for this to happen. Incomes generally increase fairly slowly. Most consumers will substitute one superior good for another (e.g., pork for beef), but generally not on a one-for-one basis.

We have discussed the relative volatilities of supply and demand as they relate to the configuration of the price–quantity scatter chart. We suggested that the deviations from a regression line through the scatter diagram are most probably the result of year-to-year changes in one or more of the *ceteris paribus* conditions. The reason that demand and supply are consistently defined in terms of *ceteris paribus* conditions is that those conditions are of very real importance. Changes in any of the *ceteris paribus* conditions will cause either demand, supply, or both to shift.

ANTICIPATING THE IMPACT OF *CETERIS PARIBUS* CONDITIONS OF SUPPLY _____

If supply, in the case of agricultural products, is generally more volatile than is demand, it follows that the *ceteris paribus* conditions of supply must be more subject to change than are those of demand. Thus, anticipating the impact of changes in the *ceteris paribus* conditions of supply must be critical to forecasting the ultimate intersection of demand and supply (and hence the price) for some future period. Included among the *ceteris paribus* conditions of supply would be:

1. Cost of resources
2. Weather
3. Level of fixed resources
4. Other production and profit opportunities for owned resources
5. Technology
6. Numbers of producers
7. Institutional arrangements (farm programs, etc.)

As was suggested in Chapter 2, the basis for any supply relationship is the production function. Let's examine each of these *ceteris paribus* conditions of supply in terms of the production function and the cost of production relationships that are derived from the production function, analyzing the impact upon the market supply function.

COST OF RESOURCES _____

The lower portion of Figure 9.4 shows the rate at which a single variable resource X_1 can be combined with some set of fixed resources (X_2, ..., X_n) in the production of Y. The solid line labeled $TVIC_{PXa}$ shows the cost initially associated with the use of the variable resource X. The dotted line labeled $TVIC_{PXb}$ shows that cost after the price for the variable resource has risen. The solid lines in the rest of the figure are associated with the initially lower resource price while the dotted lines are associated with the new higher price.

The technical production relationships are not affected by the price of resources—$10 ammonium nitrate has exactly the same productive potential as does $5 ammonium nitrate. But the level at which that resource will be **utilized** in producing a product of a given value per unit is very much influenced by the resource price. So whereas the rational range of

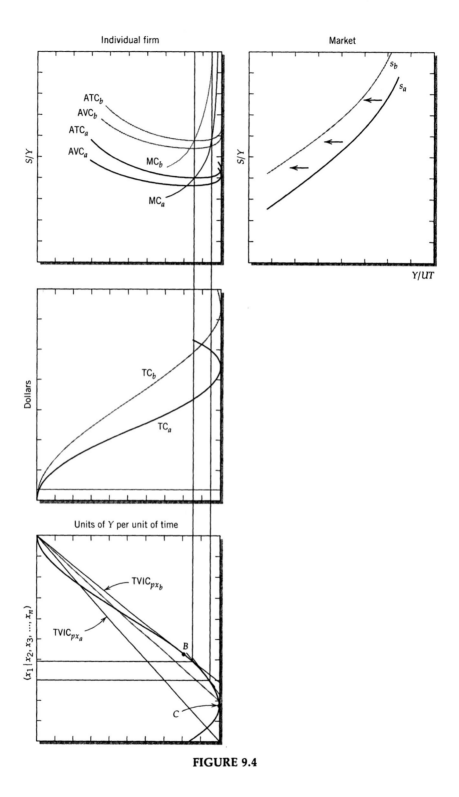

FIGURE 9.4

production (between points *B* and *C* in the lower diagram) is not affected by the resource price, the total variable cost is very much affected. The entire average and marginal cost structure for the firm shifts upward. That portion of marginal cost, which lies above average variable cost, defines the quantities of product that the firm is willing and able to offer for sale at various prices, that is, the marginal cost curve traces out the supply function for the individual firm.

It is very clear that the firm is less willing to supply product at *any* price for that product than was the case prior to the resource price increase. Under the atomistically competitive conditions faced by most agricultural producers, the market supply function is the horizontal summation of all the individual firm supply functions. Thus, the market supply function would shift as a result of a change in the price for a variable resource.

WEATHER AND LEVELS OF FIXED RESOURCES ————————————————

The impact of weather on an agricultural supply function is very much the same as would be the impact of a change in the level at which some fixed resource such as family labor might be available. The solid lines in Figure 9.5 are all associated as are the dashed lines.

If Mama Nature should in her infinite wisdom withhold the weather resource (or if a 19-year-old son should leave home for college), the net result would be that a new production function (TPP_b) would emerge. Because of the poor weather or the reduced availability of family labor, the productivity of the variable resource X_1 would be reduced. The end result of this would be an upward shift in the firm's production cost structure and a resulting shift to the left in both the individual and market supply functions.

When Mama Nature decided to be more of a lady, or if the kid flunked out of college and returned home, the result would be a return to the higher production function (TPP_a) and a corresponding shift in the supply function.

The issue of availability of fixed resources does give a very important additional dimension to both the individual and market supply functions. In the very long run (during which we all die), essentially no productive resources are fixed. In the very short run—the market period—virtually all resources are fixed (hence, supply function is vertical). But in the more intermediate planning horizons, there are a number of variable resources such as feed, seed, fertilizer, fuel, and so on. There are other resources such as land and management that are fixed. There is a third category of resources such as machinery and equipment that

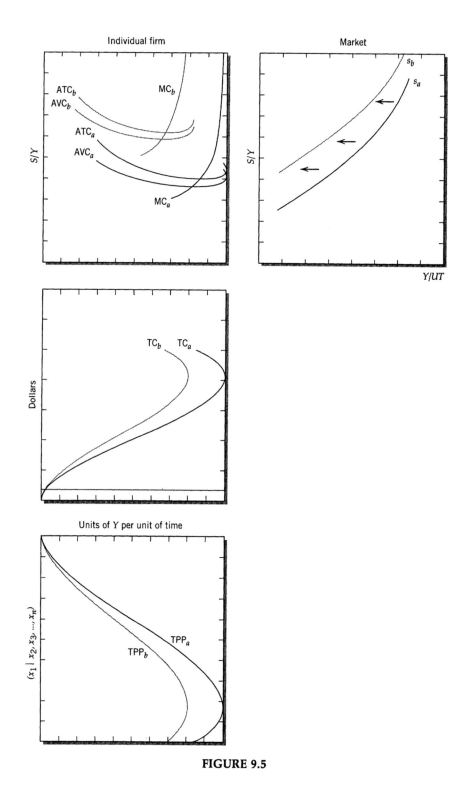

FIGURE 9.5

are "sort of" variable or "sort of" fixed. These pseudofixed resources tend to be "blocky" or "discrete" in nature (discrete means that the item is available only in whole units, that is, it is not easily divisible. It is difficult, for example, to buy a tenth of a tractor. A tenth of a ton of fertilizer, by way of contrast, presents no problem). A further difficulty associated with these pseudofixed resources is that whereas these resources *can* be varied, the price at which they are acquired is very different from the price at which they may be salvaged.

Figure 9.6 presents a factor–factor situation in which the variable resource X_1 can be acquired and salvaged at the same price. The alternative resource X_2 can be acquired at one price, but salvaged only at a substantially lower price. The least cost combination of resources for any given level of output is defined by the points on the isoproduct curves at which the marginal rate of factor substitution is equal to the inverse ratio of factor prices:

$$\frac{\Delta X_2}{\Delta X_i} = \frac{P_{x1}}{P_{x2}} \qquad (9.1)$$

Geometrically, the marginal rate of factor substitution (i.e., the rate at which X_1 and X_2 will replace one another in maintaining a given level of product) at any point on a particular isoproduct curve is defined by the slope of the curve at that point ($\Delta X_2 / \Delta X_1$). The inverse ratio of factor prices may be defined simply by dividing some arbitrary production budget (B) by the prices for each of the two resources. The point at B/P_{x1} on the horizontal axis of Figure 9.6 defines the quantity of X_1 that could be acquired for an expenditure of B. The point at B/P_{x2a} on the vertical axis defines the quantity of X_2 that could be acquired for that expenditure. The solid line connecting these points is an isocost line that defines all of the various combinations of these resources that could be purchased for a cost outlay of B.

The slope of the line between B/Px_1 and B/Px_{2a} defines the inverse ratio of factor prices. Lines parallel with this line and tangent to the isoproduct curves define the least cost combinations of resources for each level of output when it is necessary to acquire the intermediate resource X_2. The locus of these points of tangency defines the path along which production would be expanded in response to increased product prices.

This process may be repeated, using the salvage value for X_2 (the dashed lines in Figure 9.6) to define the least-cost combinations of resources under circumstances in which the intermediate-term resource has already been acquired. The locus of these points of tangency would define a path along which production might be reduced in response what are perceived by the manager to be "permanent" changes in product price.

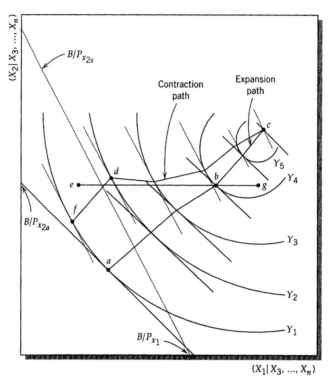

FIGURE 9.6

If a manager had determined that the price of product Y made Y_4 the appropriate level of output, output would be expanded to point b along the expansion path, acquiring more of both X_1 and X_2. Now suppose the price of the product declines such that some level of output between Y_1 and Y_2 becomes the profit-maximizing level of output. The manner in which this adjustment in output occurs is heavily dependent upon the nature of the manager's judgment regarding the probable duration of this lower price. If he expects the change to be temporary, his adjustment will be along the b–e path, maintaining the level of the intermediate-term variable resources and making the full adjustment through reductions in the levels at which short-term variable resources are employed.

If the manager perceived the price change to be more permanent in nature, the adjustment would be of a very different sort. Rather than making the entire adjustment through reductions in the usage of X_1, he would move from point b on the Expansion Path to point d on the Contraction Path by reducing the usage of X_1. From this point, he would move from point d down the contraction path toward point f, salvaging

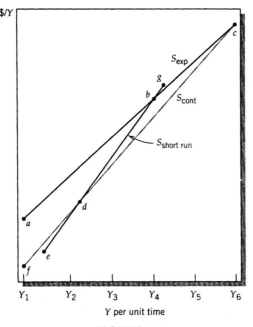

FIGURE 9.7

some of his intermediate-term resource and reducing his usage of both resources.

The impact of this situation upon the supply function is shown in Figure 9.7. The letters designating the points in Figure 9.6 and 9.7 are identical for the same levels of output. This demonstrates the reality that supplies of most farm products are reduced along a path very different from that along which they are expanded. The supply function along which supplies are reduced is typically less elastic than is the expansion supply function. That is, because of the problems associated with asset fixity, a much larger price change is generally required to get output reduced by a given quantity than is required to get it expanded by that amount.

OTHER PRODUCTION AND PROFIT OPPORTUNITIES FOR RESOURCES _____

How does one go about analyzing the expected impact of a change in the income opportunity associated with another product, the production of which can be accomplished using the same set of resources? Turkeys, for example, may be produced in facilities designed for broilers with only very minor modifications in those facilities. Corn can be produced with the same land, machinery, equipment, and human resources as can soybeans. Oats or barley can compete for the same resources as can wheat. The major difference between these enterprises with a given set of resources is the short-term resources upon which the operating funds are spent. That is, seed wheat may be purchased with the same funds that would be utilized to purchase seed oats or seed barley. While there may be some differences in the quantities of other short-term resources utilized in these enterprises, these resources are the same and can be purchased with the operating funds.

For purposes of illustration, let's assume that we have two products— Y_1 and Y_2, between which we can allocate some given set of resources. Since operating funds can command all of the short-term resources, let's use operating capital as the variable resource—a surrogate for all of the short-term variable resources commanded by operating capital. The rate at which operating capital may be combined with other resources and transformed into product Y_1, i.e., the production function for Y_1, is shown in the upper-left quadrant of Figure 9.8. The production function for Y_2 is shown in the lower-right quadrant of that figure.

The lower-left quadrant of Figure 9.8 shows the level of operating capital available and the available alternative allocations of that operating capital. That is, both axes in this quadrant measure operating capital. The distances $0-j$ and $0-a$ are exactly equal and represent exactly the same level of operating capital. A straight line from point a to point j in this quadrant defines the options the manager has regarding the allocation of this variable resource between the two products.

If the manager should decide to utilize all of this resource on Y_2 to the exclusion of Y_1, the result would be allocation a in the lower left quadrant, which would translate to a on the Y_2 production function and a in the upper-right quadrant, showing "a" level of Y_2 and zero Y_1. If he should choose allocation b, a different combination of Y_2 and Y_1 would now be produced, as shown by the points labeled b in the four quadrants. A reallocation to c or any other point would similarly restructure the combination of the two products produced.

As the variable resource continues to be reallocated between Y_1 and Y_2, the product–product relationship in the upper-right quadrant of Figure 9.8 is defined. This product–product relationship will, of course, be recognized as the production possibilities curve to which most students are introduced in their basic course in either micro- or macroeconomics.

Since the upper-right quadrant of Figure 9.8—the production possibilities curve—is the portion of the figure that is ultimately relevant to the question of how the supply function for one good may be impacted by changes in the profitability of another, let's extract this portion of the

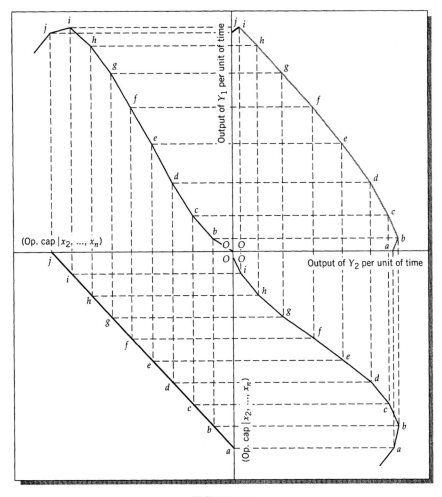

FIGURE 9.8

figure for further examination (Figure 9.9). The profit maximizing combination of Y_1 and Y_2 is defined by the position where the marginal rate of product transformation is equal to the inverse ratio of product prices:

$$\frac{\Delta Y_1}{\Delta Y_2} = \frac{P_{y2}}{P_{y1}} \qquad (9.2)$$

Geometrically, the marginal rate of product transformation (i.e., the rate at which reallocation of resources can change the combination of products produced) at any point on the production possibilities curve is defined by the slope of the curve at that point ($\Delta Y_1/\Delta Y_2$). The inverse ratio of product prices can be defined simply by dividing some arbitrary

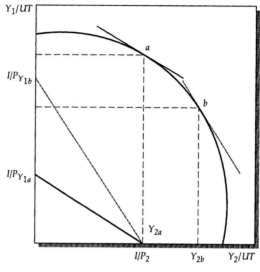

FIGURE 9.9

income target (I) by the prices for each of the two products in order to measure the quantities of each of these goods that would be required to generate that arbitrary level of income. The solid line from I/Py_{1a} to I/Py_2 in Figure 9.9 is an isoincome line defining all the combinations of the two products that would generate I in income. The slope of this line defines the inverse ratio of product prices (Py_{2a}/Py_1). A line parallel with

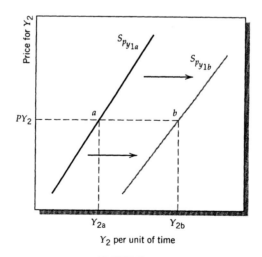

FIGURE 9.10

this isoincome line and tangent to the production possibilities curve defines the profit maximizing combination for these prices for Y_1 and Y_2 at point a.

This process may be repeated for a new, lower price for Y_1 (Py_{1b}), and the new profit maximizing position will be identified at point b. It is clear from this analysis that a reduction in the price of Y_1 generates a reallocation of resources from Y_1 to Y_2, such that the output of Y_1 is reduced and that of Y_2 is increased, even though the price for Y_2 is unchanged. The impact on the supply function for Y_2 is shown in Figure 9.10.

TECHNOLOGY _____

The impact of an increase in technology simply implies that a given set of resources will produce more than was previously the case and that a higher level production function has emerged. Analytically, this is identical with the weather or fixed resource impact shown in Figure 9.5. Technology may be defined as a fixed resource. Thus, a change from TPP_b to TPP_a in Figure 9.5 would be associated with a downward shift in per unit costs that would translate into an increase in the market supply function.

INSTITUTIONAL ARRANGEMENTS _____

Like technology, institutional arrangements might be defined to be a fixed resource. If an institutional arrangement such as a 20 percent "set aside" for land employed in the production of a commodity such as wheat were to be imposed, a farmer with 600 acres of wheat land could only plant 500 acres of wheat and still realize the benefits of the farm programs. Thus, his fixed resource of land has effectively been reduced from 600 to 500 acres (or alternatively, it now requires 1.2 acres of the fixed land resource to produce one acre of wheat). Analytically, the situation is identical with that shown in Figure 9.5.

Great effort has been expended to provide a theoretical framework within which to anticipate the sorts of impact that changes in the *ceteris paribus* conditions of supply might be expected to have on a market supply function and hence upon market price. A fundamental understanding of these relationships is crucial to any empirical estimate of a market supply function that is to be used in a price analysis for forecasting purposes. When real data are collected for use in an analysis, the only guide an analyst has for assessing the probable quality of the information is the economic theory that suggests the direction of impact that should be expected from any variable.

An analyst who is attempting to forecast the supply of pork and finds a negative relationship between the data regarding the size of the corn crop and the data regarding the volume of pork produced in the subsequent year knows that this relation does not make sound economic sense. There is most probably an error in the data collected or a gross error in the processes of the analysis. Knowledge of economic theory will provide guidance in reassessing both the data and the analysis.

Economic theory is also useful in guiding the analyst regarding what data to collect. Continuing with our hog supply example, information regarding the availability and cost of concentrate feeds is an obviously useful variable for analysis of supply. The inventory of various types of hog production facilities provides information regarding upper limits on possible production. The corn–hog price ratio would provide insight into whether producers are likely to earn greater profits by marketing corn directly or by marketing corn through livestock. Impending changes in farm programs have obvious implications for grain production, and hence for hog production.

CHAPTER **10**

Supply–Demand Relationships— Demand

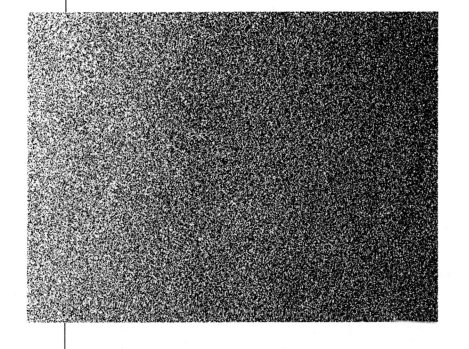

I n Chapter 9, we recognized that the source of any change in prices resulting from a supply adjustment was a change in one of the *ceteris paribus* conditions of supply. We identified and analyzed seven different *ceteris paribus* conditions of supply:

1. Cost of resources
2. Weather
3. Levels of "fixed" resources
4. Numbers of producers
5. Alternative opportunities for owned resources
6. Technology
7. Institutional arrangements

We saw how production functions and factor–product models in their various combinations and permutations were basic to any supply relationship. We examined the manner in which a change in each of the *ceteris paribus* conditions of supply caused shifts in supply via an impact upon the factor–product model—of the factor–factor and product–product models, which are fundamentally nothing more than combinations of sets of factor–product analyses.

From the analysis in Chapter 9, we could postulate supply to be:

$$\hat{Q} = f(\hat{P}, RC, W, FR, PrNo, Op_{alt}, T, IA) \tag{10.1}$$

where:

$\hat{Q}$ is the quantity expected to be supplied
$\hat{P}$ is the price expected at the time the product will be ready for market
RC is the cost of resources
W is weather
FR is the level of fixed resources present
$PrNo$ is the number of producers
Op_{alt} is the alternative opportunities for resources
T is technology
IA is institutional arrangements

If we were going to estimate this function through the use of a regression equation using time series data, we might postulate the relationship to be:

$$\hat{Q} = a + b_1\hat{P} + b_2RC + b_3W + b_4FR + b_5PrNo + b_6Op_{alt} + b_7T + b_8IA \tag{10.2}$$

190

Some of these variables—weather and technology, for example—would undoubtedly be dropped from the analysis because there are no data series that provide a dependable measure of weather over broad production areas. (These are the sorts of variables that we use trends and cycles to estimate.) But we saw in the case of our supply analysis that economic theory provided us with a framework within which we could anticipate the algebraic sign of the various b values. We recognized that an unexpected sign on one of these b values was a signal for an immediate reassessment of both our data and our analysis.

The same general analytical approach we used for supply is appropriate for analyzing market demand. Shifts in demand occur if and only if there are changes in the *ceteris paribus* conditions of demand. Among those *ceteris paribus* conditions of demand would be:

1. Consumer income
2. Consumer tastes and preferences
3. Price and availability of alternative goods
4. Consumer habits
5. Numbers of consumers, and
6. Institutional arrangements
   a. International trade arrangements
   b. Monetary and fiscal policy
   c. etc.

Thus, we might postulate a price-dependent demand relationship for product A to be:

$$\hat{P}_A = f(Q_A, P\&Q_{alt}, I, \text{etc.}) \qquad (10.3)$$

where:

$\hat{P}_A$ is the expected price of product A.

Q_A is the quantity of A available.

$P\&Q_{alt}$ is the price and availability of alternative goods.

I is income.

etc. represents all the other ceteris paribus conditions of demand.

As in the case of supply, we could postulate a form in which we would estimate this demand function, recognizing that economic theory would provide the benchmarks by which we could anticipate at least the direction of influence exerted by each of these *ceteris paribus* conditions.

A basic model that is fundamental to demand analysis is the indifference map (Figure 10.1). The shape and configuration of the indifference curves provide basic information regarding a consumer's state of tastes and preferences between two goods. When that consumer's budget for

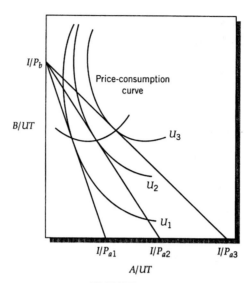

FIGURE 10.1

these two goods—an indicator of income—is divided by the prices for the two products, the maximum quantities of each of these accessible to this consumer are defined. That is, the area below a line from I/P_b to I/P_{a1} in Figure 10.1 defines the portion of the consumer's utility surface that is accessible under these price and income conditions. Since the consumer's objective is to achieve the maximum utility (or satisfaction) permitted by the income and price constraints, he/she will choose the combination of products A and B that occurs at the point of tangency between this budget constraint and the indifference curve U_1. That is, of all the combinations of products available, this is the one that provides the highest attainable level of satisfaction.

If the price of product A declines by half to P_{a2}, the doubled quantity of A that can be purchased with a given level of income allows an enlarged portion of the utility surface to become available. Quite predictably, our sample consumer moves to a higher indifference curve, substituting the now less expensive product A for some B. If the price declines still further, to P_{a3}, he/she moves to a still higher indifference curve, increasing consumption of **both** goods. The locus of points tracing out the combinations of goods this consumer will select as the price for A changes (in the absence of any other changes—i.e., *ceteris paribus*) defines the price-consumption curve. Mathematically, the price-consumption curve may be defined:

$$\frac{\Delta B}{\Delta A} = \frac{P_a}{P_b} \tag{10.4}$$

In "Economese," points along the price-consumption curve are found where the marginal rate of product substitution is equal to the inverse ratio of product prices. In English, points along the price-consumption curve are found where a dollar's worth of one good will replace exactly a dollar's worth of the alternative good in maintaining a given level of satisfaction.

Whereas the price-consumption curve is not a demand function *per se,* a demand function can be very readily derived from this curve (Figure 10.2). All that is necessary is to chart the various quantities of product *A* purchased against the prices associated with those quantities. (The lower portion of Figure 10.2 is simply the inverted mirror image of Figure 10.1. This inversion and imaging allows the same *A* axis to be common to both the upper and lower portions of the diagram.) Since market demand is simply the horizontal summation of the individual demands for all consumers participating in the market, deriving a mar-

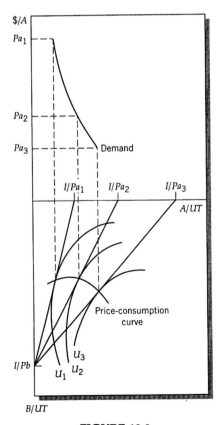

FIGURE 10.2

ket demand would be a matter of adding up those individual demand curves.

Three of the *ceteris paribus* conditions of market demand are incorporated into the individual demand function derived in Figure 10.2. Income, tastes and preferences, and the price of alternative goods are all held constant. Let's examine these for an indication of the appropriate expectations regarding impact upon market demand.

THE IMPACT OF TASTES AND PREFERENCES _____

The shape and configuration of the indifference curves provide insights regarding the state of consumer tastes and preferences. In Figure 10.3, the consumer's tastes and preferences have shifted away from product *A* toward product *B* as demonstrated by the two indifference curves *U* and *U'*. The adjustment from point *m* to point *n* illustrates a reduction in this consumer's willingness to purchase product *A*, even though prices and incomes are unchanged. This would show up in the upper portion of Figure 10.2 as a shift to the left in the position of the demand curve for product *A*.

There are a number of reasons why consumers' tastes and preferences might change. The discovery of unhealthful associations with products such as tobacco might cause such shifts. The emergence of previously unavailable products such as the microwavable poultry entrees or the poultry-based luncheon meats might cause shifts away from less con-

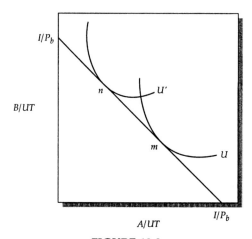

FIGURE 10.3

venient meat products. The so-called fitness craze has probably caused some shift in preference toward fresh fruits and vegetables.

As a practical matter, quantitative measures of changes in consumer tastes and preferences are virtually impossible to achieve. Since these changes are typically very gradual, the most effective method for dealing with them is probably through trend analysis.

THE IMPACT OF INCOME ———————————————

A change in income simply makes available a larger portion of the consumer's utility surface. That is, an increase in income from I_1 to I_2 in the case of Figure 10.4 for any given combination of product prices simply shifts the budget line upward and to the right. The consumer would adjust the combination of goods purchased from point m to point n, increasing consumption of both goods. But the demand for A, shown in the upper portion of Figure 10.2, would have shifted to the right, showing the consumer's willingness and ability to increase his purchases of A at any given price as a result of his increased income.

In the case of Figure 10.4, both A and B are superior or normal goods. There is, however, a category of goods that we call inferior goods that many consumers will avoid if their income is sufficient to permit it. If A were an inferior good such as hog lard or dry beans, the increase in

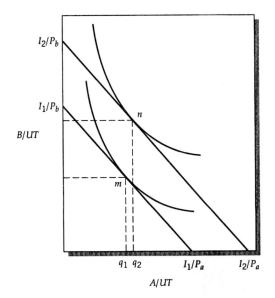

FIGURE 10.4

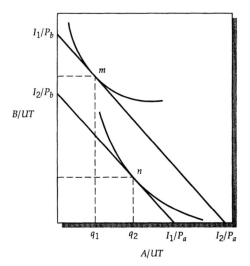

FIGURE 10.5

income would still make a broader range of combinations of goods available (Figure 10.5). But the consumer would reduce consumption of the inferior good A in response to the enlarged income, while substantially increasing the consumption of the superior good B, adjusting from point m to point n. Thus, the demand function for inferior good A would have shifted to the left in response to the increased income. Reductions in income, of course, in the case of both Figures 10.4 and 10.5 should have the reverse effects.

CHANGES IN THE PRICE OF
ALTERNATIVE GOODS _____

The impact of a change in the price of an alternative good is shown in Figure 10.6. In this case, the increase in the price of the alternative product B from P_{b1} to P_{b2} has reduced the maximum total purchase of B attainable from a given income or budget. The resulting shift in the line defining the combinations of products available under these new conditions has reduced the portion of the utility surface to which the consumer has access. The consumer's adjustment from point m to point n, reducing consumption of the relatively more expensive product and increasing the consumption of the other in response to an increased

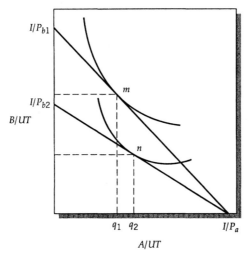

FIGURE 10.6

price for one of them, suggests a relationship of substitutability between the goods. Thus, as a result of the increased price for *B*, the quantity of *A* our consumer is willing and able to buy at the price of P_a has increased. Our demand for product *A* in the upper portion of Figure 10.2 would have demonstrated a shift to the right as a result of the increased price for the substitute *B*.

We know from our experience in courses in economic principles that not all goods are substitute goods. Whereas some pairs of goods do indeed tend to be substitutes (chicken and pork, for example), others such as shoes and shoe laces or gasoline and tires tend to be "complements." That is, as the consumption of one of these changes, the consumption of the other is likely to change in the same direction. Figure 10.7 illustrates the adjustment in consumption of product *A* in response to a change in the price of a complement good *B*. The increase in the price of *B* from P_{b1} to P_{b2} is similar to that in the case of substitutes. But because of the complementary relationship between the products (indicated by the different shape and configuration of the indifference curves), the adjustment from point *m* to point *n* shows a reduction in the use of **both** products in response to an increase in the price of only one.

There is, of course, a third type of relationship between goods, or more precisely an **absence** of relationship. These goods would be independent. In the case of independent goods, the adjustment in the combination of goods purchased would occur entirely in terms of the good, which has experienced a price change.

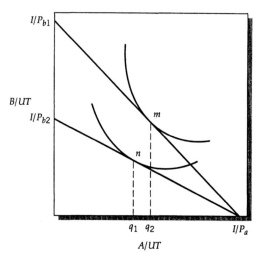

FIGURE 10.7

Price Effects Versus Income Effects

It will have been noted that we have consistently discussed consumer response to changes in the *ceteris paribus* conditions of individual consumer demand in terms of how large a portion of the consumer's utility surface (or indifference "map" of that surface) could be accessed, given prices and income. Any time there is a change in price, a consumer with a given level of income experiences a change in the **purchasing power** of that income. Whereas the **dollar** value of income may be unchanged, the fact that the portion of the indifference map that is attainable has changed means that there has been a change in the consumer's **real** income.

The previously discussed adjustments in the combinations of goods purchased in response to changes in price may be analyzed for separating those adjustments into the portion that truly results from the change in price and that which is a response to the adjustment in real income. In Figure 10.8, the price of the product A has risen from P_{a1} to P_{a2}, with consumer tastes and dollar income remaining unchanged. The budget line, which defines the array of attainable combinations of A and B, has rotated downward as a result (from I/P_b–I/P_{a1} to I/P_b–I/P_{a2}). The adjustment in purchases from point *m* to point *n*, reducing consumption of **both** products, is as was previously discussed.

We could compensate this consumer for the impact of the price change upon purchasing power by providing just enough supplemental

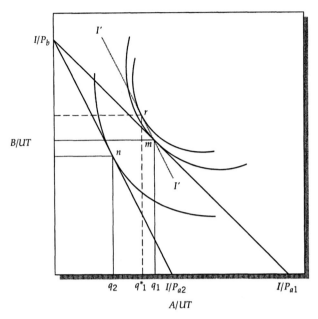

FIGURE 10.8

income to allow for the purchase of the original combination of products at point m (shown by the dotted line I'–I', which maintains the new price relationship). But if this action were taken, the consumer would no longer be content to purchase combination m. Rather, combination r, would be chosen, allowing, a still higher level of satisfaction to be achieved. That is, given the new price relationship between products A and B, and an income sufficient to indulge in combination m, the consumer would reduce consumption of A in favor of B. So the reduction from q_1 to q_1^* (since real income is the same for the two combinations that yield these two quantities) is the result of the increased price for product A. The reduction from q_1^* to q_2 would be the result of the real income impact of the price change.

The real income impact of price change is not inconsequential. One of the best illustrations of this reality is the multinational oil companies and the OPEC cartel doubling crude oil prices in 1974–75 and the subsequent tripling of those already doubled prices in 1979–81. Given the very large U.S. per capita consumption of energy, the adjustments in U.S. consumer buying habits forced by the dramatically increased energy costs were substantial and very far-reaching. The shift from the large, luxurious "gas guzzler" types of automobiles to the smaller, more efficient models was obviously related to the increased cost of energy.

Most people would not intuitively draw inferences from increased energy costs to demand for meats. But when it is recognized that meats comprise the largest single expenditure category in the grocery costs for most families and that groceries comprise the largest single expenditure over which most families can exert immediate discretionary control, the oil–meat connection is not so far-fetched. There is very convincing evidence that the apparent decline in consumer demand for meats—and particularly for beef[1]—since the mid-1970s is closely linked with the income impacts of increased energy costs.

CONSUMER HABITS _____

Analyzing the impact of consumer habit upon the individual demand curve is identical with the analysis of changes in tastes and preferences. Habit has been treated as a separate category of *ceteris paribus* condition of demand because habitual patterns of consumer behavior are not necessarily associated with like or dislike for a certain product. Rather, habitual patterns of consumption—those that may well have been established in childhood—cause some consumers to ignore the existence of certain products.

A good example of habitual consumption patterns is the consumer in Middle America who may *like* fish perfectly well—and perhaps even prefer it to some alternative sources of dietary protein. But that consumer's mother (or grandmother) in the land-locked Midwest did not have access to fresh fish. Frozen fish was not available. As a result, fish very rarely appeared at family meals. Even though technology has more recently made fresh fish and high quality frozen fish available in almost any community with as many as 20,000 people, many Midwestern families who find fish in no way objectionable don't even think of this product when planning menus. These family consumption patterns tend to be perpetuated simply through force of habit.

Similar patterns of habit may be observed in other arenas. Most of us develop habitual patterns of performing our duties. If those duties include buying for a business organization, those habits may well show up as dimensions of a demand function. Continuing with our food example, an examination of the menus for almost any group feeding operation such as a public school lunchroom, a hospital or a university dining hall will generally reveal a pattern in the frequency with which certain dishes appear. Even though ground beef may be less expensive this week, if liver and onions are due, students are very likely going to be presented with liver and onions rather than meat loaf, notwithstanding

---

[1] See John W. Goodwin, "Sources of Change in Beef Demand," *Arkansas Farm Research*, Vol. 36, No. 2, Arkansas Agricultural Experiment Station, Fayetteville, Arkansas, May–June 1987.

the reality that many people consider one serving of liver per person per lifetime to be adequate.

We have seen that analyzing the impact of changes in the *ceteris paribus* conditions of the individual demand function is a fairly straightforward process. Since the market demand function is simply the horizontal summation of the demand functions for all the individuals participating in that market, the *ceteris paribus* conditions associated with the individual demand functions are carried along in the process of summation to be included as dimensions of the market demand function. If the numbers of consumers participating in the market should change, then the total market demand would obviously shift to the right (in the case of an increase in the number of market participants).

The impact upon market demand resulting from changes in institutional arrangements would depend upon the type of arrangement under consideration and the type of change. Such changes are associated with the market demand function, and are reflected in the individual demand functions by way of impacts either upon prices or incomes. For example, an increase in the personal income tax rate would reduce the disposable income for consumers paying the higher taxes and would appear in the indifference analysis from which individual demand functions are derived as a downward shift in the budget line. This would result in a reduction in the demand for consumer goods, unless the increased collection of taxes were to be used to enhance the incomes of lower-income people.

In the event that the increased revenue were to be used to transfer income from high- to low-income consumers, one would normally expect the change to be associated with reduced demand for inferior goods such as lard, dry beans, and corn meal and with increased demand for items such as vegetable oils, animal proteins, and fresh fruits and vegetables. If, on the other hand, the increased revenue were to be used for public goods such as improved weapons systems, highways, and public health, the market demand for the items which are ingredients for those public goods would increase.

CHAPTER 11

Demand and Elasticity[1]

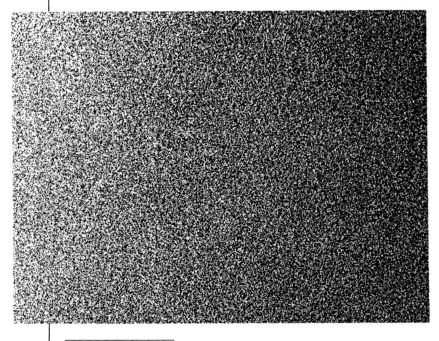

---

[1] Many of the materials in this chapter have been drawn from John W. Goodwin, *Agricultural Economics*, Reston Publishing Co., a Prentice-Hall Company, Reston, Virginia, 1977.

When we discussed the supply relationships, we recognized the importance of the time dimension. We saw how the supply function within certain time frames was not a reversible function because of differences in the prices at which intermediate-term production assets could be acquired and those at which those assets could be salvaged. There is a similar phenomenon in certain demand relationships that arises from the fact that the total effect of an economic change may not be accomplished immediately but rather be distributed over some extended period of time.

From the left-hand portion of Figure 11.1, we can see that the equilibrium quantity exchanged has been reduced from q_1 to q_2 as a result of a shift in the supply function. But rather than moving directly from q_1 to q_2 as is suggested by the left-hand portion, consumers make the adjustment more gradually. The right side of the diagram in Figure 11.1 suggests one of the numerous possible paths of response over which the response might be distributed. This idea of a delayed response on the part of consumers (or producers) to some economic change is not unlike the concept of the cobweb theorem, which also postulates a lagged response. The term that has been coined to describe the lagged adjustment over some period of time is "distributed lags."

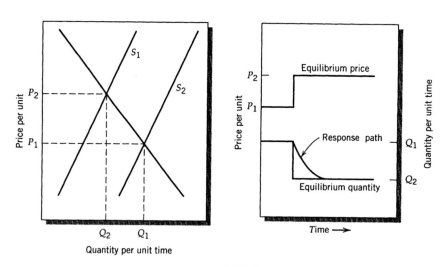

FIGURE 11.1

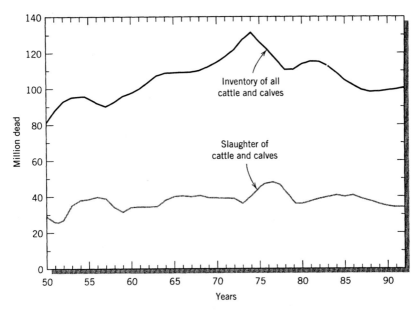

FIGURE 11.2. Total bovine slaughter compared with December 31 inventory of all cattle and calves, by years, United States, 1950–92.

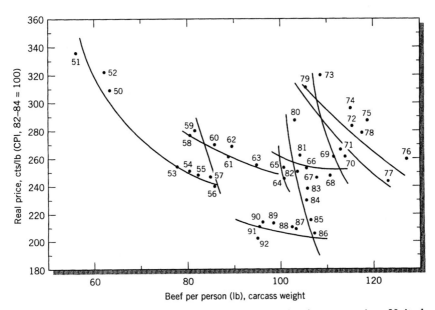

FIGURE 11.3. Real retail beef price and per capita beef consumption, United States, 1950–92, with estimated free-hand demand relationships.

A classic case of the distributed lag in response to price changes may be seen in the case of the pattern of beef consumption during the post-World War II period (Figures 11.2 and 11.3). As the availability of beef was cyclically expanded, consumers would readily increase beef consumption in response to very modest reductions in real prices. But when the availability of beef was cyclically reduced, consumers were not nearly so ready to accept the change. Very minor reductions in per capita beef availability were met with stubborn resistance and a rapid bidding up of real beef prices as consumers vied to maintain their level of beef consumption.

Once prices reached a level (typically 20–25 percent above the prices that were observed at the end of the increasing consumption phase of the previous cycle) that encouraged the beef industry to embark on the next expansionary phase of the cattle cycle, consumers would again absorb the increased availability of beef with very modest incentives in the way of price reductions. The statistical analysis of this phenomenon suggested that consumers would complete their adjustment to a reduced beef price in less than three months.[2] But adjustments to reduced availability of beef and higher beef prices required more than *seven years*! That is, *consumption was not reduced along the same price-quantity demand path as it was increased.* The response pattern was not reversible. This nonreversible consumer response pattern is analogous to the nonreversible production response we observed earlier in the case of supply. Following the disruptions of the energy crises in 1974–75 and again in 1980–81, the demand for beef began to shift downward, but the lagged responses were still evident.

The delayed (or lagged) response on the part of consumers to economic change may very possibly be a major part of the reason for some apparent differences in price elasticity estimates for agricultural products derived by various researchers over the past 30 years. In the case of beef, for example, Brandow's[3] 1957–59 analysis showed a beef price elasticity of demand of −0.68. George and King[4], using the 1946–65

---

[2] See John W. Goodwin, Reuven Andorn and James E. Martin, *The Irreversible Demand Function for Beef*, Technical Bulletin T-127, Oklahoma Agricultural Experiment Station, Stillwater, Oklahoma, June 1968

[3] G.E. Brandow, *Interrelationships Among Demands for Farm Products and Implications for Control of Market Supply*, Pennsylvania State University, Agricultural Experiment Station Bulletin 680, August 1961.

[4] P.S. George and G.A. King, *Consumer Demand for Food Commodities in the United States with Projections for 1980*, Giannini Foundation Monograph No. 26, California Agricultural Experiment Station, March 1971.

period, showed a beef price elasticity of −0.42, whereas Heien[5] using 1947–79 data, showed an elasticity of −0.96. All of these estimates suggest a relatively price inelastic demand, and all were negative in sign (meaning consumption was reduced as prices increased). But there are still some rather large apparent differences among the three.

An examination of the relationships shown in Figure 11.3 for the various time periods used by these researchers can be very revealing. The 1955–57 period used by Brandow was at the end of the 1951–56 phase of increasing per capita availability of beef when consumers were encouraged by very modest price reductions to absorb a substantial increase in availability. Thus, the response of consumers over this period was much less inelastic than would have been the case had 1957 been the initial year of the analysis rather than the terminal year.

George and King's longer-term analysis over the 1946–65 period took into account three complete cycles of increasing and decreasing per capita beef availability, allowing a more complete picture of consumer response and a rather different estimate of price elasticity of demand. Heien's analysis of the 33-year period from 1947–79 includes four complete cycles of increasing and decreasing per capita beef availability plus a part of a fifth. Thus, the elasticity estimate of −0.95 is colored to some degree by the fact that a partial cycle was involved at the end of the period.

During the 1980–86 period, when the full impact of income shocks resulting from the two energy crises and the altered focus of monetary policy came into play, beef demand appears to have become highly inelastic with respect to price. Very minor increases in per capita beef availability were associated with major reductions in real beef prices. Another way of interpreting this would be that beef demand was rapidly falling along the path described by the postulated 1980–86 relationship. Since 1986, beef demand appears to have stabilized with a relationship not unlike that observed earlier, albeit at a substantially lower level.

ELASTICITY DEFINED _____

What does price elasticity of demand have to do with the analysis and forecasting of agricultural prices? One leading economist has noted that the primary purpose for the concept of elasticity is to scare the hell out of

---

[5] Dale M. Heien, "The Structure of Food Demand: Interrelatedness and Duality," *American Journal of Agricultural Economics*, Vol. 64, No. 2, May 1982.

undergraduate economics students. Another has observed that elasticity is not only useless, it is dangerous. But these views, although they undeniably contain some element of truth, are somewhat overstated.

What, precisely, is elasticity? In the simplest of terms, elasticity is merely an indicator of the relative responsiveness (or sensitivity) on the part of producers or consumers to changes in factors such as price or income. A more formal definition of elasticity is the percentage change in quantity purchased (in the case of demand) or the quantity offered for sale (in the case of supply) in response to a 1 percent change in some other factor.

Arc Elasticity

We can measure the price elasticity of demand by dividing the percentage change in the quantity by the percentage change in price for a small segment or "arc" along a given demand curve. Algebraically, the relationship might be expressed as:

$$\epsilon = \frac{\Delta Q/Q}{\Delta P/P} \qquad (11.1)$$

where:

Q is quantity purchased, and
P is the price for the product

The algebraic formulation is shown geometrically in Figure 11.4. The change from point A to point B along the demand curve is the arc for

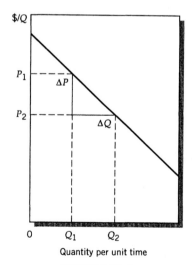

FIGURE 11.4

which we measure the elasticity. The change from Q_1 to Q_2 represents ΔQ in our formula, and the change from P_1 to P_2 represents ΔP. If our initial situation were at point A, and if the values of Q_1, Q_2, and P_1, P_2 were as shown below,

Point A	Point B
$Q_1 = 20$	$Q_2 = 25$
$P_1 = \$8$	$P_2 = \$7.50$

then our calculation of the elasticity of demand with respect to price moving from point A to point B would be:

$$\epsilon = \frac{Q_1 - Q_2/Q_1}{P_i - P_2/P_1} = \frac{\Delta Q/Q_1}{\Delta P/P_1} = \frac{20-25/20}{8 - 7.50/8} = \frac{5/20}{-0.50/8}$$

$$= \frac{1}{4} \times \frac{8}{-50} = \frac{-8}{2} = -4.0 \qquad (11.2)$$

if, however, we were to calculate the elasticity for moving from point B to point A, the estimate would be:

$$\epsilon = \frac{Q_2 - Q_1/Q_2}{P_2 - P_1/P_2} = \frac{\Delta Q/Q_2}{\Delta P/P_2} = \frac{25-20/25}{7.50 - 8/7.50} = \frac{5/25}{-0.50/7.50}$$

$$= \frac{1}{5} \times \frac{7.50}{-0.50} = \frac{7.50}{-2.50} = -3.0 \qquad (11.3)$$

Obviously, there is something amiss when we get two different estimates of elasticity for the same arc. The key to our difficulty lies in the fact that our percentages are different depending upon the point we select as our initial situation. This shows that our calculation of the elasticity for the arc between A and B is merely an approximation. The greater the size of the arc between A and B, the greater will be the difference in our two estimates, and the less will be the confidence that may be placed in either. Therefore, *it is imperative that the arc be small* (or as Alfred Marshall says, that the change in price be small[6]) if the resulting estimate of elasticity is to have any degree of reliability.

We can modify our basic elasticity formula to eliminate the discrepancy that arises from selecting either of the two end points of the A-B arc as the initial situation. This modification is accomplished by including *both* Q_1 and Q_2 and P_1 and P_2 in the calculation of the percentages such that:

$$\epsilon = \frac{(Q_1 - Q_2)/(Q_1 + Q_2)}{(P_1 - P_2)/(P_1 + P_2)} \qquad (11.4)$$

---

[6] Alfred Marshall, *Principles of Economics*, 8th ed. (London: Macmillan and Company, Ltd., 1920), Book III, Chapter IV.

Thus, the calculation for our example would be:

$$\epsilon = \frac{20 - 25/20 + 25}{8 - 7.50/8 + 7.50} = \frac{-5/45}{0.50/15.50} = \frac{-5}{45} \times \frac{15.50}{0.50} \qquad (11.5)$$
$$= \frac{-77.50}{22.50} = -3.44$$

The modified formula gives us an approximation of the elasticity within the arc from A to B in Figure 11.4. This represents an average of sorts for the two estimates that result from the basic formula. Further, the modification eliminates the problem of the discrepancy that arises from that formula: No matter which end of the arc is selected as the initial situation, the resulting estimate of elasticity is the same.

It should be pointed out that both the numerator and the denominator in the elasticity formula represent percentages. Thus, the elasticity estimate itself is a pure number. The algebraic sign of the elasticity estimate tells nothing more than the *direction* of the relationship. In our example, the sign is negative because the slope of the demand function in Figure 11.4 is negative. That is, within the arc between points A and B, if the price *increases* by 1 percent, we would expect the quantity taken to *decline* by approximately 3.44 percent. Since a 1 percent change in price is associated with more than 1 percent change in the quantity taken, demand is relatively elastic with respect to price *within the arc*.

If the absolute value (that is, the value without regard to algebraic sign) of the elasticity coefficient is between zero and one, it indicates a relatively inelastic relationship. If the absolute value is greater than one, the relationship is relatively elastic. The absolute value of the elasticity coefficient can range between zero and infinity for any given demand curve, *but it cannot pass through zero unless the curve exhibits a "U" shape* (that is, unless the demand curve reverses direction, such as sloping downward to the right and then beginning to slope upward and to the right, elasticity cannot pass through zero). If the elasticity coefficient should be exactly equal to one, elasticity is said to be *unitary*. That is, a 1 percent change in price will be associated with exactly a 1 percent change in the quantity taken.

Demand curves will often exhibit all three ranges of elasticity (elastic, inelastic, and unitary) within a single curve. This is always true in situations in which demand is a straight line. The selection of an arc along a given demand curve will frequently determine the value of the elasticity coefficient. Most demand curves are elastic with respect to price at relatively high prices and inelastic at relatively low prices. This suggests that as price for a product falls, sales will increase to some saturation point at which consumers are virtually "filled up" with the product. When this is the case, further price cuts will not induce buyers to increase purchases by relatively as much as the price has been cut (i.e., demand is inelastic). Conversely, when prices are already high, further price increases will induce buyers to either seek out substitute goods or to do without the product, causing the reduction in sales to be relatively greater than was the increase in price (in this case, demand is elastic).

Since both the elastic and inelastic ranges can occur within a single demand curve, it is obvious that as consumers pass from the elastic into the inelastic range, they must pass through some point (or range) of unitary elasticity.

Point Elasticity

In our analysis of the arc computation of elasticity, we saw the importance of keeping the arc small. Since we have seen how a straight-line demand curve includes all three ranges of elasticity, we know that the elasticity on the two ends of the arc must necessarily be different. It follows that there is a unique elasticity associated with each and every point within the arc. The arc elasticity computation, as modified, results in an average elasticity estimate that approximates the elasticity for all points within the arc. By keeping the arc small, the distortions that result from this averaging are minimized. If, however, we make the arc so small that it is impossible to distinguish point *A* from point *B*, we have in effect reduced our arc to a single point and can make a much more precise estimate of the elasticity coefficient.

The arc for which elasticity is to be calculated has been made so small in Figure 11.5 that the end points of the arc have become a single point. The quantity that consumers would consume if the product were free (i.e., if the price were zero) is measured by *ON* along the quantity axis. The level that price would need to reach before consumers would forego all consumption of the commodity is measured by *OD* along the price axis. Our straight-line demand curve, then, passes through points *D* and *N*, and has a negative slope of *−OD/ON* (the mathematical formula for calculating slope is "rise over run.") The problem we face is calculating the elasticity at some point along the demand curve such as at point *A*.

Our basic formula for calculating elasticity relates the percentage change in quantity to the percentage change in price such that:

$$\epsilon = \frac{\Delta Q/Q}{\Delta P/P} \tag{11.6}$$

Equation 11.6 may be rewritten:

$$\epsilon = \frac{\Delta Q}{Q} \times \frac{P}{\Delta P} = \frac{\Delta Q}{\Delta P} \times \frac{P}{Q} \tag{11.7}$$

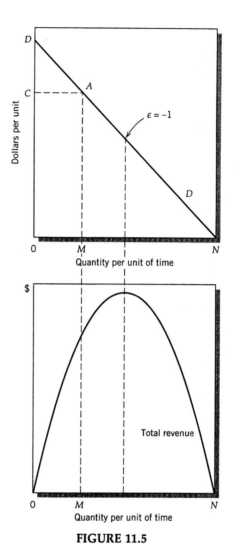

FIGURE 11.5

Since our demand curve is a straight line, any segment of that line has the same slope. But the final fraction in the identity represented by Equation 11.8 is the inverse of the ratio in our rewritten elasticity formulation. Thus:

$$\frac{OD}{ON} = \frac{MA}{MN} = \frac{\Delta P}{\Delta Q} \tag{11.8}$$

If we invert all of the fractions in Equation 11.8, we get $ON/OD = MN/MA = \Delta Q/\Delta P$. We can now substitute MN/MA for $\Delta Q/\Delta P$ in our elasticity formula. Since the slope of the demand function is negative, we know that the sign of MN/MA must be negative.

$$\epsilon = \frac{\Delta Q}{\Delta P} \times \frac{P}{Q} = -\frac{MN}{MA} \times \frac{P}{Q} \qquad (11.9)$$

Our original price, measured by MA, and our original quantity, measured by OM, may now be substituted into our elasticity formula such that:

$$\epsilon = \frac{\Delta Q}{\Delta P} \times \frac{P}{Q} = -\frac{MN}{MA} \times \frac{MA}{OM} \qquad (11.10)$$

We can rid ourselves of the two MA's through cancellation and find that the elasticity for any point along a linear demand function may be calculated by:

$$\epsilon = -\frac{MN}{OM} \qquad (11.11)$$

If the distance from M to N exceeds that from O to M, we can safely say that we are in the elastic range of the curve. Conversely, if OM is greater than MN, we are in the inelastic range.

The point elasticity calculation may be made for a curvalinear demand function as easily as for a linear one. All that is necessary is to draw a straight line tangent to the curve at the point where elasticity is to be measured (Figure 11.6). The ends of the tangent are extended until they intersect both the price and quantity axes. Then the elasticity computa-

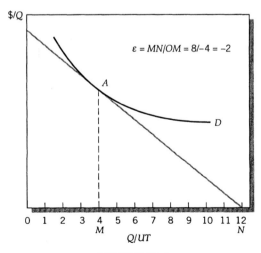

FIGURE 11.6

tion is made from the tangent in precisely the same manner as for a linear demand curve, that is, by calculating the *MN/OM* ratio.

An important dimension of the elasticity concept from an agricultural producer's or policy maker's point of view has to do with the total revenues generated at various points on a demand curve. If the demand for a product is price inelastic, increases in the available volume of the product will be associated with *reductions* in the total revenue generated (Figure 11.7). Since virtually all U.S. agricultural products are produced

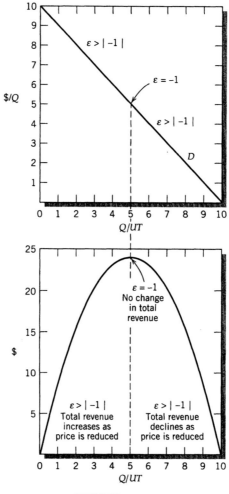

FIGURE 11.7

and sold in the inelastic portion of the market demand function, increased values of the total product at any given point in time can occur if and only if there is a reduction in total output! The only way agriculture can generate an increase in total revenues is to reduce the volume of sales!

PRICE FLEXIBILITY ———————————————————————

Price elasticity of demand is concerned with the responsiveness of consumers in the quantities they will purchase in response to a price change. But the price forecaster is frequently concerned with the volatility that might be expected in prices as a result of a change in the quantity of product made available for sale. Since elasticity measures the *quantity* response to a price change, the *inverse* of elasticity would measure the responsiveness of price to a quantity change. *Price flexibility* is the term used to describe the inverse of the elasticity relationship.

$$\text{(Price flexibility } (PF) = \frac{1}{\epsilon} \qquad (11.12)$$

If the price elasticity of demand for a product were −0.2, the price flexibility would be:

$$PF = \frac{1}{-0.2} = -5 \qquad (11.13)$$

That is, a 1 percent increase in the quantity made available would be associated with a 5 percent reduction in price. In the inelastic range of the demand curve, the absolute values of price flexibilities are substantially greater than one, meaning that a 1 percent change in quantity will generate a price change in excess of 1 percent. Thus, in the inelastic range of the demand curve, prices are much more volatile than are quantities, and quantities are much more volatile than are prices in the elastic range of demand.

The fact that most agricultural products are produced and sold in the inelastic range of the market demand function explains why agricultural prices tend to be extremely volatile and why the anticipation of changes in those prices is of major importance in the management of any firm whose business involves producing, processing, or marketing farm products.

When we discussed the lagged consumer response in beef demand, we recognized that the different lengths of the time periods involved in elasticity estimates were typically associated with different estimates of elasticity. In general, demand for agricultural products will be relatively more price elastic for periods within the storage life of a product than for periods that exceed the storage life. Also, demand for agricultural products is typically more price elastic over long periods of time than over shorter periods of time that still exceed the storage life of the product.

Storage of products can and typically does "smooth out" temporary gluts or shortages of product availability. When a glut of product reduces price to a point that owners of storage facilities can anticipate a positive price margin between the current period and some future period, the demand for storage purposes is added to the demand for immediate consumption. This activity prevents prices from falling as low as would have been the case in the absence of purchases for storage. When prices rise, the sales from storage are added to current producer marketings, preventing prices from rising to levels as elevated as they might otherwise have achieved. This "smoothing" effect yields a greater apparent degree of price elasticity than would be the case for periods over which the storage activity is not an option. That is, slaughter of meat animals can be delayed for a short time in anticipation of better prices. Fresh meat may be stored from week to week against anticipated price improvements. But these sorts of adjustments from year to year are out of the question. Thus, one would normally expect weekly or monthly demand to be more price elastic than annual demand.

Although weekly or monthly demand for a product may tend to be relatively more price elastic than annual demand, demand relationships over multiyear periods *also* tend to be relatively more elastic than annual demand. The reason for this relative increase in elasticity over longer periods is the greater opportunity for adjustment that exists with extended periods of time. A one-year increase in price may not allow a consumer enough time to make much adjustment in the quantity of a product used, whereas a multiyear period permits a great deal of adjustment opportunity. A vivid example of this situation is provided by the Energy Crisis of 1974–75.

At the onset of the energy crisis, U.S. consumers were by and large committed to very high levels of energy usage. Most U.S. automobiles were full-sized "gas guzzlers." Since energy had been quite inexpensive for a long period of time, the insulation in most residential construction was limited. Very limited attention had been given to the heat loss from homes or commercial buildings that were poorly sealed. About all consumers could immediately do in the face of rapidly increasing energy costs was to carpool, reduce the winter temperatures of their buildings and increase the summer temperatures, reduce the intensity of lighting in hallways and less frequently used areas, and pay the inflated price for a very necessary dimension of their existence.

Over the longer period, a great many energy-reducing adjustments were made. Americans could and did increase the levels of insulation in buildings. They improved the level of weather proofing to reduce heat loss. They replaced conventional furnaces and air conditioners with more energy efficient models and with heat pumps. They replaced gas guzzlers with smaller, more fuel-efficient vehicles. They developed more efficient internal combustion engines. They shifted electrical generation more toward the use of coal than petroleum. The end result was a substantial reduction in the rate of increase in per capita energy usage.

In general, elasticity measures have been developed for any *ceteris paribus* condition of demand that is measured in monetary terms. Conceptually, these measures are identical to the price elasticity measure we have already discussed. Income elasticity of demand is simply the percentage change in quantity purchased in response to a 1 percent change in the level of consumer income. Normal goods have positive income elasticities, suggesting that most consumers will buy more of that good if incomes rise. Inferior goods have negative income elasticities, suggesting that consumers will replace that good with more desirable goods if their incomes permit them to do so.

Cross-price elasticity is the percentage change in the purchased quantity of one good in response to a one percent change in the price of another. Complement goods have negative cross-price elasticities. The negative cross-price elasticity associated with complement goods suggests that an increase in the price of one of the complement goods will be associated with a reduction in the purchases of the other. (Perhaps more precisely, an increase in the price of one good, such as gasoline, will be associated with a reduction in the consumption of that good. The reduced consumption of the first good, gasoline, would be associated with a reduction in consumption of a complement good such as tires.) The positive cross-price elasticity associated with substitute goods is indicative of the reality that an increase in the price of a good will be associated with increased purchases of the other good as consumers substitute it for the now relatively more expensive good.

In general, elasticities of demand will be greater for goods that require a substantial portion of total income than for those that represent only a very minor portion of total income. Elasticities will be greater for luxury goods than for goods that are perceived to be absolute necessities. Greater availability of close substitutes will be associated with increased elasticities.

Tables 11.1 and 11.2 show price and income elasticity estimates that have been empirically derived for selected agricultural commodities over the past 25 years. Interestingly, these elasticities appear in general to have been remarkably stable. Heien's price elasticity estimates, published in 1982, for pork, chicken, and eggs are almost identical with those estimated by Brandow 20 years earlier. This recognizes the reality

TABLE 11.1. Estimates of Price Elasticities of Demand for Selected Commodities

Commodity	Brandow Farm Level (1955–57)	George and King Farm Level (1946–65)	Heien Mkt Level Not Specified (1947–79)	Huang Retail Level (1953–83)
Beef	−0.683	−0.416	−0.956	−0.617
Pork	−0.457	−0.241	−0.511	−0.730
Chicken	−0.737	−0.602	−0.797	−0.531
Eggs	−0.232	−0.225	−0.263	−0.145
Butter	−0.665	−0.461	−1.926	−0.167
Margarine	—	−0.693	−0.304	−0.267
Fresh milk	−0.144	−0.324	−0.539	−0.258
Potatoes	−0.108	−0.150	−0.392	−0.369
Wheat flour	—	−0.244	—	−0.109
Corn meal	—	−0.220	—	−0.147
Onions	—	−0.115	—	−0.196
Dry vegetables	−0.227[a]	−0.453	—	−0.125
Ice cream	−0.115	−0.451	—	−0.121
Fresh vegetables	—	—	−0.347	—
Processed vegetables	—	—	−0.856	—
Bread	—	—	−0.294	—
Wheat	−0.021	—	—	—
Rice	−6.038	—	—	—
Corn	−0.033	—	—	—

[a] Dry beans only

Source. G.E. Brandow, *Interrelations Among Demands for Farm Products and Implications for Control of Market Supply*, Pennsylvania State University, State College, Pa. Agricultural Exp. Sta. Bul. 680, August 1961; P.S. George and G.A. King, *Consumer Demand for Food Commodities in the United States with Projections for 1980*, Giannini Foundation Monograph 26, California Agricultural Experiment Station, Berkeley, CA. March 1971; Dale M. Heien, "The Structure of Food Demand: Interrelatedness and Duality," *American Journal of Agricultural Economics*, Vol. 64, No. 2, May 1982; Huang, K.S., *U.S. Demand for Food: A Complete System of Price and Income Effects*, ERS, USDA, Technical Bulletin No. 1714, Washington, DC, 1985.

TABLE 11.2. Estimates of Income Elasticities of Demand for Selected Commodities

Commodity	Brandow Farm Level (1955–57)	George and King Farm Level (1946–65)	Heien Mkt Level Not Specified (1947–79)	Huang Retail Level (1953–83)
Beef	0.47	0.29	1.27	0.445
Pork	0.32	0.009	0.33	0.442
Chicken	0.37	−0.037	0.33	0.364
Eggs	0.16	−0.076	−.39	−0.028
Butter	0.33	0.318	−2.29	0.023
Margarine	—	−0.022	0.64	0.111
Potatoes	0.08	0.008	−0.81	0.159
Rice	—	−0.651	—	−0.366
Wheat flour	—	−0.685	—	−0.122
Corn meal	—	−1.143	—	—
Dry beans	—	−0.914	—	0.585
Fluid milk	0.16	0.001	−0.55	−0.221

Source. G.E. Brandow, *Interrelations Among Demands for Farm Products and Implications for Control of Market Supply,* Pennsylvania State University, Agricultural Exp. Sta. Bul. 680, August 1961; P.S. George and G.A. King, *Consumer Demand for Food Commodities in the United States with Projections for 1980,* Giannini Foundation Monograph No. 26, California Agricultural Experiment Station, March 1971; Dale M. Heien, "The Structure of Food Demand: Interrelatedness and Duality," *American Journal of Agricultural Economics,* Vol. 64, No. 2, May 1982; Huang, K.S., *U.S. Demand for Food: A Complete System of Price and Income Effects,* ERS, USDA, Technical Bulletin No. 1714, Washington, DC, 1985.

that food consumption patterns change very gradually and only over long periods of time. The elasticity estimates for butter are the most dramatically different over the quarter-century time period for these estimates. This reflects the maturing of a generation that was never really exposed to butter. Many young Americans today appear to actually *prefer* margarine to butter.

CHAPTER 12

Estimation of Demand and Supply— Multiple Graphic Correlation

In Chapters 9, 10, and 11, we discussed in a generic sense the supply and demand relationships that we might expect for agricultural products. We recognized that the quantity supplied for any given time period was a function of the price that producers expected to receive at the time they were making production decisions, plus the impact of any changes in the *ceteris paribus* conditions that might cause the supply function to shift. The impact of these *ceteris paribus* conditions of supply along with the price expectations of producers would give an indication of the producers' expectations of *profitability*, which is really the bottom line of the supply relationship. Greater expectations of profitability will typically be associated with greater quantities of the product produced and offered for sale.

Algebraically, this supply relationship might be expressed:

$$QS_t = a + b_1 P_t + b_2 RC_t + b_3 T_t + \cdots + b_n IA_t \qquad (12.1)$$

where:

QS_t is the quantity supplied in the time period t,

P_t is the producer expectation of the prices to be received in time period t,

RC_t is the cost (which will to a major extent reflect availability) of resources in the time period t,

T_t is the level of technology in time period t,

IA_t is the configuration of institutional arrangements in time period t, and

the dots between the commas in the equation represent the parameters associated with other supply shifters.

Probably the two most critical elements in this algebraic expression of the supply relationship are the expected price and the cost of resources since these are the two major ingredients of profit expectations. The influence of technology is likely to be fairly minor from one year to the next since technological adaptation tends to be fairly gradual in its impact. But over the long periods of time involved in time series analysis, technology can be quite significant. The same thing is true of the levels of quasi-fixed resources and the numbers of producers. The *ceteris paribus* condition of institutional arrangements tends to be quite discrete in its impact and can generally be used to block or group the years of data that are associated with varying sets of institutional arrangements.

When we discussed the supply and demand relationships, we recognized that the quantity of product offered for sale was generally easier to forecast than was the price. This is true for a variety of reasons. Once agricultural production decisions are made and implemented, it is almost impossible to reverse them. Indeed, it is difficult even to modify them in any significant way. Because of this, the quantities available for market are largely exempt from the mass consumer psychology that can make demand relationships so volatile. Further, there are generally fewer measurable variables that can affect supply relationships during any given time period than is the case for demand. Thus, the estimate of supplies is typically quicker and simpler than is the estimate of demand. For this reason, if supply and demand are to be estimated separately, it is generally better to start with the supply relationship.

TREND ESTIMATE OF EXPECTED PRODUCTION AND PRICE ————————————

As an example of an effort to define the supply relationship, let's consider the case of turkeys over the 1960–92 period. The basic information for a supply analysis for turkeys is shown in Table 12.1. There has been a strong upward trend in production (Figure 12.1) and a strong downward trend in real prices (Figure 12.2) over this period. However, the trend in per capita production appears to be increasing at an increasing rate. This suggests that one of several factors is at work:

1. Real costs for the major ingredients for turkey production may have declined.
2. Technology may have made those ingredients progressively more productive such that real production costs have declined, *regardless* of the prices for ingredient costs.
3. Some combination of the two factors above encouraged turkey producers to continue to expand.

Thus, a second trend for the final 12 years of the production data is presented in Figure 12.2 showing the much greater rate of expansion during the more recent period. Had a trend for the final seven years of data been used, the growth rate would have been greater yet.

Based on the trends alone, we would have expected a 1993 per capita turkey production of 21.3 pounds live weight using the 1960–92 trend or of 26.7 pounds using the 1981–92 trend. We would have expected a real farm price for turkeys of 27.1 cents per pound (38 cents per pound in 1993 dollars). But there is obviously more than the simple trends in price and production at work here. There are some rather dramatic departures from the trend in both production and price, and the departures from

TABLE 12.1. TURKEYS—Supply Relationships, United States, 1960–90

Year	Turkey Production Mil lb (live wt)	U.S. Population (mil)	Farm Price for Turkeys (cts/lb)	CPI 1982–84 = 100	Prev Yr Real Price for Turkeys at Farm (cts/lb)	Per Cap. Turkey Production (lb live)	Diviations from Trend in Turkey Prod/Cap[a] (lb)	Change in per Capita Prod from Prev Yr (lb)	Prev Yr Turkey Feed Price Ratio
1960	1,489	180.7	25.4	29.6		8.2			
1961	1,87	183.7	18.9	29.9	85.77	10.2	0.6	1.9	5.6
1962	1,626	186.5	21.6	30.2	63.18	8.7	0.7	−1.5	4.4
1963	1,686	189.2	22.3	30.6	71.41	8.9	0.5	0.2	4.4
1964	1,826	191.9	21.0	31.0	72.84	9.5	0.7	0.6	4.9
1965	1,915	194.3	22.2	31.5	67.71	9.9	0.7	0.3	4.8
1966	2,123	196.6	23.1	32.5	70.37	10.8	1.3	0.9	5.1
1967	2,343	198.7	19.5	33.4	71.19	11.8	1.9	1.0	5.1
1968	2,015	200.7	20.5	34.8	58.41	10.0	−0.3	−1.8	4.4
1969	2,029	202.7	22.4	36.7	58.93	10.0	0.7	0.0	4.5
1970	2,197	205.1	22.6	38.8	61.11	10.7	−0.3	0.7	4.8
1971	2,256	207.7	22.1	40.5	58.21	10.9	−0.6	0.1	5.0
1972	2,424	209.9	22.2	41.8	54.57	11.5	−0.3	0.7	4.6
1973	2,452	211.9	38.2	44.4	53.07	11.6	−0.6	0.0	4.5
1974	2,437	213.9	28.0	49.3	85.97	11.4	−1.2	−0.2	4.4

Year									
1975	2,277	216.0	34.8	53.8	56.78	10.5	-2.4	-0.9	3.3
1976	2,606	218.0	31.7	56.9	64.66	12.0	-1.4	1.4	4.0
1977	2,562	220.2	35.5	60.6	55.69	11.6	-2.1	-0.3	3.7
1978	2,654	222.6	43.6	65.2	58.59	11.9	-2.2	0.3	3.8
1979	2,957	225.1	41.1	72.6	66.84	13.1	-1.3	1.2	4.6
1980	3,076	227.7	41.3	82.4	56.63	13.5	-1.4	0.4	4.2
1981	3,264	230.0	38.2	90.3	50.12	14.2	-1.1	0.7	3.6
1982	3,175	232.3	39.5	96.5	42.32	13.7	-2.0	-0.5	3.1
1983	3,336	234.5	38.0	99.6	40.93	14.2	-1.8	0.6	3.3
1984	3,386	236.7	48.9	103.9	38.14	14.3	-2.1	0.1	3.0
1985	3,702	238.8	47.2	107.6	47.08	15.5	-1.3	1.2	3.9
1986	4,147	241.6	44.4	109.6	43.88	17.2	0.0	1.7	4.5
1987	4,895	243.8	34.3	113.6	40.51	20.1	2.6	2.9	4.1
1988	5,059	246.4	36.9	118.6	30.20	20.5	2.6	0.5	3.2
1989	5,454	248.5	40.0	124.2	31.13	21.9	3.7	1.4	3.0
1990	5,805	249.9	38.3	130.7	32.22	23.2	4.6	0.3	3.2
1991	5,884	252.8	37.7	136.2	29.30	23.3	4.2	0.05	3.2
1992	6,109	255.4P	37.6	140.4P	27.68	24.0	4.6	0.7	3.3
1993	—	—	—	—	26.78	—	—	—	3.1

[a] Trend in Per Capita Production:

$Q_i = 6.36 + 0.426T_i$, where $T_i = 1$ in 1960. $R^2 = 0.81$, $S_y = 2.04$, $S_b = 0.037$

P Preliminary Data

SOURCE: Mark R. Weimar and Shauna Cromer, *U.S. Egg and Poultry Statistical Series, 1960–89*, ERS, USDA, Statistical Bulletin No. 816, September 1990; *Livestock and Poultry Situation and Outlook Report*, ERS, USDA, various issues since 1989.

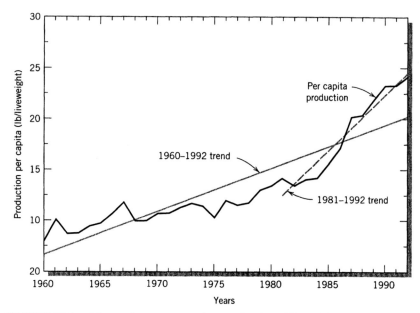

FIGURE 12.1. Live turkeys, per capita production, United States, with 1960–92 and 1981–92 trends.

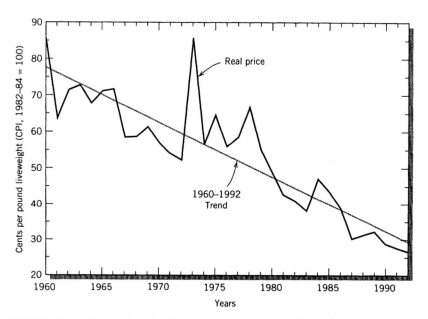

FIGURE 12.2. Real prices for live turkeys with trend, United States, 1960–92.

SOURCE: Mark R. Weimar and Shauna Cromer, *U.S. Egg and Poultry Statistical Series, 1960–89*, ERS, USDA, Statistical Bulletin No. 816, and *Livestock and Poultry Situation and Outlook Report*, ERS, USDA, various issues since 1989.

trend in price do not always correspond precisely with opposite departures from trend in production.

APPROACHES TO SUPPLY ANALYSIS _____

One would ordinarily begin the supply dimension of a price analysis with some estimate of the expected price. Probably the most naive of price expectations is that prices for the coming year will be the same as prices received during the past year. That is, immediate past prices may be used by producers as a forecast of future prices.

If we chart per capita turkey production over the 25-year period from 1961 through 1985 against the real turkey prices received by farmers the previous year (Figure 12.3), we would ordinarily expect to get a supply function of sorts.[1] But the configuration of the charted data in no way resembles a supply function. Indeed, the appearance is of a negative rather than a positive relationship between the previous year's price and the current year's production.

If the data are grouped, the 1962–69 period gives a relationship that is consistent with economic logic, as do the data for the 1970–79 period (with 1974 excluded as an "outlier"). The data for the 1982–86 period also show the positive relationship between turkey output and the previous year's price. The observations for 1980 and 1981 could have been grouped with the information on either side of these years without doing major violence to either of these relationships, but this is most probably a transitional period between these two relationships. A similar observation may be made regarding the data for 1987, with the 1988–92 data forming still a fourth supply relationship. (The data for 1991 and 1992 might be viewed as the beginning of another transitional period similar to 1980–81.) Over the entire 1960–92 period, the supply shifting impact of rapidly improving technology and/or declining resource costs obscures the positive relationship between these variables that economic logic would lead one to expect. That is, technology has caused the prices required to generate a given level of per capita turkey production to become progressively lower and lower.

Perhaps there is another way to get at the supply relationship. The major cost item in turkey production is feed cost. The "turkey-feed" price ratio measures the value of turkeys in terms of the value of feed. That is, a turkey-feed price ratio of 4.1 indicates that 1 pound of turkey commands the same monetary value as does 4.1 pounds of feed. Thus,

---

[1] It should be noted that Figure 12.3 shows the dependent variable—per capita turkey production—on the vertical axis, with the independent variable of the previous year's price on the horizontal axis. Most conventional supply–demand charts reverse these axes.

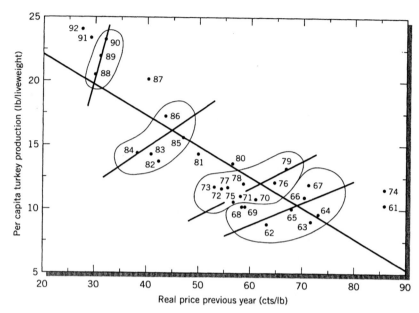

FIGURE 12.3. Relationship between real live turkey prices the previous year and per capita production of turkey United States, 1961–92.

the turkey-feed price ratio for any year is indicative of the cost of the primary resource relative to the value of the product. The price ratio in no way reflects technological change in the rate at which feed may be converted to turkey. But in the *absence* of technological change, the turkey-feed price ratio should give some indication of the *profitability* of turkey production during any given year. Relatively high turkey-feed price ratios would be expected to be associated with favorable profits. Lower ratios would be associated with less favorable profits.

The use of the turkey-feed price ratio is really an example of combining two supply variables into a single variable. The cost of the feed resource for any given year is combined with the product price for that year to give an indication of profitability. That indication of profitability is then used as an expectation of profitability in the subsequent year.

A chart of the turkey-feed price ratio against per capita turkey production in the following year still does not conform with economic logic (Figure 12.4). Whereas the apparent negative relationship between the two variables is somewhat less precisely defined than was observed in the case of previous year prices and production, the apparent relationship is negative nevertheless. If the economically logical relationship is to emerge from the data, it is again necessary to group blocks of years. The blocks of years are somewhat different than was the previous case, and 1974 is no longer an outlier. This suggests that whereas real turkey prices were unusually high in 1974, the 1974 aberration was most probably a result of unusually high prices for both corn and soybean meal—the primary ingredients in turkey rations—in the aftermath of the 1972–73 Russian Grain Deal.

The fact that the previous year turkey price and the previous year turkey-feed price ratio exhibit similar relationships with per capita turkey production eliminates the cost and availability of resources as a cause for the apparently illogical relationship. The only factor remaining as a possible explanation is steadily improving technology.

When we discussed trends in Chapter 4, we recognized that one of the reasons for long-time directional drifts in production and/or prices for agricultural products was continuing adaptation of new technology. There are at least two ways we can test for the impact of technology. One is to use the deviations from the trend in production as the dependent variable to be explained. The other is to use year-to-year changes in production as the dependent variable (generally called "first differences" in the language of price analyst), since the impact of technological change is generally not particularly significant from one year to the next.

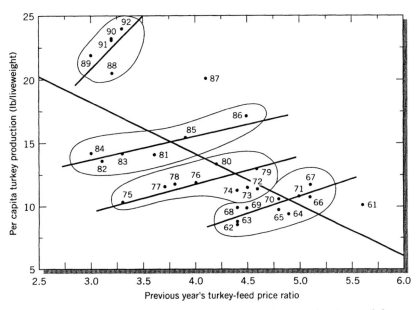

FIGURE 12.4. Relationship between per capita turkey production and the previous year's turkey-feed price ratio, United States, 1960–92.

Deviations from Trend in Supply Analysis

When we use deviations from the trend in production as the dependent variable, the relationship between those deviations and the previous year turkey-feed price ratio exhibits the positive relationship that economic theory suggests we should expect (Figure 12.5). There is a 27-year grouping of the data prior to 1987, with a second grouping of data for the years subsequent to 1987, both of which show a generally positive relationship. Since there are so few years involved in the second grouping, it would be difficult to state precisely what the relationship might be.

There was a dramatic rearrangement of the institutional factors beginning on January 20, 1981, that may account for some of the separation of these groups of years. But the new value-added turkey products such as turkey "ham," turkey "franks," and turkey "salami," which became commercially available during the 1980s, coupled with cost-reducing technological improvements is probably a reason for much of it.

If one were satisfied that most of the explainable variation in the deviations from the 1960–92 trend (which in itself explains 77 percent of the total variation in per capita turkey production) has been explained by this variable, one could construct "drift" lines as guides for the analy-

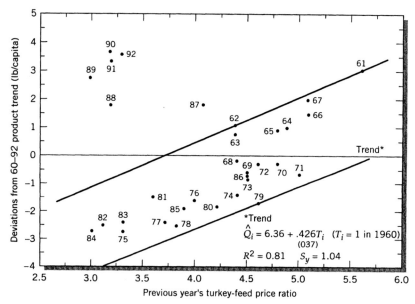

FIGURE 12.5. Relationship between deviations from the 1960–92 trend in per capita turkey production and the previous year's turkey-feed price ratio, United States, 1960–92.

sis. These drift lines could be constructed around the two groups of data in the scatter diagram.

Drift lines are simply lines connecting the extremes on either side of any central tendency observed in the scatter of points. For example, if one were using the entire data set in the scatter of data relating the previous year turkey-feed price ratio to the deviations from the trend in turkey production, 1962, 1982, and 1984 appear to be generally in line with each other, with 1963, 1981 and 1983 only slightly below this line. Thus, a line through these points could be interpreted as the upper limit of any relationship defined by the variables. But the years from 1987 through 1992 are clearly outliers from the group of years that appear to exhibit a generally consistent relationship between the two variables.

Using the drift lines constructed and the average values of the two variables (0 for the deviations from the trend and 4.1 for the turkey-feed price ratio) as guides, one could construct a line through the data that would appear to be most descriptive of the entire scatter. However, since the most recent six years of data are clearly outside the thrust in Figure 12.5 there is little point in going further in attempting to define a "best" line of relationship between the drift lines.

We have previously recognized that there was an increase in the rate of expansion in turkey production in the very early 1980s—hence, the reason for our two production trend calculations in Figure 12.1. Thus, it is appropriate to examine the deviations from the 1981–92 trend as well (Figure 12.6). Whether these deviations reveal any real pattern is arguable. The trend itself describes more than 90 percent of the variation in per capita turkey production over the 1981–92 period. Thus, there is not a great deal of variation left to be explained. The positively sloping drift lines shown in the figure have been drawn in this fashion because economic theory tells us that the relationship should be positive. However, a negatively sloping upper drift line could be defined by the 1981, 1987, and 1986 observations, and the 1982, 1992, and 1985 observations could be used to establish a negatively sloping lower drift line. Thus, any conclusions based on Figure 12.6 regarding probable per capita future turkey production should be treated *very* cautiously.

Having recognized that great caution should be used in drawing inferences from Figure 12.6, let's proceed with our analysis for purposes of understanding how data with less dramatic trend characteristics might be used. We know from the data in Table 12.1 that the turkey-feed price ratio in 1992 was 3.1. If we locate 3.1 on the horizontal axis of Figure 12.6 and draw a vertical line from that point, we can identify from our line of best relationship that U.S. per capita live turkey production in 1993 might be expected to be about 0.5 pounds below the levels of 1992—or about 23.5 pounds per person. The drift lines would give us an estimate of the range of errors we might reasonably expect from this estimate.

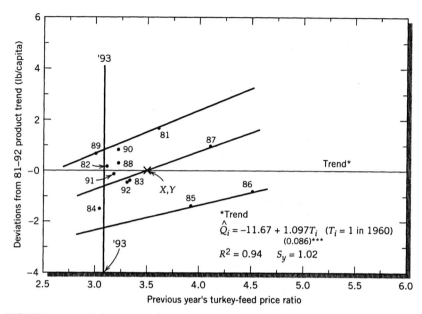

FIGURE 12.6. Relationship between deviations from the 1981–90 trend in per capita turkey production and the previous year's turkey-feed price ratio, United States, 1961–92.

That is, we might expect the output of turkeys to be as much as 1.7 pounds below this 23.5-pound estimate or as much as 1.3 pounds above it.

"First Differences" in Supply Analysis

The analysis of first differences in turkey production as related to the turkey-feed price ratio is conducted in much the same fashion as the analysis of deviations from the trend. The first differences are calculated simply by subtracting the previous year value of the variable in question from the current year value. That is, the first difference in per capita turkey production for 1975 would be the 1975 production of 10.5 pounds per person less the 1974 production of 11.4 pounds per person—a difference of −0.9 pounds per person. This decline in production per person would be related to the turkey-feed price ratio of 3.3 in 1974. That is, limited profitability (or perhaps losses) in turkey production as a result of a low turkey-feed price ratio would be expected to be associated with a reduction in turkey production in the subsequent period.

The logic for using first differences in an analysis of supply or demand is much the same as that for using a moving average trend in the analysis of cycles. Current circumstances are linked with the circumstances of a year ago, and, in turn, are linked with those of the future. When there is a long-term factor such as technological growth that obscures the relationships between variables, the use of year-to-year change can frequently "strip" the obscuring movement from the data to a degree sufficient for analyzing the relationships in question.

When the scatter diagram of first differences in turkey production and the turkey-feed price ratio is examined (Figure 12.7), we can see that the grouping of blocks of years is not nearly so dramatic as was the case of the trend deviations analysis, but the grouping does occur. In this case, the grouping appears to be for the years prior and subsequent to 1980—a year that marks the very early part of the second Arab oil boycott and the beginning of the period when the focus of U.S. monetary policy was shifted from an objective of controlling interest costs toward an objective of controlling economic inflation. These events rearranged many relationships in the American economy, but especially the relationships in the production cost structure of U.S. agriculture, and *most* especially for animal agriculture.

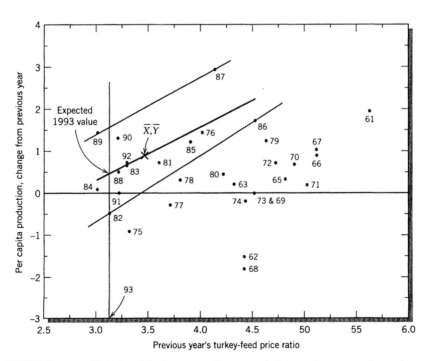

FIGURE 12.7. Relationship between the annual change in per capita turkey production and the previous year's turkey-feed price ratio, United States, 1981–92.

The income shocks associated with energy forced consumers to re-structure their buying patterns, particularly regarding meat consumption. The massive increases in real interest rates impacted on *all* agricultural production. The more heavily leveraged the segment and the higher the cost, the greater the impact. Thus, beef and pork were both impacted more heavily than were the poultry meats, giving poultry some advantage. These realities, coupled with the ongoing technological growth and the development of further processed poultry products enhanced the poultry situation still further.

As in the case in which the deviations from the production trend were analyzed, the options for the first differences analysis are to use the entire range of data in the scatter diagram or to partition the diagram based on the block groupings. Since the onset of the second Energy Crisis and the refocusing of monetary policy represent such a dramatic disruption of many economic relationships and since there are 12 full years of data in that most recent grouping, the earlier data can probably be ignored. The drift lines would align 1987, and 1989 as the upper limit of the scatter and 1982, and 1986 for the lower limit. These drift lines and the average values of the two variables for the 10-year period (+0.8 for the annual change in per capita production and 3.45 for the turkey-feed price ratio) can be used as guides to define a line describing the "best" relationship between the variables. (It should be noted that the line of best relationship in Figure 12.7 does not necessarily bisect the space between the drift lines. The concentration of values toward the lower drift line draws the upper end of the line of best relationship toward that lower drift line.) The 1992 turkey-feed price ratio (3.1) can then be used directly to estimate the increase or decrease in per capita turkey production that might be expected in 1993.

Our drift lines suggest that the turkey-feed price ratio of 3.1 in 1992 would have been expected to trigger an increase in live turkey production of from about −0.5 to 1.5 pounds per capita in 1993. The "most probable" estimate, suggested by the line of relationship through the means of the two variables, would be for an increase of about 0.5 pounds. Thus, with a 1992 output of 24 pounds per capita, the expectation would be for 1993 live turkey production to range between 23.5 and 25.5 pounds per capita, with a most probable level of about 24.5 pounds.

There may be additional variables that might have impacted upon turkey supplies expected in 1993, but the estimates we have already derived give a fairly clear picture. All of our estimates based upon supply analysis provide a more accurate estimate of expected 1993 turkey production than would the simple linear trend for the 1960–92 period, and probably a better estimate than would the trend for 1981–92 (Table 12.2). The trend values alone suggest that 1993 turkey production would have been expected to be 21.3 or 26.7 pounds per capita. The analysis of

TABLE 12.2. Comparison of Results of Alternative Approaches to Estimating Expected 1991 Live Turkey Production per Capita

Estimation Approach	Expected 1991 Live Turkey Production		
	High	Most Probable (Pounds per Capita)	Low
Linear Trend			
1960–92		21.3	
1981–92		26.7	
Supply Analysis Approach:			
Deviations from Production Trend against Turkey-Feed Price Ratio			
A. Entire 1961–92 Period		Cannot define. Most recent six years of data are clearly outliers from the remaining 27 years.	
B. Only 1981–92 Period	24.8	23.5???	21.8
First Differences in Production against Turkey-Feed Price Ratio	25.5	24.5	23.5
USDA Preliminary Estimate of Actual 1993 Production		24.1	

deviations from the long-term trend as related to the previous year's turkey-feed price ratio are really not relevant since the most recent data are clearly outliers from that trend. The deviations from the shorter-term trend suggests that 1993 production would have been about 3.0 pounds below the 1993 trend value. The first-difference analysis of turkey production as related to the previous year's turkey-feed price ratio suggested that 1993 per capita turkey production could have been expected to be 0.5 pounds above the 24.0 pounds produced in 1992.

Which, if any, of the estimates of expected 1993 per capita live turkey production should ultimately be used as a forecast of 1993 turkey output depends upon the judgment of the price analyst. If the analyst can justify why one of the estimates is more probable than the others, he might adopt that estimate and ignore the others. He might simply average the estimates or use the high and low estimates as a range, using the midpoint of the range as the most probable value. Supply analysis approaches that place greater emphasis on more recent information (the deviations from trend and the first differences analysis) generally prove to be superior to those that place less emphasis on recent data. The preliminary USDA estimate of actual 1993 live turkey production was

24.1 pounds per person. The average value of the four estimates (the two trends, deviations from the shorter-term trend, and first differences) is 24.16 pounds—not a bad approximation of the value actually observed in 1993.

APPROACHES TO DEMAND ANALYSIS _____

We have recognized that the probable market quantity available is generally easier to predict than market prices because of the enormous price volatility introduced by psychological market responses to factors such as news reports regarding weather conditions and international trade. For this reason, we estimated expected market quantity supplied separately. Now that we have an estimate of the market quantity available, we can use this estimate in combination with a demand analysis that is yet to be conducted to get an estimate of expected market price.

When we discussed the demand relationship in Chapters 10 and 11, we recognized that market prices for a product are a function of the quantity available, plus the influence of the demand-shifting *ceteris paribus* conditions. Among the *ceteris paribus* conditions for demand that we specified are:

1. Numbers of consumers, for which we can compensate by converting variables such as market quantities and income to a per capita basis (this is the reason for estimating our turkey production on the per capita basis rather than on a basis of total tonnage).
2. Prices and availability of alternative goods (substitutes or complements).
3. Consumer income.
4. Consumer tastes and preferences.
5. Consumer habits.
6. Institutional arrangements
   a. International trade regulations (tariffs)
   b. Monetary and fiscal policy
   c. etc.

As in the case of supply, this demand relationship may be expressed algebraically:

$$P_t = a + b_1 QS_t + b_2 Y_t + b_3 AG_t + \cdots + b_n IA_t \qquad (12.2)$$

where:

P_t is the expected price in the time period t,

QS_t is per capita quantity supplied in the time period t,

Y_t is consumer income in time period t,

AG_t is the quantity (or price) of an alternative good in time period t,

IA_t is the configuration of institutional arrangements in time period t, and

The dots between the plus signs in the demand equation represent parameters that might be associated with other demand shifters such as consumer tastes and preferences, consumer habits, or additional substitute or complement goods.

It should be noted that QS_t in the coming time period (i.e., 1993) is the market quantity supplied that we estimated earlier in this chapter. Thus, the algebraic expression of supply could be substituted into the demand equation, incorporating the market supply and market demand variables into a single equation designed to predict the market price. The market price, of course, is one of the end results of the intersection of the market supply and demand functions. It is not uncommon—particularly in the age of computers—to statistically estimate this single equation based on time series data. It can also be estimated graphically, but in graphic analysis, it is generally easier to estimate the market quantity supplied separately from the estimate of price.

To illustrate the manner in which we might estimate the demand for an agricultural product, let's continue with our turkey example. Table 12.3 includes price and per capita quantity information for variables that might be expected to be associated with the demand for turkeys. The *ceteris paribus* condition of numbers of consumers has been dealt with by converting the relevant data series to a per capita basis in order to correct for population growth. The *ceteris paribus* condition regarding price and/ or availability of alternative goods is addressed by information regarding the per capita production of other major meats. Real per capita disposable consumer income information is provided for addressing the income issue. The remaining demand shifters are not readily measurable. Thus, there will almost inevitably be some variation in price that cannot be explained by the measurable variables.

It will be noted in Table 12.3 that there are preliminary values for 1993. These values are the values actually reported for these variables in 1993. In a forecasting situation, actual values may not always be available. However, the U.S. Department of Agriculture and the U.S. Department of Commerce have historically been fairly accurate in their forecasts of these variables. These published forecasts can be used in the estimation of an expected price or the analyst can conduct his/her analysis to predict these values.

The starting point for our turkey demand analysis is to construct a scatter diagram of price-quantity points for each year during the time period in question (Figure 12.8). This scatter diagram conforms very

TABLE 12.3. TURKEYS—Real Farm Prices, Per Capita Production, and Other Factors Potentially Affecting Turkey Demand

Year	Farm Turkey Price (cts/lb)	Per Cap Income ($)	CPI (1982–84 = 100)	Real Farm Price Turkeys (cts/lb)	Per Cap. Turkey Production (lb lv wt)	Jan 1 Stg of Turkey (mil lb)	Real Income per Cap ($)	Per Cap Pork Prod (lb)	Per Cap Chicken Prod (lb)	Per Cap Beef Prod (lb)
1960	25.4	1,938	29.6	85.8	8.2	149.2	6,544	77.0	28.0	85.1
1961	18.9	1,984	29.9	63.2	10.2	160.1	6,633	74.3	30.0	87.8
1962	21.6	2,066	30.2	71.4	8.7	263.1	6,830	74.8	30.0	88.9
1963	22.3	2,139	30.6	72.8	8.9	203.3	6,987	76.6	30.7	94.5
1964	21.0	2,284	31.0	67.7	9.5	217.5	7,364	76.1	31.1	99.9
1965	22.2	2,436	31.5	70.4	9.9	207.4	7,721	65.8	33.4	99.5
1966	23.1	2,605	32.5	71.2	10.8	200.1	8,028	65.1	36.1	104.2
1967	19.5	2,751	33.4	58.4	11.8	267.1	8,240	71.1	37.2	106.5
1968	20.5	2,945	34.8	58.9	10.0	366.9	8,466	72.3	37.5	109.7
1969	22.4	3,130	36.7	61.1	10.0	317.1	8,539	70.3	39.1	110.8
1970	22.6	3,489	38.8	58.2	10.7	191.9	8,986	71.7	40.4	113.6
1971	22.1	3,595	40.5	54.6	10.9	218.9	8,877	77.1	40.3	112.7
1972	22.2	3,837	41.8	53.1	11.5	223.1	9,172	68.7	41.8	115.5
1973	38.2	4,284	44.4	86.0	11.6	208.1	9,641	62.4	40.5	108.8
1974	28.0	4,667	49.3	56.8	11.4	281.0	9,465	67.0	40.7	115.7
1975	34.8	5,291	53.8	64.7	10.5	275.0	9,831	54.5	40.2	118.8
1976	31.7	5,477	56.9	55.7	12.0	195.2	9,622	58.2	42.8	127.6

Year									
1977	35.5	5,965	60.6	58.6	11.6	203.4	9,844	60.2	44.2	124.0
1978	43.6	6,621	65.2	66.8	11.9	167.9	10,149	60.2	46.7	117.9
1979	41.1	7,331	72.6	56.6	13.1	175.1	10,101	68.6	50.6	105.5
1980	41.3	8,421	82.4	50.1	13.5	240.0	10,220	73.0	50.1	103.4
1981	38.2	9,243	90.3	42.3	14.2	198.0	10,239	69.0	51.6	104.2
1982	39.5	9,724	96.5	40.9	13.7	238.4	10,075	61.3	53.1	104.3
1983	38.0	10,340	99.6	38.1	14.2	203.9	10,379	64.8	53.8	106.4
1984	48.9	11,257	103.9	47.1	14.3	161.8	10,838	62.6	55.7	106.2
1985	47.2	11,872	107.6	43.9	15.5	125.3	11,037	62.0	58.9	98.6
1986	44.4	12,508	109.6	40.5	17.2	150.2	11,412	58.2	61.2	100.2
1987	34.3	13,094	113.6	30.2	20.1	178.2	11,529	59.0	65.8	96.0
1988	36.9	14,123	118.6	31.1	20.5	266.2	11,913	63.7	67.6	95.1
1989	40.0	14,973	124.2	32.2	21.9	249.9	12,059	63.6	72.2	92.5
1990	38.3	16,174	130.7	29.3	23.2	236.0	12,375	61.4	77.2	90.6
1991	37.7	16,658	136.2	27.7	23.3	306.0	12,231	63.0	77.9	90.5
1992	37.6	17,346	140.4[p]	26.8	24.0	264.0	12,355	67.4	81.6	90.2
1993	—	17,900[f]	145.3[a]	—	24.1[a]	300.0	12,319[f]	66.8	83.8[f]	91.1[f]

[p] Preliminary
[f] USDA forecast
[a] Assumes 3.5% inflation in 1993
[b] From previous analysis

SOURCE: Mark R. Weimar and Shauna Cromer, *U.S. Egg and Poultry Statistical Series, 1960–89*, ERS, USDA, Statistical Bulletin No. 816, September 1990; *Livestock and Meat Statistics, 1984–88*, ERS, USDA, Statistical Bulletin No. 784, September 1989; *Livestock and Poultry Situation and Outlook Report*, ERS, USDA, various issues since 1988.

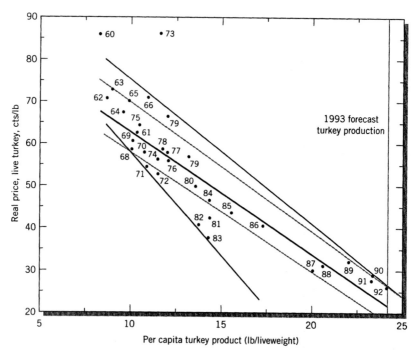

FIGURE 12.8. TURKEYS—production per capita and real farm prices, United States, 1960–92.

comfortably with the economic logic that suggests that as the availability of the product increases, the price at which the entire quantity can be sold declines. The grouping of years that we observed in the case of our supply analysis is readily apparent in the case of the demand scatter diagram, with the 1960s in the upper-left part of the scatter, the 1980s and 1990s in the lower right, and the 1970s between the two. The 1980s and 1990s are clearly separated into the periods before and after 1986, but the configuration of these groupings is entirely compatible with what economic theory tells us we should expect.

When we consider the trends in price and production of turkeys, which we saw earlier, this scatter diagram suggests that both of these trends are due largely to changes in the *ceteris paribus* conditions of *supply*. That is, while there have been massive changes in the supply relationships for turkeys since the mid-1960s, the demand relationships appear to have remained relatively stable.

We can construct drift lines, with the upper limit being defined by a line compatible with the points describing 1966, 1978, 1989, 1990, and 1992. The lower limit would be defined by a line compatible with the points for 1968, 1971, 1982, and 1983. It should be noted that these drift lines exclude the information for 1973. We have already discussed how the 1972–73 Russian Grain Deal caused substantial economic disruptions particularly in animal agriculture, and that information during this aberrant period can conveniently be ignored. Even though the 1960 observation falls very near the upper drift line, that observation is so far out of line with the rest of the price information that we should exclude 1960 from the analysis as well.

The position of the 1982 and 1983 observations suggests that these two years may well be outside the main thrust of the demand data as do the observations for 1966 and 1978. Therefore, auxiliary drift lines shown by the dashed lines in Figure 12.8 have been constructed to gather the data a bit closer.

Using the drift lines we constructed, the average price (51.7 cents per pound), and the average per capita annual production (13.8 pounds) over this 33-year period, we can construct a single line that we judge to be the "best" description of the relationship between these two variables. Based on this information alone, we could use our "average" 1993 live turkey production estimate of 24.1 pounds per person and decide that other things being equal, we would expect a real price for turkey in 1993 of about 22 cents per pound live weight, plus 5 cents or minus 3 cents (using the auxiliary drift lines to calculate the potential error).

We have already eliminated from our analysis the information for 1960 and 1973 because of the extreme aberrations of those years from the rest of the data. But the range of potential error from our best estimate gives us a range of potential price in the best of circumstances about a third as large as the total price in 1992. Under the worst case, using the initial set of drift lines, this error is potentially larger than our *entire* 1992 price. Is there a way to reduce this range, or at least to estimate whether the price is likely to be in the upper or lower portion of it? Our auxiliary drift lines suggest that any error in our 1993 estimate would be most likely to fall in the upper part of the error range.

The first step to improving our confidence in our 1993 expected price estimate is to measure the unexplained residual of price. That is, our best estimate of the relationship between per capita turkey production and the real price of live turkeys is defined by our line. But the data for 1966, 1978, and 1989, 1990, 1991, and 1992 are substantially above this best estimate while those for 1968–72 and for 1981–83 are well below. The price–quantity relationship we defined explained a major part of the 1966, 1978, 1989–92 prices, but considerably less than all of them. On the other hand, that relationship *more* than explained—or *overexplained*—the prices for the 1968–72 and 1981–83 periods. Is there another variable(s) that will account for some of these unexplained residuals?

Just how much residual price variation is there to be explained? This can be estimated best by using a 3″ × 5″ card, and drawing a zero line across the middle of it to represent the line of relationship that we have constructed (Figure 12.9). That card should be identified as the measure of "first residuals" of real prices from the turkey price–quantity relationship. Then, being careful to maintain the card in a *vertical* position, mark off along the edge of the card the positive and negative unexplained price differences from the line, identifying each tick mark with the year with which it is associated. It is important to maintain the vertical position of the card since each of the price observations is associated with a specific quantity of product. If the card is allowed to tilt, the quantity measured on the line will be different from that associated with the unexplained price residual.

Once the first price residuals for all observations have been measured and identified, a second variable that our knowledge of economic theory suggests might influence the price for turkeys can be selected for testing (Figure 12.10). In our example, we have selected per capita commercial beef production. Beef is not only a substitute meat, beef also represents the largest single portion of total meat consumption. Further, some of the new turkey products—turkey hamburger, for example—compete

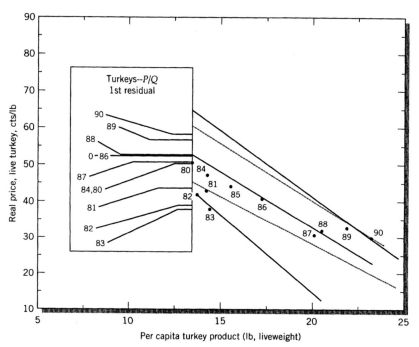

FIGURE 12.9.   TURKEYS—Measuring residuals between actual real prices and the portion of price explained by per capita turkey production, United States, 1960–92.

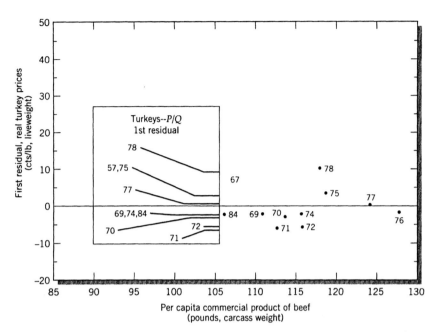

FIGURE 12.10. TURKEYS—Charting first residuals against a second variable.

directly with beef. Chicken or pork might have also been selected. A horizontal line across the middle of the chart should be drawn to represent the line originally drawn to define the relationship between prices and quantities. This line is identified as 0, with positive and negative measures of the price residuals on the vertical axis. It is important that the price scale of this second chart be identical with that of the original price–quantity scatter diagram since all price residuals have been measured in that original scale. It is to be recommended that the horizontal scale be as large as the size of the graph paper and the range of the data for the second variable will permit. This large scale simplifies visual identification of any relationship between the residual prices and the second determinant variable.

Using the annually identified values for the second variable to locate the horizontal placement of the data, the residual price for each year should be plotted and identified. In Figure 12.10, the 1984 price residual of negative 2.7 cents is marked at the 106.2 pounds of commercial beef production per capita observed in 1984. Again, it is important to maintain the vertical position of the card with the zero line on the card coinciding with the zero line on the chart. This insures that the quantity of beef with which the 1984 residual turkey price is associated is, in fact, plotted at 106.2 pounds of beef.

When all of the residual prices have been charted against the values of the second variable, drift lines may again be constructed to enclose the data (Figure 12.11). In our example of beef production against the first residual of turkey prices, the lower limit would be defined by the values for 1982 and 1983. The upper limit would be defined by the values for 1966 and 1978. You will recall that we questioned whether the 1966, 1978, 1982, and 1983 observations should be retained as a part of the analysis when we constructed our first price–quantity scatter diagram. When we chart our first residuals of price against per capita beef production, it will be noted that these years continue to be at the extremes— further evidence that these may be aberrant observations to be ignored in the construction of our drift lines. For this reason, a second set of auxiliary drift lines have been constructed in Figure 12.11.

Using the drift lines and the average value for per capita beef production (105.1 pounds) as a guide, a line best describing the relationship between the new variable and the first residual of prices can be drawn. In the case of our example, the relationship is negative, suggesting that low levels of per capita beef production would tend to be associated with positive first residuals of turkey prices and that high levels of per capita beef production would be expected to be associated with negative first

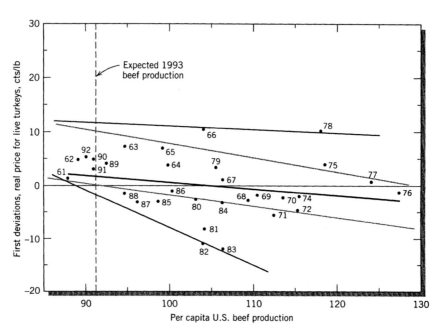

FIGURE 12.11. First residuals in real farm prices for turkeys as related to per capita U.S. beef production.

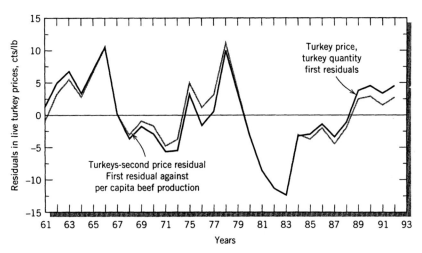

FIGURE 12.12. Residuals in real live turkey prices: first residual from price/per capita turkey production. Second residuals from first residual/per capita beef production.

residuals. This sort of relationship is, of course, entirely compatible with the expectations fostered by economic theory. The line of relationship we have drawn suggests that the 91.1 pounds of beef per capita produced in 1993 would be expected to add about 2 cents per pound to the 1993 real turkey price of 22.0 cents we might expect on the basis of expected turkey production alone. Thus, with our two variables, 1993 real live turkey prices should be about 24.0 cents per pound (about 35 cents in terms of 1993 dollars, reinflating the price with the 1993 Consumer Price Index value of 145.3[b]).

To test whether the beef production residual should be retained as a part of the analysis, we can measure the second-order price residuals in precisely the same fashion as we measured the first-order residuals. If there is an increased concentration of values around the zero line, the "fit" of the analysis has been improved. Although the range of the deviations has not been reduced materially, there are numerous observations that are drawn closer to the zero line (Figure 12.12). Ideally, both the range and the concentration would be brought closer to the zero line. The second residuals for 1961–74 are in fact concentrated closer to the zero line than were the first residuals, as are those for 1988–90. However, the second residuals for 1975–78 and for 1985–88 are a bit further from the zero line than were the first residuals. Also, the *range* of

---

[b] The 145.3 estimated CPI for 1993 assumes a 3.5 percent rate of inflation.

the deviations is enlarged just a bit (in 1977) by the beef production variable. Thus, the judgment of the analyst might be either to use a different variable with the first residuals to improve the fit or to try the second residuals against that variable. For the moment, let's retain the per capita beef production in the analysis and move on to another variable.

We can repeat this effort, using the second price residuals against another variable such as January 1 cold storage holdings of turkey (Figure 12.13). Obviously, the turkey that is left over in one year added to the production of the next year makes up the total supply available to consumers in that year. Turkey that was produced and frozen in late 1992 is a pretty acceptable substitute for turkey that was produced and frozen in early 1993. Thus, high levels of carryover would be expected to be associated with negative price residuals (i.e., would be expected to reduce prices in the coming year) and low levels of carryover would be associated with positive price residuals. This negative relationship does, in fact, show up in the drift lines that result from charting the second-order residuals against beginning inventories of stored turkey. How-

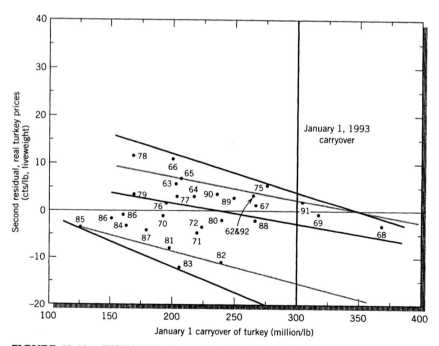

FIGURE 12.13. TURKEYS—Second residual in real price against January 1 cold storage holdings of turkey.

ever, it is difficult to justify much negative slope in the line of best relationship since there are so few observations in the high levels of turkey carryover. The disagreement between the drift lines and the line of best relationship suggests that perhaps an analysis of first differences might be appropriate in analyzing turkey demand. If one uses the information in Figure 12.13, the relatively large January 1, 1993, inventory of 300 million pounds suggests that 1991 real farm prices for turkeys could be expected to be as much as 15 cents per pound lower or 2–3 cents per pound higher than would be the case if turkey storage were at its long-term average level of about 220 million pounds.

When the third residuals of price are compared with the first and second residuals (Figure 12.14), it quickly becomes apparent that the cold-storage carryover of turkey from year to year doesn't do a great deal to improve the multiple graphic correlation analysis of turkey demand. The third residual is superimposed on the second.

If we were to stop at this point, our expectation of 1993 real farm turkey prices would be 22 cents on the basis of our live turkey per capita production expectation of 24.1 pounds per person. To this, we would add 2 cents for the lower than usual production of beef and would probably ignore the larger than usual cold storage carryover of turkey. Thus, our total real price expectation for live turkeys would be 24 cents per pound in 1993. If we reinflate this estimate by the expected 1993 Consumer Price Index value of 145.3, we get an expected 1993 farm turkey price of

$$\frac{22.5 \times 145.3}{100} = 34.87 \text{ cents per pound} \qquad (12.3)$$

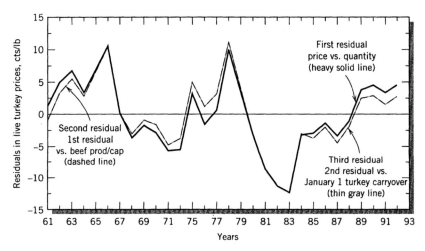

FIGURE 12.14. First, second, and third residuals in real turkey prices.

(about 35 cents per pound), which is about 2.7 cents below the price of the previous year. Remember, however, that there were consistently wide ranges of potential error associated with our drift lines. Further, the indications were that the errors were much more likely to fall above the line of best relationship than below. Thus, our 35-cent estimate is much more likely to be below than above the actual price observed in 1993. Our forecast price (which we recognize as probably being low) of 35 cents is by no means exact, but it does tell us that the price for turkeys in 1993 most likely would be somewhat lower than in 1992.

Using First Differences to Estimate Demand

In Figures 12.1 and 12.2, we saw that there were very strong trends in both prices and production of turkey. The 1960–92 trend in per capita live turkey production was:

$$\text{Expected per capita production of live turkeys} = 6.36 + 0.426T_i, \quad \text{where } T_i = 1 \text{ in 1960} \quad (12.4)$$
$$(0.037)$$
$$R^2 = 0.81 \qquad S_y = 2.04$$

It will be remembered that per capita turkey production in the 1980s increased much more rapidly than the trend over the total period would suggest. For that reason, we constructed a second trend for the 1981–92 period:

$$\text{Expected per capita production of live turkeys} = -11.67 + 1.097T_i, \quad \text{where } T_i = 1 \text{ in 1960} \quad (12.5)$$
$$(0.08)$$
$$R^2 = 0.94 \qquad S_y = 1.02$$

The 1960–92 trend in real farm prices for live turkeys was:

$$\text{Expected real price for live turkeys} = 78.8 - 1.477T_i, \quad \text{where } T_i = 1 \text{ in 1960} \quad (12.6)$$
$$(0.145)$$
$$R^2 = 0.77 \qquad S_y = 7.9$$

Since there was no major change in the nature of the price trend, we didn't bother to calculate one for a more recent period. That is, we recognized that the major changes in the turkey market situation were on the supply side of the market.

The statistical properties of these trends suggest that the nonmeasurable factors such as technology, new product development, and so on, are highly significant. We saw how the trend in production overshadowed the influence of the supply variables, causing our supply analysis to appear to be contrary to economic logic until we used either devia-

tions from the production trend or a first-differences approach to remove the impact of technology.

The extraordinarily strong upward trend in turkey production during
the 1981–92 period may have accounted entirely for the somewhat
weaker downward trend in real turkey prices. The configuration of the
scatter diagram in Figure 12.8 suggested that much of the downward
trend in real prices for live turkeys was associated with the upward
trend in production. But the positioning of the observations since 1986
suggests that new product development in recent years has been a real
factor in the demand for turkey. We can test just how critical it may be to
account for the trend in prices by using first differences in both production and price and for the other demand variables. That is, by linking
each year to the year preceding it, and then to the year following, we
remove much of the visual distortion associated with the trend.

Table 12.4 shows the first differences (changes from the values for the
previous year) for a variety of variables that might influence demand for
turkey over the 1960–92 period. Preliminary reported and USDA forecast values for 1993 are shown at the bottom of the table. You will note
that our projected change in turkey production for 1993 is based on the
24.1 pounds per capita derived from the supply analysis conducted
earlier in this chapter.

The initial scatter diagram based upon first differences, with the drift
lines and a postulated line of best relationship already constructed is
shown in Figure 12.15. It will be noted that the observation for 1961 has
been excluded from the analysis, as have those for 1973 and 1974. You
will recall from our previous demand analysis (Figure 12.8) that we
eliminated 1960 and 1973 from the analysis as aberrant years. Since the
first-difference analysis is based on year-to-year calculations, any aberrant year of information forces the elimination of any observation for
which the aberrant year is an element. Thus, an aberrant year forces the
elimination of two years of information rather than one. This loss of data
is one of the limitations of the first-differences approach.

The mean values of the two data series falls in the lower-right quadrant of Figure 12.15, reflecting the reality of an upward trend in production and a downward trend in real prices. The line of best relationship
happens to pass very near the intersection of the zero lines of first
differences. This is due to chance rather than to any particular compul-
sion to place the relationship in this position.

When we use our 1993 forecast of the change in per capita turkey
production (an increase of 0.1 pounds over the observed 1992 production level), our relationship suggests that on the basis of expected production alone, real farm turkey prices in 1993 would be expected to be
about a cent below 1992. The range established by the drift lines suggests that the real price could be as much as 9 cents above or 8 cents

TABLE 12.4. TURKEYS—Changes from the Previous Year (First Differences) in Values for Selected Variables Potentially Affecting Turkey Demand and Prices

Year	Real Farm Price Turkeys (cts/lb)	Per Cap Turkey Prod (lb Lvwt)	Jan 1 Stg of Turkey (Mil lb)	Real Income per Cap ($)	Per Cap Pork Prod (lb)	Per Cap Chicken Prod (lb)	Per Cap Beef Prod (lb)	Per Cap Red Meat Prod (lb)
1960								
1961	−22.6	2.0	10.9	89	−2.7	2.0	2.7	0.0
1962	8.2	−1.5	103.0	198	0.5	0.0	1.1	1.6
1963	1.4	0.2	−59.8	157	1.8	0.7	5.6	7.4
1964	−5.1	0.6	14.2	377	−0.5	0.4	5.4	4.9
1965	2.7	0.3	−10.1	357	−10.3	2.3	−0.4	−10.7
1966	0.8	0.9	−7.3	306	−0.7	2.7	4.7	4.0
1967	−12.8	1.0	67.0	213	6.0	1.1	2.3	8.3
1968	0.5	−1.8	99.8	226	1.2	0.3	3.2	4.4
1969	2.2	0.0	−49.8	73	−2.1	1.6	1.1	−1.0
1970	−2.9	0.7	−125.2	447	1.4	1.3	2.8	4.2
1971	−3.6	0.1	27.0	−109	5.4	−0.1	−0.9	4.5
1972	−1.5	0.7	4.2	295	−8.4	1.5	2.8	−5.6
1973	32.9	0.0	−15.0	469	−6.3	−1.3	−6.7	−13.0
1974	−29.2	−0.2	72.9	−176	4.6	0.2	6.9	11.5

Year								
1975	7.9	-0.9	-6.0	367	-12.5	-0.5	3.1	-9.4
1976	-9.0	1.4	-79.8	-209	3.7	2.6	8.8	12.5
1977	2.9	-0.3	8.2	222	2.0	1.4	-3.6	-1.6
1978	8.2	0.3	-35.5	305	0.0	2.5	-6.1	-6.1
1979	-10.2	1.2	7.2	-49	8.5	3.9	-12.4	-3.9
1980	-6.5	0.4	64.9	120	4.3	-0.5	-2.1	2.2
1981	-7.8	0.7	-42.0	19	-4.0	1.5	0.8	-3.2
1982	-1.4	-0.5	40.4	-164	-7.8	1.5	0.1	-7.7
1983	-2.8	0.6	-34.5	304	3.6	0.7	2.1	5.7
1984	8.9	0.1	-42.1	459	-2.2	1.9	-0.2	-2.4
1985	-3.2	1.2	-36.5	198	-0.6	3.2	-7.6	-8.2
1986	-3.4	1.7	24.9	375	-3.8	2.3	1.6	-2.2
1987	-10.3	2.9	28.0	117	0.8	4.6	-4.2	-3.4
1988	0.9	0.4	88.0	384	4.7	1.8	-0.9	3.8
1989	1.1	1.4	-16.3	146	0.0	4.6	-2.6	-2.6
1990	-2.9	1.3	-13.9	23	-2.2	5.0	-1.9	-4.1
1991	-1.6	0.1	70.0	-54	1.6	.7	-.1	1.5
1992	-.9	.7	-42.0	124	4.4	3.7	-.3	4.1
1993	—	.1f	36.0	-36f	-.6f	2.2f	-.9f	-1.5f

f Forecast

SOURCE: Mark R. Weimar and Shauna Cromer, *U.S. Egg and Poultry Statistical Series, 1960–89*, ERS USDA, Statistical Bulletin No. 816, September 1990; *Livestock and Poultry Situation and Outlook Report*, ERS, USDA, various issues since 1989.

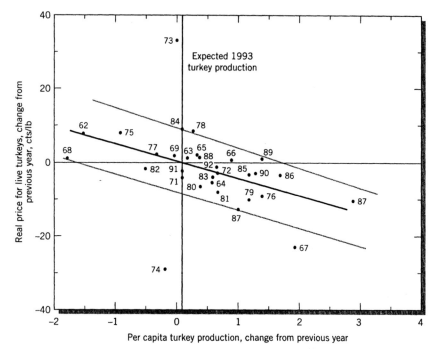

FIGURE 12.15. TURKEYS—Real farm prices related to per capita production measured in changes from the previous year, United States, 1961–92.

below this estimate. Another variable may be useful in reducing this range.

If we use the change in the per capita availability of red meats as a second variable, the scatter diagram for the first residual of real farm prices for turkeys against the change in red meat availability is shown in Figure 12.16. We can measure the second-order price residuals from the relationship defined by this variable. When we compare the changes in price expected on the basis of the addition of the per capita change in red meats with the price change expected on the basis of change in turkey production alone (Figure 12.17), it is very clear that the change in the availability of red meats does little to improve our estimate. Indeed, the *direction* of the expected change in price is incorrect in two of the most recent years of data. That is, the actual and expected price changes are on opposite sides of the zero line. Thus, we should most probably eliminate the red meats from consideration and use our first residuals against an alternative variable.

The first residual of prices is measured against the change in the January 1 cold storage holdings of turkey in Figure 12.18. The drift lines

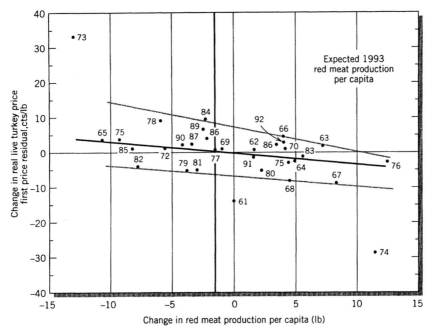

FIGURE 12.16. TURKEYS—First residuals of the change in price against change from the previous year's per capita red meat production.

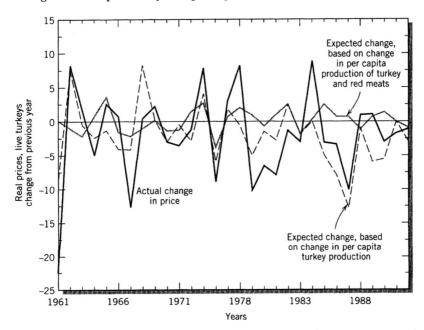

FIGURE 12.17. TURKEYS—Actual and expected change from previous year's price, based on per capita production of turkey and red meats.

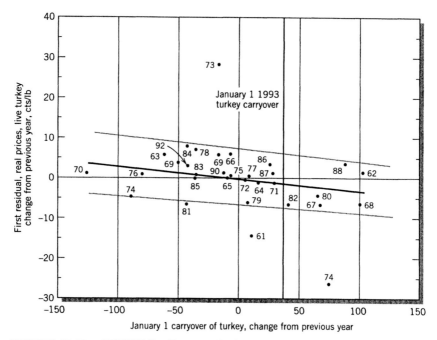

FIGURE 12.18.   TURKEYS—First residuals of the change in price against the change from the previous year's January 1 cold storage holdings of turkey.

suggest that the change in turkey carry-over might reduce the range of possible error a bit—particularly on the top side. When the line of best relationship is drawn, the increased level of January 1, 1993, cold storage holdings of turkey would be expected to reduce the 1993 real farm turkey price by an additional cent per pound.

The progressive residuals of price through the process of our analysis are shown in Figure 12.19. In general, the use of the January 1 cold storage holdings of turkey against our first price change residual does not make a great deal of change in the picture we saw earlier. It does give some slight improvement in the concentration and range of the price residuals—particularly in the more recent years. Whether the improvement is sufficient to justify the retention of the variable is up to the judgment of the analyst. This process can be continued, accepting or rejecting explanatory variables according to their impact upon the concentration and range of residuals.

The combined effect of the expected change in 1993 turkey production and the change in January 1, 1993 cold storage holdings of turkey would be about 2 cents (1.0 + 1.0) below the 24-cent real price observed in 1992, or 22 cents per pound. If we use the expected 1993 Consumer Price

Index value of 145.3 to reinflate the 22-cent-per-pound real price into terms of 1993 dollars, the expected 1993 cash price for live turkeys would be about 32 cents per pound—5 cents below the cash price of 37.2 cents observed in 1992. This 32-cent estimate compares with the 35 cents per pound derived from our previous direct price approach to estimating turkey demand. Which of these approaches is "superior" would be dependent upon the judgment of the analyst.

A troubling aspect of both the multiple graphic correlation approaches to demand for turkeys is that the expected values for the most recent years of data are so erratically different from what actually occurred. While the general pattern of prices is really pretty well described by the variables we have selected (Figure 12.20), the accuracy leaves much to be desired. Major directional changes (that is, changes in cyclical direction) in price may be called a year early or a year late. Part of this problem is undoubtedly associated with the reality that only six to eight months are required for turkey producers to begin to respond to economic incentives. Thus, quarterly data would perhaps improve the analysis materially.

A second possible explanation for the wide range of potential errors in our demand analysis is that there may have been a substantial structural

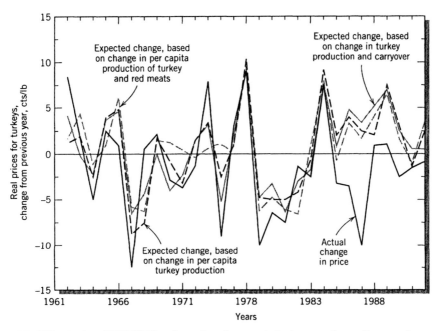

FIGURE 12.19. TURKEYS—Actual and expected changes from the previous year's price, based on selected variables.

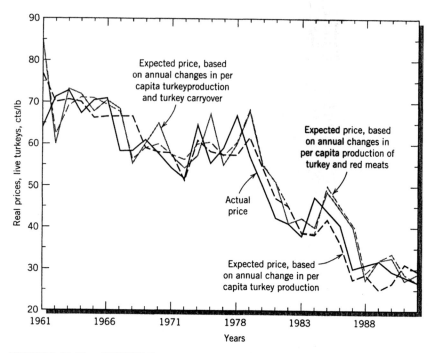

FIGURE 12.20. TURKEYS—Actual and expected prices, utilizing data expressed as change from the previous year, selected demand variables.

change in the demand for turkey that we do not yet have enough data to define. This potential structural change in demand is a real possibility. We know that there has been a massive increase in the development of turkey-based products during the 1980s. The emergence of turkey cold cuts, turkey hamburger, microwavable turkey entrees, and so on, may well have created structural demand changes that will allow increased quantities of turkey to be sold at higher prices.

One thing that should be made abundantly clear regarding the use of multiple graphic correlation in the estimation of demand and supply is that it involves a large element of "artistic" judgment on the part of the analyst. Each successive iteration of the process allows the eye of the analyst to identify and ignore aberrant observations. With some experience, many price analysts can become astonishingly accurate in the free-hand definition of relationships between variables. The multiple graphic correlation forecasting technique inherently assumes that the impacts of various explanatory variables upon the dependent variable of interest are isolated from one another. Each subsequent variable introduced deals only with the unexplained residual variation. The approach does not permit comparisons of interactions between variables. That is, if the influences exerted by two explanatory variables overlap, the overlapping influence is not captured, rather, it is all ascribed to the variable that was first selected. This might be considered an advantage in that the redefinition of the dependent variable as an unexplained residual variation with the introduction of each new explanatory variable eliminates—or at least ameliorates—some of the statistical problems of autocorrelation and multicollinearity frequently encountered in the use of time series data.

A disadvantage of the multiple graphic correlation approach is that it does not provide any means for definitively measuring the probability of potential errors. Since the slope associated with each of the relationships depends upon the eye of the analyst, there is no s_b statistical measure for significance and confidence in the accuracy of the slope. Since the drift lines are the only means for establishing potential errors in the level of the estimates, the analyst's judgment in identifying aberrant observations can make very large differences in the range of any potential error. There is no s_y statistical measure for establishing the probable range or degree of error. Nevertheless, the multiple graphic correlation approach does provide a means for analyzing supply and demand relationships with no more investment than a pencil, a straight edge, and some graph paper. It also provides the advantage of the analyst gaining a feel for the data that can be extremely helpful in other approaches to price analysis.

CHAPTER **13**

Estimation of Demand and Supply— Regression Revisited[1]

---

[1] The author is indebted to a colleague, Dr. Bruce L. Dixon, for his review and constructive suggestions regarding materials in this chapter.

The multiple graphic correlation approach to estimating demand and/or supply presented in Chapter 12 offers several advantages—among them the use of universally available, inexpensive materials and the development of the analyst's ability to sense the implications of changes in various data series. The development and honing of an analyst's artistic skills with data should not be underrated. However, this approach can lend itself to the generation of rather heated arguments among analysts, since different analysts using exactly the same data may come to marginally different conclusions. These differences of opinion are, of course, much of the stuff from which markets, and ultimately prices, are made.

Multiple regression analysis provides an alternative method for estimating demand and/or supply relationships. The multiple regression approach offers an estimation procedure that is more systematic and is therefore less dependent upon the artistic skills of the analyst. This does not imply that one approach is necessarily superior to the other. It simply means that the approaches are different regarding their requirements for equipment and analytical skills. The end results (i.e., the forecasts) developed through either approach are likely to be quite similar. The multiple regression approach does offer the advantage of providing some statistical measures of significance and reliability of the parameters (i.e., the coefficients associated with the independent variables) developed and of the reliability of the expected values of the dependent variable.

Conceptually, multiple regression is the same as the simple regression idea presented when we estimated trend models in Chapter 5. The only real difference is in the multidimensional character of the multiple regression process as compared with the two-dimensional character of the simple regression problem. In the simple regression problem, each observation of the dependent variable was hypothesized to have been related to an associated (or a "paired") observation of some independent variable. The objective of the simple regression analysis was to estimate that relationship by minimizing the squared vertical deviations of the observed values of the dependent variable from the value expected on the basis of the estimated relationship. That is, the sum of the squared deviations between the observed values of the dependent variable and the regression line was minimized in calculating numerical values of the parameter estimates.

Multiple regression retains the objective of minimizing the sum of the squared deviations between the observed values of the dependent variable and the calculated regression line. But it adds additional dimensions to this concept through supplementing the information provided by a single independent variable with additional information in the form of additional independent variables. Each additional independent variable included in the analysis, if the regression model is correctly specified, would be expected to reduce the s_y. That is, the sum of the squared vertical deviations from the regression line would be expected to be reduced as variables are added, subject to the constraints imposed by the degrees of freedom.

To illustrate the manner in which multiple regression might be used to estimate a supply or demand function, let's return to our example of turkey demand from Table 12.3 in Chapter 12. The scatter diagram in Figure 13.1 presents the paired observations of real prices for live turkeys and the per capita production of live turkeys over the 1960–92 period with the 1960 and 1973 observations eliminated as aberrant observations. The negative relationship between quantity and price normally associated with demand curves is very clear in Figure 13.1. Either a linear or a semilogarithmic regression line can be fitted to these data. Both of these explain more than 80 percent of the variation in real live turkey prices, but the semilogarithmic function has both a higher R^2 and a smaller S_y. Thus, the semilogarithmic function is marginally better. (The figures in parentheses below the estimated b parameters are the standard errors of those parameters. The asterisks adjacent to the stan-

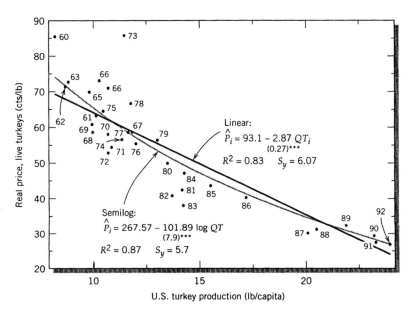

FIGURE 13–1. TURKEYS. Real Price-Quantity Relationships Based on Linear and Semilogarithmic Demand Hypotheses, U.S., 1960–92.

dard errors signify the level of statistical significance on a two-tailed test: *-90 percent level, **-95 percent level, ***-99 percent level.)

When the expected values for turkey prices using these alternative functions are calculated (Figure 13.2), it is very clear that the semilogarithmic relationship between price and quantity provides expected values that are generally closer to the real prices actually observed. However, there are long periods—1962–67, for example—during which the expected prices are consistently above or below the actuals. Can an additional variable be introduced that will improve the fit during these periods?

Recall that there was a strong downward trend in real turkey prices over the 1960–90 period and an even stronger upward trend in turkey production. The interaction between these two trends in the semilogarithmic estimate explains 87 percent of the variation in turkey prices over the period. Thus, only 13 percent of the variation remains unexplained. When other variables such as turkey carryover, availability of beef, pork, or chicken, or per capita disposable real income are added to the equation, each parameter (i.e., the b value) associated with its variable is not significantly different from zero at a 90 percent probability level. When

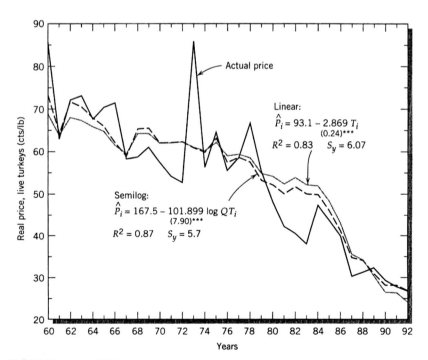

FIGURE 13.2. TURKEYS—Actual versus expected real prices, based on linear and semilogarithmic demand relationships, United States, 1960–92.

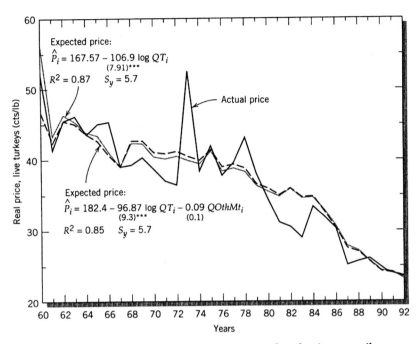

FIGURE 13.3.   TURKEYS—Actual versus expected real prices, semilog quantity of turkey per capita and per capita production of all competing meats, United States, 1960–92.

the per capita availability of pork, beef, and chicken are *combined* into a single variable, the substitute "Other Meats" variable still does not offer a significant improvement in the fit of the equation (Figure 13.3).

The competing meats variable does draw the expected prices a bit closer to the prices actually observed during the latter half of the 1960–92 period. However, the circumstance of long periods during which expected prices either consistently exceed observed prices or remain consistently below them persists. What is probably happening in this situation is that the very strong trends in price and turkey production have created a situation in which the quantity variable grossly overshadows the influence of all other variables in explaining turkey prices. The most obvious way for dealing with this situation is, as we saw when we were working with multiple graphic correlation, to utilize first differences for all variables.

The actual real prices for live turkeys and the first difference in those real prices are shown in Table 13.1. Since 1960 and 1973 have been defined previously as aberrant years (outliers), these years have been omitted from the table. Also, since 1960 and 1973 would be elements of the calculation for the price *change* from the previous year, 1961 and 1974

TABLE 13.1. TURKEYS—Comparative Variances in Real Live Prices and the Annual Change in Prices, U.S., 1960–90

Year	Real Price, Turkeys		Real Price, Change from Previous Year	
	Actual Price (cts/lb)	Squared Deviation from Mean (cts/lb)	Price Change (cts/lb)	Squared Deviation from Mean (cts/lb)
1960				
1961				
1962	71.3	441.00	8.1	100.00
1963	72.9	510.76	1.6	12.25
1964	67.7	303.09	−5.2	10.83
1965	70.5	408.04	2.8	22.00
1966	71.1	432.64	0.6	6.25
1967	58.4	65.76	−12.7	116.45
1968	58.9	74.46	0.5	5.86
1969	61.0	116.79	2.2	16.63
1970	58.2	62.52	−2.9	1.00
1971	54.6	18.26	−3.6	3.01
1972	53.1	7.67	−1.5	0.16
1973				
1974				
1975	70.6	412.09	7.5	89.11
1976	58.9	73.96	−11.7	96.04
1977	62.5	146.41	3.5	29.16
1978	72.0	470.89	9.6	132.25
1979	63.0	161.29	−9.0	50.41
1980	56.9	43.56	−6.1	17.64
1981	46.4	15.21	−10.5	73.96
1982	43.4	47.61	−3.0	1.21
1983	39.4	118.81	−4.0	4.41
1984	49.1	1.44	9.7	134.56
1985	45.4	24.01	−3.7	3.24
1986	41.2	82.81	−4.2	5.29
1987	31.3	361.00	−9.9	64.00
1988	32.5	316.84	1.2	9.61
1989	33.8	272.25	1.3	10.24
1990	30.8	380.25	−3.0	1.21
1991	28.8	462.25	−2.0	0.01
1992	27.6	515.29	−1.2	0.49
Total	1,460.0	5,906.00	−53.7	917.30
Average	50.3		−1.9	
Variance		145.7		31.9
Standard Deviation		13.49		5.64

264

are also omitted from the table. The means of both the actual price and the annual change in price for the remaining years are calculated at the bottom of the table. These mean values are then deducted from the observed values, and the differences (i.e., the deviations) are squared for purposes of calculating the variance. The sums of the squared deviations are then divided by two less than the total number of observations $[(n - 2) = 27 - 2 = 25]$ to calculate the variance. Back in Chapter 5, we learned that the variance and standard deviation were measures of dispersion about the mean. These measures provided an indication of just how widely dispersed the observations of the variable in question might be.

When we calculated the R^2 statistic, we measured the degree to which our variance had been reduced by measuring the dispersion from the *regression* line rather than the mean. A similar calculation regarding the degree of reduction in the variance that is associated with the use of the *change* in price rather than the price itself provides a measure of the variation that is explained by the annual price change, which is similar to the R^2 statistic. This calculation may be made:

$$\frac{(181.9 - 31.9)}{181.9} = \frac{150.0}{181.9} = 0.825 \tag{13.1}$$

That is, 82.5 percent of the total variation in the real price of live turkeys over the 1960–92 period has been removed through the use of the annual price change technique. Only 17.5 percent of the total variation in real prices for live turkey remains to be explained. Thus, a regression equation based on first differences that exhibits an R^2 statistic of 0.50 would be explaining 50 percent of the remaining 17.5 percent variation in turkey prices or 8.75 percent of the total variation. If this 8.75 percent is added to the 82.5 percent of the variation removed by the use of annual price change, the analysis is explaining 91.25 percent of the total price variation.

We can use the first difference data we developed in Table 12.4 in Chapter 12 to pursue our analysis of the annual changes in real prices for live turkeys. When we regress the annual change in real turkey prices on the annual change in per capita turkey production (Figure 13.4), we can see that the annual change in turkey production does explain 35 percent of the year-to-year change in live turkey prices, or about a third of the 17.5 percent of unexplained variation. The standard error of the estimate is only 4.9 cents per pound, compared with a raw standard deviation of 5.64 cents. The *b* value associated with the change in production is highly significant at the 99 percent level. Thus, the change in per capita turkey production is important in explaining changes in real turkey prices.

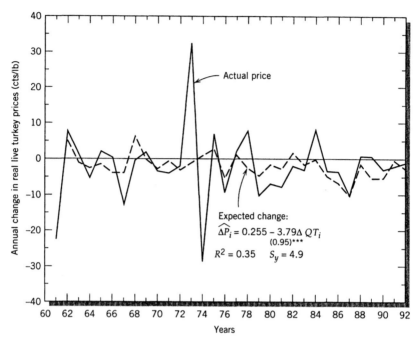

FIGURE 13.4. TURKEYS—Annual change in real price: actual versus expected, based on annual change in per capita turkey production, United States, 1960–92.

There are clearly some periods during which there is more than change in turkey production at work. For example, from 1967 to 1968 and from 1979 to 1983, the regression relationship based on the annual change in turkey production suggests that live turkey prices should have been considerably higher than was actually the case. In 1965, 1977, 1978, 1984 to 1986, and 1988 to 1990, actual prices were *higher* than this relationship suggests. Thus, there must be some missing variable(s) that would improve our understanding.

When we conducted our multiple graphic correlation analysis of turkey demand, we used the January 1 cold storage holdings of turkey as an explanatory variable. The addition of beginning carryover stocks of turkeys yields the following regression equation:

$$\Delta P_1 = 0.52 - 4.28 \Delta QT_i - 0.0245 \, \Delta IT_i$$
$$ (1.05)^{***} (0.018) (13.2)$$
$$R^2 = 0.39 S_y = 4.9$$

where:

ΔP_i is the expected change from the previous year's price

ΔQT_i is the change from the previous year's per capita turkey production in pounds

ΔIT_i is the change from the previous year's January 1 inventory of turkey in cold storage, in millions of pounds

The addition of the change in turkey carryover does increase the R^2 statistic a bit, and the algebraic sign of the estimated parameter is correct. But the b value associated with the turkey carryover variable is statistically nonsignificant. That is, because of the low statistical significance, a different sample from the same population might yield a coefficient with a positive sign. Further, the magnitude of the s_y statistic is unchanged. Thus, it is clear that change in turkey carry-over doesn't do much to explain the change in live turkey prices. Whether the variable should be retained in the analysis is subject to the judgment of the analyst, but there are no compelling statistical reasons for doing so. Therefore, for the time being, let's drop it from consideration.

If we replace the change in beginning turkey carry-over variable with the change in the availability of red meats (Figure 13.5), we find that the R^2 statistic is increased from 0.35 to 0.46 and the standard error of the

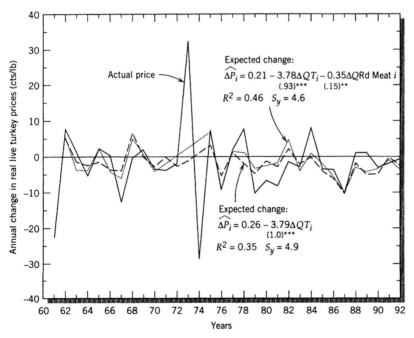

FIGURE 13.5. TURKEYS—Annual change in real price: actual versus expected, based on annual change in per capita production of turkey and all red meats, United States, 1960–92.

estimate is reduced from 4.9 to 4.6 cents per pound. Further, the parameter associated with the new variable is significant at the 95 percent
level. The expected year-to-year changes in real live turkey prices *do*
generally move closer to the actual changes than was the case when we
used the change in turkey production alone. Thus, it is clear that the
variable is likely an important component of the model. We do, however, still have some of the long periods during which the equation
either overestimates or underestimates the actual change in price. Is
there an additional variable that might improve our estimate?

Chicken is also a substitute meat, so perhaps the addition of the
change in the per capita production of chicken would improve the fit of
our equation in explaining the change in live turkey prices. The regression equation that includes the change in per capita production of
chicken is:

$$\Delta P_1 = -1.39 - 5.16\,\Delta QT_i - 0.263\,\Delta QRM_i + 1.21\,\Delta QCh_i$$
$$(1.32)^{***} \quad (1.63) \qquad\qquad (0.84) \qquad\qquad\qquad (13.3)$$
$$R^2 = 0.50 \qquad S_y = 4.5$$

where:

ΔP_i is the expected change from the previous year's price

ΔQT_i is the change from the previous year's per capita live turkey
production in pounds

ΔQRM is the change from the previous year's per capita production of
red meats (pork and beef) in pounds

ΔQCh_i is the change from the previous years per capita production of
chicken, in pounds

The addition of chicken to the analysis does not improve the fit of the
regression equation. It actually degrades it. Not only is the paramater
associated with chicken nonsignificant, that associated with red meats is
no *longer* significant. Worse, the algebraic sign associated with the *b*
value for chicken is positive. The positive sign suggests that turkey and
chicken are complementary goods rather than substitutes. In other
words, the price of turkey would be expected to increase as the availability of chicken is increased. This is clearly nonsense. Therefore, the quantity of chicken variable should be immediately discarded.

The only variable remaining in Table 12.4 to help in explaining the
change in turkey prices is the change in consumer income (Figure 13.6).
The addition of the income variable improves both the R^2 and the s_y and
all of the *b* values in the equation have the expected signs and are
significantly different from zero. An examination of Figure 13.6 reveals

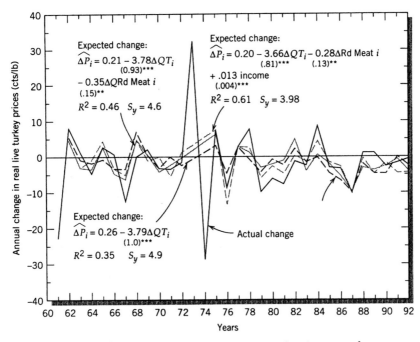

FIGURE 13.6. TURKEYS—Annual change in real price: actual versus expected, based on annual changes in per capita production of turkeys and red meats and per capita real income, United States, 1960–92.

that the change in income does, in fact, improve the levels at which expected price changes describe actual changes.

When the expected values from the various first-difference regression analyses are converted back to terms of expected real prices (that is, when the expected change from the previous year's real price is added to that previous year's price), the result is shown in Figure 13.7. The first difference estimates of expected real prices compare pretty accurately with the prices actually observed over this 30-year period. This is particularly true for the model that postulates the expected change in real price as a function of the expected changes in per capita production of turkey and red meats and in per capita disposable real income. This estimate leaves something to be desired during the most recent years of the sample, but even in these years the first-difference analysis is superior to the analysis based on the undifferentiated basic data (Figure 13.8). If the 82.5 percent of the variation in real live turkey prices that was accounted for by the first-difference calculation is added to the 61 percent of the remaining 17.5 percent unexplained variation, the total R^2 would be 0.93 (0.61 × 0.175 = 0.107) or 10.7 percent. Thus, 10.7 per-

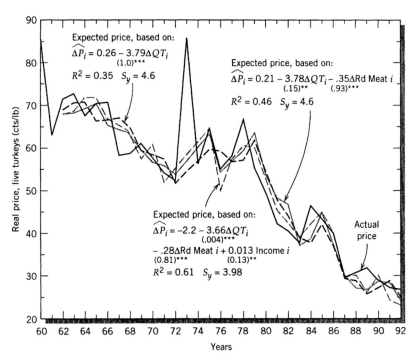

FIGURE 13.7. TURKEYS—Actual versus expected prices, based on annual changes in selected demand variables, United States, 1960–92.

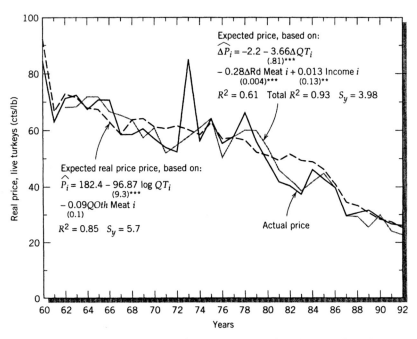

FIGURE 13.8. TURKEYS—Actual versus expected real prices, based on total values compared with annual changes in selected demand variables, United States, 1960–92.

cent + 82.5 percent = 93.2 percent of the total variation. Perhaps more important, the first-difference approach reduces the standard error of the estimate of real live turkey prices from 4.6 to 3.98 cents per pound. Thus, the first-differences analysis has reduced our error by a sixth. However, even the superior estimate based on first differences leaves much to be desired. The standard error of the estimate at 3.98 cents per pound is still about 15 percent of the more recent real prices observed. That is, two-thirds of our expected values would be within 3.98 cents of the actual values of real live turkey prices. We could expect our forecast value to frequently be at least 15 percent above or below the actual real price in one case out of three.

The true test of a price forecast is not how close the forecast may lie to the actual price that ultimately occurs. Rather, the test of the forecast is whether it leads managers to make sound managerial decisions. Not many turkey producers, processors, or sellers consistently enjoy a net profit as large as 15 percent of the value of sales. Our standard error of 3.98 cents (in *real terms*) per pound might well give us forecasts that could lead a manager to an incorrect decision. Thus, we should most probably look further in our effort to forecast live turkey prices.

GAINING DEGREES OF FREEDOM _____

Both approaches to the estimation of real live turkey prices through multiple regression analysis show their greatest limitations during the most recent 7 to 10 years of annual data. Recall that we had previously speculated that there very well might have been a significant structural change in per capita turkey demand during the 1980s, resulting from the development of a host of new turkey products. A reexamination of the price–quantity scatter diagram with a grouping of consecutive years suggests a change in demand beginning in 1984, and possibly another change in 1987 to 1988 (Figure 13.9).

With no more than nine observations with which to work, the available degrees of freedom place severe limits upon the degree to which we might be able to further utilize annual data for purposes of analyzing turkey demand. The calculation of the means of price and quantity involves the loss of two degrees of freedom. Each additional variable utilized in the analysis would involve the loss of an additional degree of freedom. The *t* ratios required for significance of parameter estimates are elevated considerably with this sort of reduction in the numbers of observations. This limitation can be dealt with through the use of quarterly data (or even monthly data, if available). Table 13.2 presents the quarterly data for turkey demand analysis.

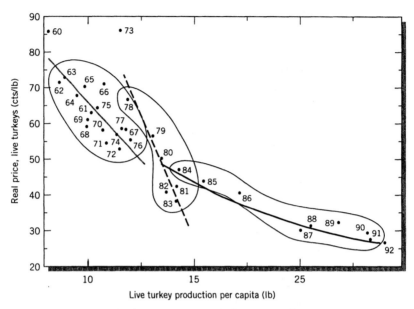

FIGURE 13.9.   TURKEYS—Intertemporal changes in demand, United States, 1960–92.

There are several advantages associated with the use of quarterly data in a supply or demand analysis. First of all, the lags between the time of managerial decisions and the time those decisions are reflected in increased supplies can be more precisely specified when the data are in quarterly form. This is particularly helpful in the case of commodities such as turkeys or broilers for which the entire life cycle of birth, maturation, and reproduction may be accomplished in a period less than a year in length. Second, seasonality of both demand and supply can be directly measured (indeed, it *must* be accounted for) within the supply and/or demand equation if quarterly data are used. Third, the "misses" in timing of major directional changes (these directional changes are generally cyclical in nature) in expected values as compared with actual values are likely to be less frequent, provided the predictive equation is correctly specified.

When the quarterly real prices for turkeys are charted, it is clear that a strong seasonal price pattern exists (Figure 13.10). Since the fourth quarter includes both the Thanksgiving and Christmas holidays, fourth-quarter real turkey prices are predictably consistently higher than other quarters during any given year. It will be remembered that we suggested there had perhaps been a change in turkey demand during the 1987–88 period. Figure 13.10 lends some credence to that suggestion in

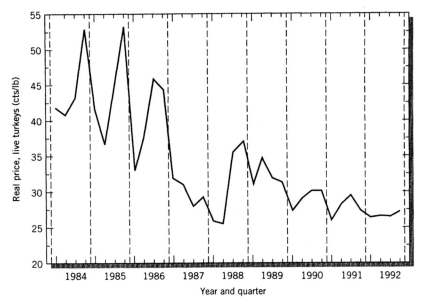

FIGURE 13.10. TURKEYS—Real live prices, by quarters, United States, 1984–92.

that the 1984–87 downward trend in prices appears to have "flattened" subsequent to 1988. Also, the magnitude of the seasonal oscillations in price appears to have been reduced.

Because of the very strong seasonal price variation illustrated in Figure 13.10, some provision must be made in any quarterly regression analysis in order to account for price seasonality. When Table 13.2 is examined carefully, it will be observed that there are three columns labeled "Seasonal Binary Variables," for which the values are either 0 or 1. Since the real live turkey price is seasonally high during the fourth quarter, that quarter has been defined to be the "base" quarter and no binary variable has been provided for it.[1] The value for the fourth quarter is thus zero for all of the seasonal binary variables.

The "zero–one" nature of the binary variables is simply an indication that consumer response to change in an independent variable such as the per capita availability of competing meats or per capita income

---

[1] If binary variables were provided for all four quarters, with the equation specified to be of the $Y_i = a + b_1X_{1i} + b_2X_{2i} + \cdots + b_nX_{ni} + e_i$ form, the result would be a singular matrix for which the determinant is 0, implying that a unique set of coefficients could not be estimated. If one wishes to directly estimate the intercepts for each of the quarters, most spread-sheet computer software packages provide an option that permits the operator to restrict the estimated a value to zero, thus eliminating the singular matrix problem.

TABLE 13.2. TURKEYS—Prices, Per Capita Production, and Other Factors Potentially Affecting Turkey Demand, by Quarters, United States, 1984–92

Year and Quarter	Nominal Price for Live Turkeys (cts/lb)	CPI (1982–84 = 100)	Real Quarterly Price for Live Turkeys (ct/lb)	Binary Variables 1st Qtr	2nd Qtr	3rd Qtr	Per Cap Prod Ready-to-Cook Turkeys (lbs)	Beginning Stocks of Turkeys (Mil lb)	Per Cap Pork Prod (lb)	Per Cap Beef Prod (lb)	Per Cap Young Chicken Prod (lb)	Per Capita Disposable Personal Real Income (Dollars, 1982–84 = 100)
1984-I	42.8	102.3	41.9	1	0	0	1.9	84.3	16.0	24.4	13.1	10,809
-II	42.4	103.4	41.0	0	1	0	2.6	83.5	15.6	24.7	14.1	10,797
-III	45.3	104.5	43.3	0	0	1	3.4	154.9	14.2	25.1	14.1	10,848
-IV	55.9	105.3	53.1	0	0	0	3.4	317.4	16.8	25.2	13.6	10,890
1985-I	43.4	106.0	41.0	1	0	0	2.1	62.6	15.3	24.1	13.7	10,932
-II	39.4	107.2	36.8	0	1	0	2.8	70.8	15.7	24.9	14.9	11,115
-III	47.8	108.0	44.2	0	0	1	3.7	174.0	14.9	25.9	14.8	10,998
-IV	58.1	108.9	53.4	0	0	0	3.7	358.1	16.0	24.3	14.1	11,106
1986-I	36.3	109.3	33.2	1	0	0	2.4	78.3	14.9	24.2	14.2	11,273
-II	41.6	109.0	38.2	0	1	0	3.1	84.4	14.9	26.0	15.3	11,490
-III	50.5	109.6	46.1	0	0	1	4.0	215.8	13.4	26.0	15.0	11,463
-IV	49.2	110.4	44.5	0	0	0	3.9	416.1	15.0	24.7	14.8	11,432
1987-I	35.5	111.5	31.9	1	0	0	2.8	105.7	14.7	23.9	15.5	11,580
-II	35.3	113.0	31.2	0	1	0	3.7	154.5	13.7	23.6	16.1	11,349
-III	32.3	114.3	28.2	0	0	1	4.6	288.2	13.9	24.9	16.3	11,496
-IV	34.2	115.3	29.6	0	0	0	4.6	485.2	16.7	24.1	16.0	11,689

1988-I	30.1	116.0	26.0	1	0	0	3.4	139.6	15.5	23.4	16.3	11,865
-II	30.1	117.5	25.6	0	1	0	4.0	214.0	15.2	23.7	16.7	11,901
-III	42.6	119.1	35.8	0	0	1	4.4	321.7	15.3	25.2	16.5	11,987
-IV	44.9	120.3	37.3	0	0	0	4.2	436.5	17.6	23.5	16.3	12,029
1989-I	37.9	121.6	31.2	1	0	0	3.3	139.3	15.8	22.6	16.8	12,146
-II	43.2	123.6	35.0	0	1	0	4.2	172.3	16.0	23.4	17.7	12,039
-III	40.0	124.6	32.1	0	0	1	4.8	315.8	15.4	24.1	17.8	12,057
-IV	39.7	125.8	31.5	0	0	0	4.9	431.2	16.8	23.4	17.8	12,091
1990-I	35.2	128.0	27.5	1	0	0	4.1	236.0	15.8	22.3	18.2	12,134
-II	37.9	129.3	29.3	0	1	0	4.6	318.0	14.6	23.0	18.7	12,098
-III	39.9	131.1	30.4	0	0	1	5.1	481.0	14.6	23.4	18.6	12,025
-IV	40.6	133.6	30.4	0	0	0	5.2	624.0	16.4	22.4	19.1	11,859
1991-I	35.3	134.7	26.2	1	0	0	4.2	306.0	15.5	21.4	18.7	11,790
-II	38.4	135.6	28.3	0	1	0	4.5	377.0	15.1	22.6	19.9	11,809
-III	40.3	136.2	29.6	0	0	1	4.8	503.0	15.4	24.0	19.6	12,265
-IV	37.4	137.7	27.2	0	0	0	4.9	667.0	17.6	23.7	19.5	12,262
1992-I	36.6	138.7	26.4	1	0	0	4.1	264.0	17.0	22.1	20.0	12,359
-II	37.3	139.8	26.7	0	1	0	4.2	393.0	15.8	22.5	20.6	12,367
-III	37.7	140.9	26.8	0	0	1	5.0	580.0	16.7	23.4	20.9	12,301
-IV	38.9	142.0	27.4	0	0	0	4.9	734.0	17.8	22.2	20.4	12,401

Source. Production and price data from Mark R. Weimar and Shauna Cromer, *U.S. Egg and Poultry Statistical Series, 1960–89*, ERS USDA, Statistical Bulletin No. 816, September 1990; *Livestock and Meat Statistics, 1984–88*, ERS, USDA, Statistical Bulletin No. 784, September 1989; *Livestock and Poultry Situation and Outlook Report*, ERS, USDA, various issues since 1989; Income Data and CPI from *Survey of Current Business*, U.S. Dept. of Commerce, various issues since 1984.

would be expected to be similar in all quarters, but that the seasonal strength or weakness in turkey demand can be accounted for simply by adjusting the value of the intercept (i.e., the constant a value that appears as the first term in the regression equation). Thus, the value of the intercept will represent the constant value for the fourth quarter. The parameter associated with any of the seasonal binary variables would define the magnitude by which the constant should be adjusted for the quarter in question.

If the parameters associated with the independent variables are expected to change with the season (e.g., if consumers are expected to respond differently to an increase in income during warm seasons than they might respond during cold seasons), the demand for each quarter should be estimated separately. In that case, the degrees of freedom limitation for any given quarter would be identical with that experienced in the use of annual data.

Figure 13.11 shows the price–quantity scatter diagram for turkeys since 1984, with the observations grouped by quarters. The seasonality in turkey demand is very clear. During the January–March quarter (the observations identified with the year and the letter w in the figure),

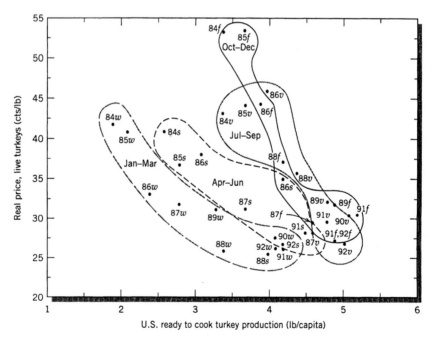

FIGURE 13.11. TURKEYS—Quarterly real price–quantity combinations, ready-to-cook turkey production per capita and live turkey prices, United States, 1984–92.

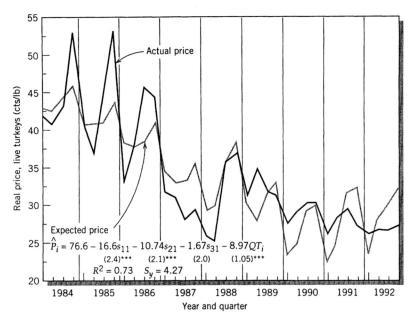

FIGURE 13.12. TURKEYS—Real prices: actual versus expected, based on per capita ready-to-cook turkey production and seasonality, by quarters, United States, 1984–92.

turkey demand is at its lowest. It strengthens—that is, demand shifts upward to the right—in the April–June quarter (the observations identified with the letter s). During the July–September period (the observations identified with the letter v), turkey demand strengthens still further as the industry prepares for the very strong Thanksgiving and Christmas demand. During the October–December quarter (the observations identified with the letter f), turkey demand is at its seasonal peak.

The predicted prices from a basic turkey demand estimate are presented in Figure 13.12. This equation simply defines real live turkey prices to be a function of the per capita production of turkey (QT_i) and seasonality (s_{1i}, s_{2i}, and s_{3i}). The estimate explains 73 percent of the variation in prices and exhibits a standard error of 4.27 cents per pound of live turkey, with the quantity variable and two of the three seasonal binaries highly significant at the 99 percent level. The third-quarter seasonal variable is nonsignificant—a not unexpected result, since the third- and fourth-quarter observations in Figure 13.11 were consistently overlapping. The estimated equation understates the seasonality of demand during the early years and overstates it during the later years of the analysis, an indication of a reduction in the seasonality of demand, and perhaps a change in the actual nature of turkey demand *per se*. This is precisely what one might expect to have resulted from the continuing development of the large numbers of turkey-based meat products during the 1980s. As additional information becomes available, an analyst should probably eliminate the information prior to 1988 when the decline in seasonality appears to have begun. It could be argued that the continuing restructuring of turkey demand associated with the emergence of further processed turkey products renders the earlier information irrelevant.

When the additional variable of beginning quarterly stocks of turkey is added to the analysis, the fit of the equation is marginally improved and the new variable is statistically significant at the 95 percent level. In addition, the third-quarter seasonal variable becomes statistically significant at the 95 percent level (Figure 13.13). When the other variables from Table 13.2 (availability of competing meats and per capita disposable real income) are added to the analysis, none of them improve the statistical fit nor are they statistically significant.

We could utilize first differences (being careful because of the seasonality issue to calculate these differences from *year to year* rather than from quarter to quarter; that is, first quarter in the current year less the first quarter of the previous year, thereby eliminating the necessity for sea-

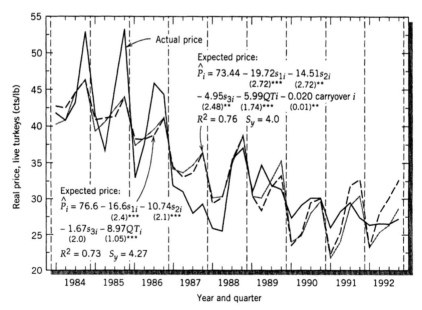

FIGURE 13.13.   TURKEYS—Real prices: actual versus expected, based on quarterly per capita production and beginning quarterly inventories of ready-to-cook turkey, United States, 1984–92.

sonal binary variables), as we did in the case of our analysis with annual data in an effort to improve the explanatory and forecasting capabilities of our estimate. An alternative approach to our problem might be to use a four-quarter moving total of per capita turkey production in our effort to improve our analysis. The rationale behind this approach would be that while many consumers consider beef to be sirloin, T-bone, prime rib, and hamburger, and pork to be cured ham, bacon, and pork chops, those same consumers consider turkey to be merely turkey. The reality that many consumers become very quickly "burned out" on turkey is illustrated by the numbers of cartoons, jokes, and quips regarding turkey left-overs during the Thanksgiving–Christmas season. A four-quarter moving total of per capita turkey production would provide a continuing measure of the volume of turkey ingested by average consumers over the past 12 months—and hence, just how sick of the stuff they may have become.

The approaches to utilizing regression analysis in the estimation of supply and demand are limited only by the imagination of the analyst. There are obviously some missing variables that might help to better explain our turkey demand equation. Whether the data regarding these variables are readily available is an altogether different question. Both of the regression equations suggest that 1993 real turkey prices would be expected to be marginally lower than was the case in 1992. A first-differences approach to the estimate might produce a much lower standard error of the estimate—even in the absence of additional variables—since the year-to-year changes shown by the actual data and the year-to-year differences in the expected values produced by the equations are not greatly different.

Appendix _____

This appendix provides information regarding the use of the computer in estimating ordinary least squares regression models for supply and demand. About the only difference from the regression instructions provided in the appendix to Chapter 5 is that the X range will include more than a single column, that is, the X range will include a column for each independent variable. It is important to realize that most spreadsheet computer software packages such as LOTUS 1-2-3 and QUATTROPRO require that the independent variables be immediately adjacent to each other. Thus, if a variable is introduced and subsequently discarded from the analysis, that column must be moved out of the body (or block) of independent variables and the X range then redefined.

Potential Errors Associated with Ordinary Least Squares Regression Analysis

The ordinary least squares regression procedure assumes certain characteristics regarding the data used for the analysis that may or may not be valid when time series data are utilized.

1. The structure of the economic relationships that create the dependent variable Y is some linear relationship between the dependent and independent variable(s) that can be described by an equation:

$$Y_i = a + b_1 X_{1i} + b_2 X_{2i} + \cdots + b_n X_{ni} + e_i$$

2. The independent variables are known and no linear relationship is present between any two or more of these independent variables.

    A violation of this assumption constitutes what is known as *perfect multicollinearity*. High but not perfect multicollinearity makes the interpretation of regression results very difficult since the standard errors associated with linearly related variables can become very large. The unexpected negative sign associated with the per capita chicken production variable when we worked with annual data may well have been the result of multicollinearity between chicken and some other variable included in the analysis.

    (Whether or not multicollinearity exists in a supply or demand equation is not the issue. With time series data, some degree of multicollinearity is most probably present. Thus, the question becomes whether the degree of multicollinearity is sufficient to cause problems of interpretation and inference.)

3. The error term (e_i) has an expected mean of zero and a constant variance.

    A violation of this latter assumption constitutes what is known as *heteroskedacity*. Heteroskedasticity in time series data occurs when the error terms in one portion of the time period have a different variance than is the case in another portion of the period.

4. Error terms (e_i) corresponding to different observations are not correlated with one another.

    A violation of this assumption constitutes what is known as *autocorrelation*. With time series data, there are frequently cases in which there will be a series of observations in which the error term for one period will be positively correlated with that for the subsequent period(s). If ordinary least squares regression is applied to data with autocorrelated error terms, the resulting standard errors are unreliable estimates of the true standard errors. Thus, inference about the coefficients is misleading if standard t tests are used. If the data are autocorrelated (or heteroskedastic), then an alternative to ordinary least squares should be utilized. The generalized least squares procedure in computer software such as SAS or SHAZAM are examples of such alternatives.

5. The errors are normally distributed. That is, when the errors are plotted in a frequency distribution, the errors will form a bell-shaped curve, with the mean of zero being the peak of the bell. Thus, the most frequently observed errors will be those closest to the mean. As the error departs further from zero, the frequency with which the error will be observed is reduced. The assumption of normality is most critical for drawing statistical inference regarding the parameters in samples with fewer than 30 degrees of freedom. For larger samples, statistical inference using the customary tests tends to be reliable even when the errors are not distributed in a precisely normal fashion.

6. The regression coefficients b_1, b_2, . . . , b_n are constant within the range of the data (i.e., they are parameters). The reason we went from an analysis of annual data to one utilizing quarterly data for a much shorter period of time was that we suspected that there had been some change in the values of the parameters over time. By using quarterly data, we were able to generate enough observations for the shorter period to escape problems with degrees of freedom.

There are a number of software packages (SAS, for example) that provide the capability for diagnosing and correcting for one or more of these statistical problems. The Durbin-Watson test, for example, is used to identify problems of autocorrelation. Once an autocorrelation problem has been identified, a generalized least squares procedure can be used to correct for the autocorrelation.

Diagnosing and correcting for autocorrelation, multicollinearity, and heteroskedacity require a much higher level of statistical training than is available in a text at the level for which this book is designed. Thus, these issues are beyond the scope of this text. Nevertheless, it is important for the student to recognize that when a regression analysis performs less effectively than the R^2, S_y, and t test values suggest should be the case, the probable cause is that one or more of the basic assumptions underlying that analysis has been violated.

CHAPTER **14**

Marketing Margins

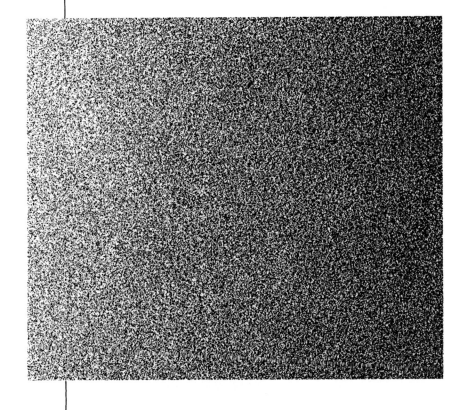

In Chapter 2, we discussed the relationships between price determination and price discovery and the differences between these two concepts. In that discussion, we recognized that prices were *determined* by the basic forces of supply and demand. But the *discovery* of the prices that were being determined was quite a different matter. We recognized that the processes of price discovery were fundamentally the same processes as for the forecasting of prices—telescoped in time. These price forecasting processes have been the primary focus of our attention throughout Chapters 3 through 12.

In Chapters 9 through 11, we examined the supply and demand relationships in some detail, preliminary to our efforts to actually estimate those relationships through the use of multiple graphic correlation in Chapter 12 and through the use of multiple regression analysis in Chapter 13. We discovered that the market supply function was simply the horizontal summation of all the individual supply functions for the various producers dealing in this market. Underlying each individual supply function was a production function—the technical relationship defining the rates at which variable resources could be combined with some set of fixed resources and thereby transformed into products. When this technical information was combined with resource price information, the cost structure for producing the good in question could be derived, and the individual firm's supply function could be defined. That individual supply function along which the firm would respond to changes in product prices was, of course, defined to be that portion of marginal cost which lay above average variable cost.

Like market supply, market demand is simply the horizontal summation of all the individual demand functions for all the consumers participating in the market. Every individual demand function is undergirded by some indifference surface that is defined by that consumer's personal tastes and preferences. Given the consumer's income (or budget), the prices for alternative goods, and a set of alternative prices for the good in question, we can use a map of the consumer's indifference surface to derive that consumer's individual demand for a product.

Figure 14.1 summarizes most of the supply and demand information we have considered. The left-hand portion of the diagram illustrates the fundamental concepts of supply for a "typical" producer while the right-hand portion illustrates those of demand for a typical consumer. The center portion of the diagram shows the market supply and demand relationships composed of the summations of all the individual relationships. The equilibrium price (P_E) is shown as are the quantities supplied

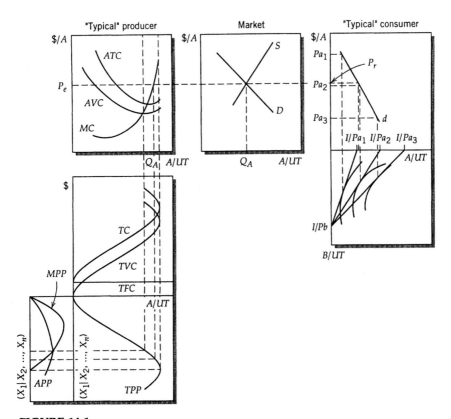

FIGURE 14.1

or demanded (the Q_A's in the three upper segments of Figure 14.1) at that equilibrium price.

We can see from Figure 14.1 that the position and shape of the individual supply function, that is, the position and shape of the marginal cost curve, is determined by:

1. The price for variable resources,
2. The level of fixed resources available,
3. The technical rate of transformation between resources and products (i.e., the position and shape of the production function), and
4. The value of alternative production opportunities.

These factors will immediately be recognized as being among the *ceteris paribus* conditions of supply.

The factors that determine the position and shape of the individual demand function in the upper-right-hand corner of Figure 14.1 will likewise be recognized as *ceteris paribus* conditions of demand. These factors are:

1. Consumer tastes and preferences (as revealed by the shape and configuration of the indifference curves),
2. Consumer income (or budget), and
3. The prices for alternative goods.

If any of these determinant conditions of individual supply or demand should change, the position, and perhaps the shape and slope, of the function would be altered.

When all of the individual supply or demand functions are summed in order to define the market relationships, there are additional *ceteris paribus* conditions that may alter the position and/or shape of the market functions. Included among these conditions are:

Demand	*Supply*
1. Number of consumers	1. Number of producers
2. The general price level	2. Institutional arrangements
3. Institutional arrangements	a. Farm programs
a. International trade	b. Financial regulations
b. Credit	c. etc.
c. etc.	3. etc.
4. etc.	

In primitive economies where producers and consumers deal directly with one another, the market equilibrium is determined as depicted in Figure 14.1, with producers receiving the same price as is paid by consumers. But in modern economies, which are based upon specialization and division of labor, marketing systems have been developed. As a result, producers and consumers deal directly with each other only in rare and isolated cases. "Farmers markets" for locally grown fresh fruits and vegetables in the farm belt, for example, represent a situation in which producers and consumers deal directly. The so-called pick-your-own farming operations near population centers represent a second example. But in terms of the total volumes of products produced and consumed, these and other examples represent no more than a microscopic fraction.

An agricultural marketing system typically performs three basic functions: *concentration, equalization, and dispersion.* The initial marketing function—concentration—pulls together a volume of product sufficient for the other two functions to be efficiently performed. Examples of marketing businesses that perform the function of concentration would include grain elevators, livestock auction markets, and feed lots.

Once the function of concentration has been accomplished, the function of equalization can begin. Some of the equalizing activities performed by the agricultural marketing system include sorting, grading, processing, and packaging. Examples of marketing businesses that engage in equalizing activities include grain milling, oil seed crushing, meat packing, canning, and freezing.

Upon completion of the equalization function, the agricultural marketing function of dispersion may be undertaken. This function includes activities such as transportation, warehousing, wholesaling, and retailing.

In the case of agricultural goods, the individual consumer operates as a *polyopsonist*—one of a great many buyers who cannot individually influence market prices. An agricultural producer typically operates as a *polyopolist*—one of a great many sellers who, like consumers, are incapable of individually exerting influence upon market prices. But this purely competitive circumstance in agriculture generally involves only the two ends of the production–marketing–consumption chain. The "middlemen" in the marketing agencies typically operate under conditions that are considerably less than perfectly competitive.

We will be examining the conditions of competition in some depth in subsequent chapters. The crux of the discussion at this point is that the providers of marketing services must receive some compensation (or some margin of payment) if those services are to be available. Since the two ends of the production-to-consumption chain in agriculture are bereft of bargaining power, the nature of this marketing margin assumes some significance with regard to quantities made available in the market and with regard to prices at various points along the production–marketing chain. Thus, our supply–demand model of Figure 14.1 requires some modification if it is to realistically portray what actually occurs in the marketplace.

The market separation of consumers and producers of agricultural goods has created the situation in which the fundamental forces of basic demand operate at a market level different from that at which the fundamental forces of supply are observed. Since consumers do their thing in the various retail outlets, basic demand is observed at the retail level. Demand for any product at the wholesale, processing, or farm levels exists **if and *only*** if there is a demand at retail. Indeed, the product purchased at retail is typically a very different product than that which is available at some lower level. The demand at all previous levels of production, processing, and so on is *derived* from the basic retail demand. Thus, retail demand *less* the relevant marketing margin(s) determines the demand at any lower level.

Conversely, the basic forces of supply occur at the farm level. Since very few American consumers are equipped to utilize most farm products in the condition in which they are sold from the farm (i.e., something must be done to a hog to prevent its biting back when bitten), and since marketing agencies must be compensated for their services, the supply at all subsequent levels is the supply at the farm level *plus* the marketing margin(s). That is, the supply at any subsequent level is *derived* from the farm supply function.

Retail prices in the marketplace are determined by the interaction between a basic demand function and a derived supply function. Farm prices are determined by the interaction between a basic supply function and a derived demand function. In the case of the intermediate market levels, the interaction is between *two* derived functions.

Figure 14.2 illustrates the modifications in our basic diagram that can include the presence of the agricultural marketing system. The dashed functions (S_r and D_f) illustrate the derived supply at retail and the derived demand at the farm level. The market quantity exchanged is smaller than was the case when producers and consumers dealt directly with one another. The farm price is lower and the consumer price is higher as a result of the need to pay for marketing services. The typical consumer of our illustration is responding to the supply information

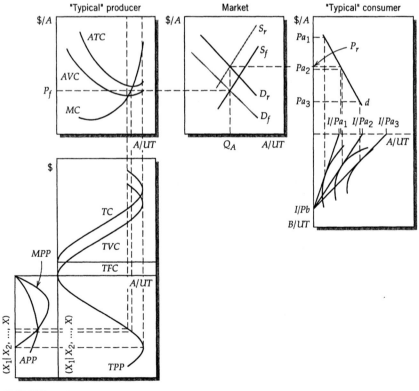

FIGURE 14.2

only after that information has been filtered through the marketing agencies. The typical producer, likewise, is responding to similarly filtered information. The difference between P_r and P_f (i.e., the farm-to-retail "price spread" or the "marketing margin") represents the "price" that is paid for the "filtering" of the information through the various concentrating, equalizing, and dispersing activities of the marketing system. The nature of this marketing margin has a wide array of implications for the production and marketing processes, and for the prices that are likely to emerge at various levels as a result of changes in the determinants of basic farm supply or basic consumer demand.

THE CONSTANT COST PER UNIT TYPE OF MARKETING MARGIN _____

Probably the easiest type of marketing margin to understand is the constant cost per unit marketing margin. This marketing margin tends to add a constant monetary value per unit of product to the price received by the basic producer. This constant cost per unit type of marketing margin is fairly typical, for example, for fresh fruits and vegetables.

One of the reasons for the existence of the constant cost per unit type of marketing margin is that the vast majority of the costs faced by the marketing agencies tend to be *variable costs* (Figure 14.3). The major costs for marketing fresh fruits and vegetables, for example, are harvesting labor, grading and sorting labor, packaging materials, and transportation—all of which vary almost perfectly with the volume of product

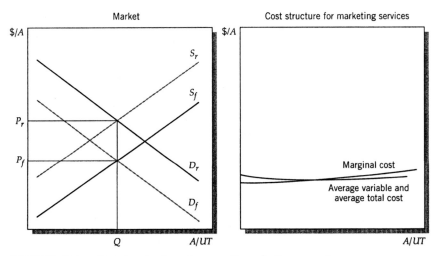

FIGURE 14.3. The constant cost per unit marketing margin.

handled. Thus, the cost structure for marketing would be of the type shown in the right-hand portion of Figure 14.3—Average Variable Costs and Average Total Costs would be almost identical and would be almost horizontal. Marginal costs likewise would be almost horizontal, implying that each added unit of product marketed would add essentially a constant amount to the total marketing cost.

There are several implications of the constant cost per unit marketing margin. Any price change associated with changes in the level of production will be charged (or credited) *entirely* to the basic producer. That is, if Mamma Nature should decide to bestow her weather bounty in favorable abundance, the price reduction resulting from the increase in per acre yields would be borne entirely by the basic farm producer. Since the marketing agencies receive a constant fee per unit for marketing services, their percentage "share" of the total retail price and most probably their net profitability would increase. If, on the other hand, Mamma Nature should decide to withhold her blessings, the opposite result would occur, with the entire retail price increase accruing to those producers who had product to sell. This is the reason that California and Texas citrus growers have been known to pray for a frost in Florida.

A second implication of the constant cost per unit marketing margin is that there is an inherent conflict of interests between producers and those persons at all subsequent market levels (Figure 14.4). We saw in Chapter 11 that the retail demand for virtually all food products is inelastic with respect to price. With a constant cost per unit marketing margin, demand for any given market quantity of product is *always* less elastic at the producer level than at subsequent levels. In the elastic range of the market demand, total revenues increase more rapidly at the retail level than at the farm level. Since the total revenue accruing to the farm level represents the basic cost to the marketing agencies, and with total revenue increasing faster for the marketing agencies than for farmers, it is in the best interest of marketing agencies to see sales expanded in this range.

Once farmers expand production beyond the point at which farm demand is unitarily elastic, total revenue at the farm level begins to decline. But total revenue at the retail level is still increasing. In the inelastic range of market demand, total revenues decline more rapidly at the farm level than at the retail level. Thus, it is in the best interest of the marketing agencies to expand sales *throughout* the range of the farm demand curve. This is a major part of the reason that marketing agencies have historically opposed acreage allotments, marketing orders, marketing quotas, or any other technique that would have enabled agricultural producers to effectively manage supplies.

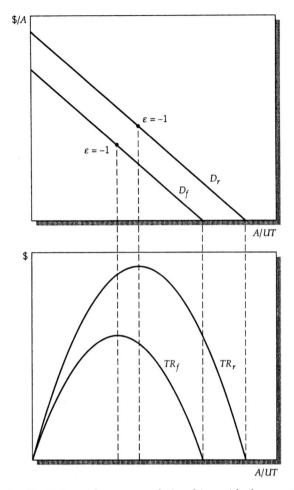

FIGURE 14.4. Elasticity and revenue relationships with the constant cost per unit marketing margin.

One advantage of a constant cost per unit type of marketing margin is that the low fixed investments generally associated with this type of marketing margin make it fairly easy for producers to band together in marketing cooperatives. There are numerous local and regional cooperatives that have been established for this purpose. Some brand names that are generally familiar to many consumers are Sunmaid raisins, Sunsweet prunes, Sunkist citrus, Diamond walnuts, Ozark Pride blueberries, and Ocean Spray cranberry products.

THE CONSTANT PERCENTAGE OF RETAIL PRICE TYPE OF MARKETING MARGIN _____

The constant percentage of retail price type of marketing margin is fairly typical for products for which the marketing process involves very large fixed investments and substantial economies of scale. An example of the constant percentage marketing margin is provided by dairy products.

Since the cost structure for marketing firms generally involves very large fixed investments, average total costs decline very rapidly as the volume of product marketed increases toward the optimal capacity (Figure 14.5). Thus, the financial penalties for operating at less than full capacity are substantial. Yet, the presence of major scale economies, which allow the larger scale of plant (AVC_2, ATC_2, and MC_2 in Figure 14.5) to operate at lower cost than the smaller scale facility (AVC_1, ATC_1, and MC_1) over the Q_1–Q_2 range of product volume encourages marketing agencies to overbuild facilities. These conflicting incentives create an environment in which the marketing agencies will absorb a part of any price reduction associated with an enlarged output in order to grant as much price concession as possible to producers in an effort to limit price disincentives for maintaining the volume of output.

The implications of the constant percentage of retail price marketing margin are that conflicts of interest between the producer level and subsequent market levels are reduced (Figure 14.6). The demand for any

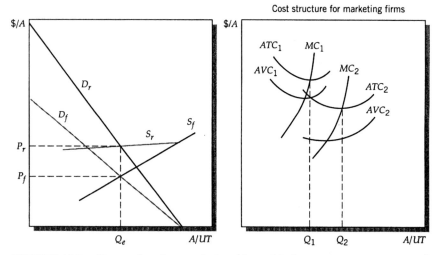

FIGURE 14.5. Demand and cost relationships with the constant percentage of retail price marketing margin.

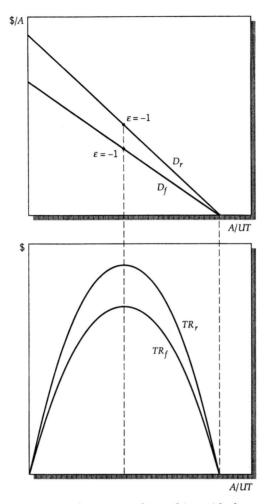

FIGURE 14.6. Elasticity and revenue relationships with the constant percentage of retail price marketing margin.

given quantity of product is equally elastic (or inelastic) with respect to price at all market levels sharing the constant percentage of retail price type of marketing margin. Maximum total revenue occurs at the same level of output for all market levels.

Since fixed investments for the provision of marketing services are very large, marketing cooperatives that collectively bargain for prices are more common than are those that actually own the facilities for concentrating, equalizing, and ultimately dispersing the product. They may frequently contract with the owners of such facilities for the utilization of excess capacity in order to strengthen their bargaining position. These collective bargaining associations are also typically very active in their

efforts to secure institutional arrangements favorable to their member-
ships. Dairy marketing cooperatives have been very instrumental in
securing price support and loan legislation and in influencing the
promulgation of regulations by which that legislation is administered.

THE INCREASING COST PER UNIT TYPE
OF MARKETING MARGIN _____

The increasing cost per unit type of marketing margin is fairly typical for
products for which marketing firms face significant levels of fixed investment costs, but have substantial variable costs as well. While economies
of scale may be available, most of these scale economies are realized at
relatively low levels of output. Meat products—and most especially the
fresh meat products—tend to exhibit increasing cost per unit marketing
margins. Under these circumstances, marketing firms will not process
products unless the price spread is sufficient to cover the cost of handling the final unit of product.

At output *a* in Figure 14.7 illustrates the situation for products with the increasing
cost type of marketing margin. Since the marginal cost for marketing
services *is* the marketing margin that must be deducted from basic retail
demand to define the prices that marketing firms are willing to pay for
various volumes of product, no product will be processed at marketing
margins below the average variable cost. That is, once raw product
prices are bid up to the point that the higher cost marketing firms cannot
cover the average variable cost of operations, those firms will close
down at least until raw product supplies increase by enough to allow the
coverage of these costs.

At output *a* in Figure 14.7, the marketing firms would be willing to
pay no more than the retail price at which the finished product could be
sold, less the marginal cost at *a*. If raw product availability should increase to *b*, the larger marginal cost at level *b* would be deducted from
the retail price associated with this level of output. In this fashion, the
farm demand for this product can be derived from the retail demand
simply by deducting the marginal cost for marketing services from the
retail demand function.

The retail supply function under conditions of the increasing cost
marketing margin is derived in much the same fashion as is the farm
demand. The marginal cost for marketing services is simply *added* to the
farm supply function. That is, the farm supply function plus the marginal cost for marketing services defines the prices at which various
volumes of product will be supplied at retail.

The implications of the increasing cost per unit marketing margins are
basically an exaggeration of the implications of the constant cost per unit

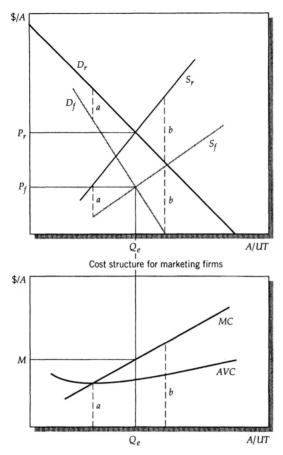

FIGURE 14.7. Demand and cost relationships, increasing cost per unit marketing margin.

margin (Figure 14.8). Not only are the retail price changes associated with changes in the volume of output charged (or credited) exclusively to the basic producers, the change in the level of marginal cost for marketing services are charged to them as well. That is, farm prices will decline *more*—both relatively and absolutely—than will retail prices when output is expanded and will increase more when output is reduced. The greatest volatility in farm prices occurs when the marketing margin is of the increasing cost type.

The increasing cost per unit marketing margin generates the situation in which the potential conflicts of interest between the various market levels are maximum. Demand is *much* less price elastic at the farm level than at subsequent market levels. Thus, raw product producers are terribly vulnerable to being "whipsawed," particularly in times of cycli-

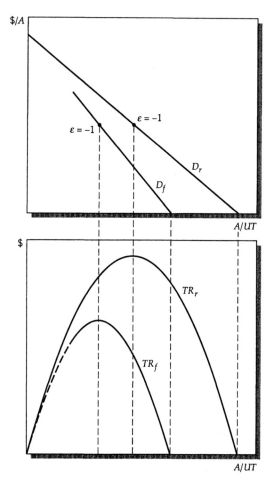

FIGURE 14.8.   Elasticity and revenue relationships with the increasing cost per unit marketing margin.

cally or seasonally increasing output. Also, they are extremely vulnerable to price impacts that result from disturbances in the marketing sector such as transportation difficulties or labor problems. If a major meat packer faces a prolonged strike, for example, the resulting increase in marginal costs for the increased volumes processed by other packers will almost inevitably be reflected in reduced livestock prices.

The nature of the marketing margin for many farm products can be readily defined from published data sources. The increasing cost per unit nature of the farm-to-carcass marketing margin for beef, for example, is very clear. From the 21 years of information included in Figure 14.9, it is clear that as the commercial production of beef increases, so does the margin realized by meat packers.

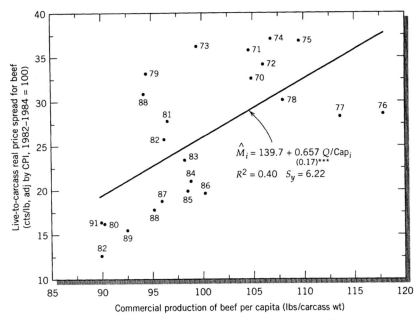

FIGURE 14.9. Relationship between per capita availability of beef and the live-to-carcass marketing margin, United States, 1970–90.

SOURCE: *Livestock and Poultry Situation and Outlook Report*, ERS, USDA, various issues since August 1990.

It could be argued that there are actually two marketing margin relationships in Figure 14.9 rather than one—one prior to 1976 and a second, lower relationship during the period subsequent to 1982. This is probably the result of the combined impact of two forces. During the late 1960s and early 1970s, there were a large number of new slaughter plants constructed in the Southern Plains cattle feeding region. These new plants created a situation of enormous overcapacity in the beef slaughter sector. This wasn't a major problem up through 1975, since there was a continuing increase in the availability of slaughter cattle. But with the massive liquidation of cattle beginning in 1975, the availability of cattle began to decline. The resulting intense competition for the available slaughter cattle placed enormous pressure on the live-to-carcass marketing margin, driving it to levels below that which might normally have been expected.

The 1979–81 period was the time of the second Energy Crisis when the OPEC countries tripled crude oil prices. With their need for refrigeration and for transportation services, meat packers perceived energy costs to be a major cost item. Given their experience with the first Oil Crisis in 1974 and 1975, it is probable that the packers overcompensated for the anticipated impact of increased energy costs. The result was a set of marketing margins that were very high relative to the volume of product available.

Even ignoring the apparent "break" in the continuity of the packer margin data, the regression relationship indicates that the volume of beef alone explains almost half the total variation in the real spread in beef prices between the live and carcass levels. If the 1983–90 period were analyzed alone, the statistical fit would be improved substantially.

CHAPTER **15**

Market Structure—Pure Competition

In our discussion of price spreads and marketing margins in Chapter 14, we recognized that the basic producers and the ultimate consumers of agricultural goods only rarely deal directly with one another. We further recognized that the people at the two extremes of the agricultural production–marketing chain have no power to negotiate prices because of the structure of the markets within which they participate. This lack of bargaining power for both producers and consumers, both of whom deal with marketing agencies that do have bargaining power, has some very real implications for the prices that occur at all market levels.

The fact that producers and consumers do not deal directly with one another causes some limitations upon the degree of communication that occurs between producers and consumers. Indeed, the *product* purchased at the consumer level is frequently perceived to be a product entirely different from that originally created by basic producers. While these perceptions of product differences are entirely valid, consumers typically have difficulty identifying the relationship between the product they buy and the product produced at the farm level. In the case of grains, oil seeds, and most livestock products, these differences in product at the farm and consumer levels are obvious. Fluid milk, for example, is very rarely utilized by consumers in the condition that it comes from the farm. Typically, that milk is pasteurized, homogenized, vitaminized, containerized, and standardized with regard to fat content prior to its consumption.

The "distance" between basic producers and ultimate consumers of farm products—distance not only in the sense of geography, but also in the form and appearance of the products—has made the communication of biological and economic realities between producers and consumers considerably less than perfect. The author's own preschool children, for example, found the container from which they observed their grandfather extracting milk to be extremely objectionable. They wouldn't drink the milk that they saw grandpa squeeze from a cow—they wanted milk from a box! As early as 1960, a Chicago housewife created a minor sensation when a television newswoman asked for her opinion regarding the dumping of milk in the gutter by Wisconsin dairy farmers protesting low milk prices. The Chicago housewife's response was that the protest was of no concern to her—she got her milk at A & P!

Even those consumer food products that appear to be much the same as those marketed from the farm (fresh fruits and vegetables, for example) are in reality very different products. These consumer products include the addition of the marketing services of sorting and grading, transportation, refrigeration, and packaging, which have been added to the product subsequent to its production at the farm level.

The price implications of the existence of the agricultural marketing system were examined in Chapter 14. But the location of the power to bargain for prices also has some significant price implications. We have already recognized that neither the basic producer nor the ultimate consumer enjoys any degree of individual bargaining power in the case of most farm products, and we have further recognized that this lack of bargaining power flows from the structure of the market in which these individuals participate. The market structure that gives rise to the absence of individual bargaining power has been given a variety of names—"pure competition," "perfect competition," "polyopoly," and "atomistic competition" are among them. While some economists strive to draw subtle differences among these terms, analytically and pragmatically, the four terms refer to essentially the same situation.

Most economists tend to limit their discussion of the conditions of competition to the differences in the conditions under which products are produced and sold. But because of the presence of the agricultural marketing system interposed between producers and consumers, the competitive conditions under which agricultural products are purchased and utilized have become every bit as much at issue as are the competitive conditions under which they are produced and sold. For this reason, we will separate our discussions of market structure into the competitive conditions under which procurement occurs and those under which sales are made.

The conditions of competition in any market may be identified by a set of Greek combining forms that indicate the numbers of market participants and the market activity in question. The suffix -opoly comes from the Greek *polein* meaning *to sell*. The suffix -opsony comes from the Greek *opsonin* meaning *to buy*. Thus, *monopoly* would be the combination of *monos* (alone) + *polein* (to sell) indicating a single seller of the good. Other combining term roots are shown in the following table.

Number of Market Participants	*Type of Market Activity*
Mono- (one)	
Duo- (two)	-opoly (selling conditions)
Oligo- (few)	-opsony (buying conditions)
Poly- (many)	

Our basic farm producer would be one of a great many sellers of the good or a *polyopolist*. Our ultimate consumer would be one of a great many buyers of the good, or a *polyopsonist*.

There are three conditions that are necessary for the existence of poly-opoly or polyopsony:

1. Insignificance of the individual buying (or selling) unit. That is, the individual buyer or seller is such a small part of the total market that no individual can through individual action affect the market price.
2. Homogeneity of product. That is, once products reach the market, it is not possible to identify them as to source. One bushel of corn is pretty much like another bushel of corn or one ice-packed, ready-to-cook broiler is pretty much like any other ice-packed, ready-to-cook broiler.
3. Absence of artificial barriers to market entry or exit. That is, products are free to move to their highest-paying buyers and resources are free to move to their highest-paying uses.

Figure 15.1 illustrates the circumstances of the polyopolist and the polyopsonist as related to a market situation, assuming a constant cost per unit marketing margin. Since the individual producer is insignificant in relation to the total market, and since the product A produced by one polyopolist is the same as that offered by any competing polyopolist, the presence or the absence of any single seller will not perceptibly affect the market supply or price. The individual can sell as much or as little as he/she wishes *at the market price* (P_f). The schedule of quantities he is willing and able to sell at a given series of prices (i.e., his *supply*) is defined by that portion of the marginal cost, which lies above average variable cost. If he requires a price above the level established by the market, his sales volume declines to zero. He will not cut prices in order to increase sales since he can already sell everything he wishes to sell at price P_f. Thus, the only portion of the market seen by the individual polyopolist is the intersection of the farm-level market supply and demand functions for

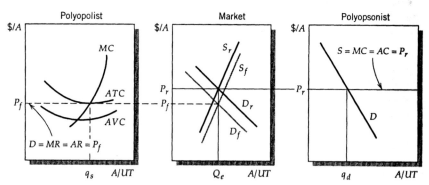

FIGURE 15.1.   Relationships between the market, polyopoly, and polyopsony (constant cost per unit marketing margin).

the product he is producing (D_f and S_f). All he sees is the market price P_f. The demand *as he perceives it* is a horizontal line at the market price level. This horizontal line (i.e., the market price) also defines the average revenue and the marginal revenue for the individual. The polyopolist will maximize profits by producing and selling q_s where marginal revenue and his individual marginal cost are equal.

Like the purely competitive seller of the product, the only portion of the market situation seen by polyopsonists is the market price for the product they buy. Since the polyopsonist is such a minute portion of the total market, any attempt to negotiate lower prices in the marketplace would be met first with incredulity and then probably with derision. If a housewife offers a price below the market price for a can of green beans (P_r), her green bean purchases decline to zero. But she can purchase as much or as little as she wishes at that market price. This market price also defines the marginal cost for each additional unit purchased as well as the average cost. She will purchase q_d, defined by the intersection of her personal demand function and the market-price-level horizontal supply function she faces.

THE EFFECTS OF POLYOPOLY ——————————————

Let's suppose that for some reason, the market demand function for the basic product has shifted from D_f to D_f^*, such that the market price faced by the polyopolist has risen from P_f to P_f^* (Figure 15.2). The immediate response of the individual polyopolist is to increase the usage of variable resources to expand output from q_s to q_s^*, maximizing profits at the point where marginal cost and marginal revenue are equal. But since one of the conditions necessary for the existence of polyopoly is that resources

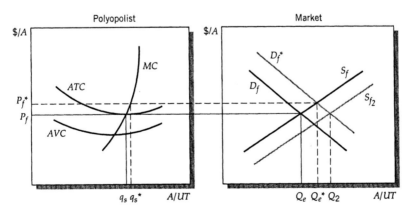

FIGURE 15.2

are free to move to their highest paying use, the new price encourages people who previously refrained from the production of this good to enter the market. If the price increase is deemed to be a permanent (or long-term) increase, existing producers may well invest in additional fixed resources to increase productive capacity. As a result of these adjustments, market supply shifts from S_f to S_f^* giving a new equilibrium market volume of Q_2 with the original market price of P_f.

The end results of the polyopolistic market structure are:

1. Products tend to be produced at the lowest possible average total cost.
2. Products tend to be priced at this same minimum average total cost.
3. Since no single firm can affect market prices and since the products produced by the various firms are homogeneous, there is no real benefit to be realized from sales promotion and advertising.
4. The largest possible degree of economic efficiency is realized under conditions of polyopoly. Each firm will operate an optimum scale of plant, producing at an optimum rate of output, insuring that the product will be produced at the lowest possible cost per unit of output, *if* the market is of sufficient size to accommodate polyopoly.
5. In order for polyopoly to exist, the total market volume must be quite large relative to the volume associated with the optimum scale of plant in order to insure the insignificance of the individual.

THE EFFECTS OF POLYOPSONY _____

If we make the same assumption of an increase in market demand (perhaps as a result of an increase in the numbers of consumers either through natural population increase or through some change in institutional arrangements that give foreigners greater access to U.S. markets), we can see the implications of a polyopsonistic situation (Figure 15.3). The change in the market equilibrium and the new higher market price is perceived by polyopsonists as simply an upward shift in the supply function they face. The inability to renegotiate prices limits their options to simply adjusting to the higher price by reducing purchases from q_d to q_d^*.

To the extent that polyopoly (pure competition in the conditions of selling) exists in this market, the adjustment process described earlier may give our polyopsonist some relief. But we have already recognized that in the case of agricultural goods, the consumers who buy as polyopsonists only rarely deal directly with the polyopolistic production sector that is equally devoid of bargaining power. Rather, *both* of these sectors

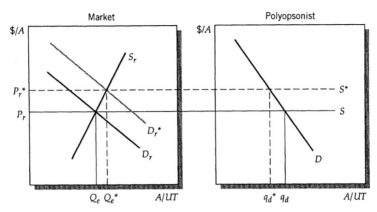

FIGURE 15.3

deal with the middlemen who typically operate in considerably less perfectly competitive circumstances—both as buyers and as sellers. These less perfectly competitive market structures will be the focus of the next two chapters.

THE IMPLICATIONS OF PURE COMPETITION _____

The fact that the purely competitive market structure gives the greatest possible degree of economic efficiency (in those markets large enough to accommodate this structure) is probably the basis for the use of polyopoly and polyopsony as the standard against which other types of market structures are measured. But it should be pointed out that there is nothing particularly sacred about "efficiency."

People who claim to be great advocates of "economic efficiency" are typically those who personally do not face the kind of market structure that promotes the greatest degree of economic efficiency. The two general groups of people who function as polyopolists—farmers and individual workers in a wide variety of categories—aren't a bit excited about the desirability of economic efficiency in their lines of personal endeavor. Rather, they are concerned about a wide array of other issues. Some of the words you hear used in discussing the needs of these groups are "equity," "fairness," "economic justice," and "job security."

It is fairly clear that the U.S. society in general may talk a good game about the need and desire for economic efficiency. But it is equally clear that Americans want any drive for economic efficiency to be constrained by a wide array of other objectives. There are numerous examples of these publicly imposed constraints. Among them are:

1. The existence of farm programs designed to limit output and to manage supplies in order to maintain farm prices and incomes at levels higher than would otherwise be the case.
2. The "Union Shop" provision that limits entry into certain skilled labor categories and hence increases earnings for those who are accepted. Analytically, this is no different than supply management for farm products.
3. The administration of sometimes quite arbitrary admission standards to limit enrollments in certain publicly supported (and admittedly expensive) professional schools such as medicine, law, and veterinary medicine. Analytically, these are no different than the Union movement in other career areas.
4. Local licensing provisions designed to limit market access for some service businesses such as plumbing, electrical wiring, and housing construction. Again, these provisions are a technique for the management of the supply of these services, designed to increase the rewards for those who do in fact possess the licenses.
5. Import constraints on items such as automobiles, electronics, shoes, and textiles. Limitation upon the numbers of suppliers allowed to participate in a domestic market is simply an effort to increase the revenues realized by domestic producers.

The imposition of these licensing constraints and other devices for limiting entry into various career areas are almost invariably justified on the basis of "protecting the public" from incompetent and unethical operators. Whether the constraints have notably improved professional competence or professional ethics is subject to some skepticism. The probability of an elevation of competence and ethical behavior would appear to be enhanced as a result of increased competition rather than by a reduction therein.

Polyopsonists have also attempted to take action to gain relief from the lack of bargaining power. The so-called Consumer Movement, which began in the early 1970s was and is one evidence of this. The very existence of the Food and Drug Administration is another. The creation of Offices of Consumer Affairs in many state governments is still another.

CHAPTER 16

Market Structure— Monopoly and Monopsony

In Chapter 15, we examined the implications of the purely competitive market structure for both buyers (polyopsonists) and sellers (polyopolists). We recognized that the lack of individual bargaining power under this purely competitive market structure set the stage for the maximum possible degree of economic efficiency with products tending to be produced at the minimum point on the average total cost function and product prices tending toward this same minimum. We also recognized that this was a serendipitous situation for everybody *except* for the polyopolists and polyopsonists who had no bargaining power.

One of the conditions necessary for the existence of the polyopolistic or polyopsonistic market structure is that the individual buyer or seller be insignificant relative to the total market. That is, the volume of product associated with the optimum scale of productive plant or with the ordinary purchasing unit must be very small when compared with the size of the total market. This is generally true for agricultural producers and for the ultimate consumers of agricultural goods. But these two groups ordinarily do not deal directly with one another. Rather, these groups generally deal with the middlemen of the agricultural marketing system.

The volumes of output associated with the optimum scales of plant at the various levels within the agricultural marketing system typically are *not* insignificant when compared with the volume of the total market. Thus, the marketing agencies generally *do* possess some significant degree of bargaining power. When an agency that possesses bargaining power negotiates prices with an individual who has no bargaining power, it is not difficult to predict the outcome of such price negotiations. Thus, the price implications for pure competitors dealing with buying or selling entities that function in a less competitive environment are fairly obvious.

MONOPOLY

The end of the competition spectrum opposite from that of polyopoly is monopoly. Three conditions are necessary for the existence of monopoly.

1. **One and only one seller of the product.** That is, as the only seller of the product, the monopolist is *totally* significant in the marketplace. The monopolist, therefore, faces the *market* demand function.

2. **No close substitutes for the product.** Hence, purchasers who do not like the price of the product in question cannot adjust by substituting other goods.
3. **Entry into the market is blocked.** This blockage of market entry may be the result of a market size so limited that the market will not accommodate more than one such business. It may be the result of the monopolist controlling the supply of an essential resource. Or it may be the result of patent ownership or some other institutional limitation such as licensing. But whatever the reason, even if profit incentives are large enough to create the desire on the part of other firms to compete with the monopolist, they are unable to do so.

Since the circumstances of monopoly are unique only on the selling side, let's for the moment assume that the monopolist buys resources as a polyopsonist. This means that his production cost structure is of the normal sort that we have studied in previous chapters, allowing us to focus our attention on the circumstances of product sales. As the sole seller in the market, the monopolist can set the price at any level he would like, *provided* he is willing to accept the limitations imposed by the market demand curve. Thus, if the monopolist chooses to set the price at P_h in Figure 16.1, his sales volume declines to zero. That is, the volume of sales that the monopolist realizes at various prices is defined by the shape and position of the market demand function.

Under conditions of polyopoly, the market supply function is the horizontal summation of all the individual supply functions. Thus the market price under polyopoly conditions would—at least in the short

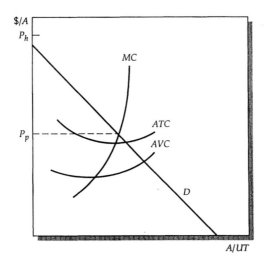

FIGURE 16.1. The market demand curve faced by the monopolist.

term—be at P_p. But how would monopolists go about making the decision regarding the profit-maximizing price for their products?

Throughout our study of price analysis, we have recognized that the objective of a profit-maximizing manager is to produce and sell every unit of product that adds more to revenue than it adds to cost, and to avoid producing any unit that adds *less* to revenue than it adds to cost. Therefore, the key to identifying the profit-maximizing position for our monopolist in Figure 16.1 would be the marginal revenue function. The demand curve faced by the polyopolist is a horizontal line at the market price level. Since the market price received by the polyopolist is independent of the volume of product offered **by that individual,** this horizontal line also defines the marginal revenue function.

The monopolist as the only seller faces the *market* demand function. If the quantity offered for sale changes, there is a corresponding change in the realized price. Since the price changes not only for the marginal unit, but also for all other units, the change in total revenue (i.e., the marginal revenue) differs from the change in price.

Table 16.1 shows the relationship between the market demand function and the levels of total revenue and marginal revenue generated at various points along that function. As price declines, the quantity sold increases. Total revenue increases at a decreasing rate up to some maximum and then begins to decline. Marginal revenue is by definition the change in total revenue that is associated with a one-unit change in the level of sales. An inspection of the figures in Table 16.1 shows that as prices change by $1, marginal revenue changes by $2. That is, the marginal revenue function exhibits a slope double that of the demand function.[1]

Since the marginal revenue associated with any demand curve possessing any degree of slope has twice the slope of the demand curve, the marginal revenue curve vertically bisects the area under the demand curve. The profit-maximizing decision facing our monopolist is illus-

---

[1] Mathematically, the demand curve in Table 16.1 may be defined:

$$D = P = AR = a - bQ$$

Total revenue would therefore be:

$$TR = Q(AR) = Q(a - bQ) = aQ - bQ^2$$

Marginal revenue, as the rate of change in total revenue associated with a one-unit change in quantity would be:

$$\frac{\Delta TR}{\Delta Q} = a - 2bQ$$

The doubling of the slope of the marginal revenue as compared with demand is demonstrated by $MR = a - 2bQ$ as compared with $D = a - bQ$.

TABLE 16.1. Relationship Between Market Demand and the Generation of Total and Marginal Revenues

Market Demand			
Price (Average Revenue)	Quantity	Total Revenue	Marginal Revenue
10	0	0	
			9
9	1	9	
			7
8	2	16	
			5
7	3	21	
			3
6	4	24	
			1
5	5	25	
			−1
4	6	24	

trated in Figure 16.2. He would select that output that equates marginal cost and marginal revenue, producing Q_e and selling at a price of P_e. Since the average total cost function includes a "normal" return to all resources (i.e., all resources receive a return equal to their next-best revenue opportunity), the "pure" profits or "economic" profits extracted by the monopolist are shown by the shaded area in Figure 16.2. These economic profits are borne by the consumers that purchase from the monopolist. Thus, *if the market is of a size sufficient to accommodate pure competition*, buyers pay a higher price for less product under

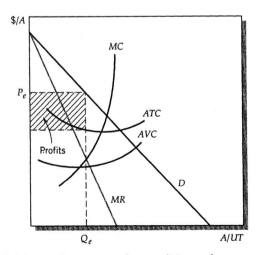

FIGURE 16.2. Pricing and output under conditions of monopoly.

conditions of monopoly. The degree of economic efficiency achieved is less under conditions of monopoly than under conditions of polyopoly, since the product is not necessarily produced and sold at the minimum point of the average total cost curve, nor is it necessarily produced with an optimum scale of plant.

Monopolies are not necessarily *always* profitable. A common situation in rural areas is that the out-migration of population has reduced the size of the market such that only one lumber yard, one farm implement business, and so on can survive. And that one business cannot generate enough revenues to recover the full cost of operations (Figure 16.3). Because of the investment in fixed resources that have very limited or even zero market value, the business will continue to operate. The reason for this, of course, is that monopolistic managers prefer to recover most of the fixed costs that they must pay whether or not they operate. Their alternative is to cease operations and lose them all.

Except in the locational sense, monopoly conditions in the selling of agricultural products is really fairly infrequent. Because of limited market size, monopoly conditions, especially for the vendors of certain services to agricultural producers, do occasionally occur in the agricultural resource sales area. Again, these monopoly conditions are typically monopolistic primarily in a locational sense.

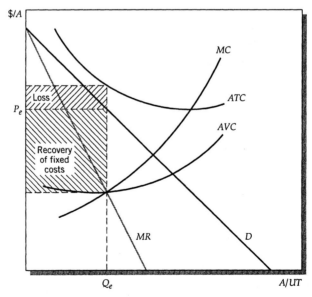

FIGURE 16.3. Pricing and output under conditions of monopoly, with loss being incurred.

There are some business situations—notably the public utilities such as natural gas, electrical distribution, and telephone service—in which the fixed investments are so large that the monopoly situation can actually provide the goods or the service more efficiently and at lower cost than can an alternative market structure. As a result, governmental entities (e.g., states, counties, or municipalities) will grant exclusive "franchises" to individual firms to provide the service (hence the term *public* utilities). This exclusive franchise is granted in exchange for an agreement to provide all the service desired at a previously agreed upon price.

The effects of a franchising agreement upon the monopoly pricing and output are shown in Figure 16.4. Left to his own devices, the monopolist would offer Q_m for sale at a price of P_m, extracting economic profits of the magnitude shown by the P_m-a-b-c rectangle. With the franchising agreement, the franchise price P_f is associated with the larger output of Q_f, and the economic profits are reduced in the amount of the difference between the P_f-P_m-a-g and b-e-d-g rectangles. In this fashion, the monopolist is relieved of the pressure of potential competitors (along with some of his economic profits) and consumers receive more product at a lower price than might otherwise be the case, since the market is not large enough for more than one of these businesses to operate efficiently. As circumstances change, the monopolist can petition to the

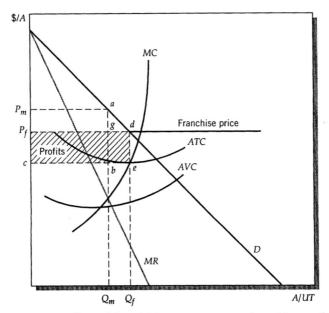

FIGURE 16.4. The effect of franchising upon monopoly pricing and output.

public body granting the franchise for relief from unduly burdensome circumstances. In most cases, this petition must be approved by a state-level Public Service Commission, Corporation Commission, or, in the case of the state of Texas, the Railroad Commission.

Monopoly as such is not necessarily evil. The monopolistic market structure does contain circumstances that in the absence of regulation may foster predatory business practices that are abusive of the interests of consumers—not to mention those of potential competitors. Contrary to popular belief, monopoly was not outlawed by the Sherman Anti-Trust Act. What was outlawed by that act was the predatory business practices that the monopoly circumstance may encourage. The much-discussed court-ordered "break-up" of the Bell Telephone companies in the early 1980s, for example, did not and was not intended to eliminate the monopolistic nature of local telephone services. Rather, that court decision was directed toward predatory practices of the Bell System in the area of long-distance service as alleged in complaints filed by firms competing for the long-distance business.

MONOPSONY ——————————————————————

The cognate of the monopoly situation, which describes a set of conditions under which products are bought, is monopsony. Monopsony is at the extreme opposite from polyopsony. Actually, the monopsony circumstance is typically concerned with the conditions under which the monopsonist purchases the resources from which products are produced. For purposes of convenience, let's assume that the operating costs of production per unit of output are constant and very close to zero. That is, we are assuming the cost of production to be exclusively the cost of the resource. In this fashion, we can focus our attention upon the impact the monopsony circumstance has on prices and quantities sold.

Two conditions are necessary for the existence of monopsony:

1. One and only one buyer of the product.
2. Access to the market is blocked. Blockage of entry into the market may be the result of very limited market size or of institutional constraints.

There are numerous real-world examples of the monopsony situation. The prohibition against the sale of certain types of uranium ore to any entity other than the U.S. government is one example of how these two conditions may be met. A similar prohibition against the sale of bulk quantities of precious metals existed for many years. In the world of agriculture, there is an occasional case of the locational monopsony in which limited market size will not accommodate more than one buyer.

Like the monopolist, the monopsonist comprises one entire side of the market. Since the market supply function for resources is faced by the monopsonist, the monopsonist is constrained by that function. That is, he can reduce the resource price to any level he may wish, *provided* he is willing to live with the level of resources that will be forthcoming at that price. Thus, the market supply function faced by the monopsonists has implications beyond the supply function itself. Table 16.2 shows the relationship between the market supply function and the generation of total and marginal costs of procurement under monopsonistic conditions. The monopsonist can secure increased volumes of the product if and only if he pays an increased price. Since the price changes not only for the marginal unit of the good, but also for all the other units, the change in the total cost incurred (i.e., the marginal cost of procurement) differs from the change in price. As the purchases grow, the price also increases. Thus, total procurement cost increases at a greater rate. Marginal procurement cost is by definition the change in total procurement cost associated with a one-unit change in the level of purchasing. In Table 16.2, as prices change by $1, marginal procurement cost changes by $2. Thus, the marginal procurement cost function exhibits a slope double that of the market supply function.[2]

Since the uniqueness of the monopsony situation is the conditions under which purchases of resources are made, let's simplify our analysis by assuming that the monopsonist sells as a polyopolist. That is, the demand function faced by the monopsonist is identical with marginal revenue, shown by a horizontal line at the market price level. We saw in Table 16.2 that the monopsonist's marginal procurement cost (MPC) exhibits a slope double that of the market supply function for resources faced by the monopsonist. Thus, the MPC vertically bisects the area to

---

[2] Mathematically, the market supply function in Table 16.2 may be defined as an average procurement cost function:

$$S = APC = a + bQ$$

Total procurement cost would therefore be:

$$TPC = Q(APC) = Q(a + bQ) = aQ + bQ^2$$

Marginal procurement cost, as the rate of change in total procurement cost, would be:

$$MPC = \frac{\Delta TPC}{\Delta Q} = a + 2bQ$$

The doubling of the slope of the marginal procurement cost as compared with the market supply (i.e., the average procurement cost) is demonstrated by $MCP = a + 2bQ$ as compared with $S = a + bQ$.

TABLE 16.2.   Relationship Between the Raw
Material Supply Function and the
Generation of Total and Marginal Costs of
Procurement for a Monopsonist

Supply Function		Total Procurement Cost	Marginal Procurement Cost
Price	Quantity		
1	0	0	
			2
2	1	2	
			4
3	2	6	
			6
4	3	12	
			8
5	4	20	
			10
6	5	30	
			12
7	6	42	

the left of the market supply function of (Figure 16.5). The monopsonist
would maximize his economic profits by purchasing that quantity where
the marginal procurement cost was equal to the marginal revenue from
sales (Q_e). The price he would pay for those resources would be P_e, with
the economic profits extracted shown by the shaded area in Figure 16.5.

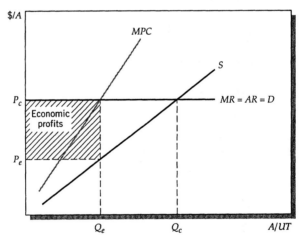

FIGURE 16.5.   Volume of purchases and pricing under conditions of monopsony.

Obviously, the economic profits extracted by the monopsonist are extracted at the expense of the producers of the resource in question. If this market were purely competitive, the quantity purchased and the market price would be determined by the intersection of the supply and demand functions at Q_c and P_c. Thus, under conditions of monopsony, raw materials suppliers face a restricted market and are very vulnerable to underpricing of resources. Some real-world examples of the monopsony circumstance as illustrated in Figure 16.5 include the share-cropper system that was once typical of agriculture in much of the American South and the so-called company town syndrome that was common in coal mining, steel, and other heavy industry. With improved transportation, greater mobility of labor, and more social programs, these situations have largely disappeared. The most common monopsony circumstances today are isolated and largely locational in nature.

The example of the locational monopsonist who sells as a pure competitor (Figure 16.5) does in fact exist in the case of the so-called Peckerwood sawmills across the American South. These small, independent sawmill operations are frequently the only outlet for hardwood saw logs in their geographic area. However, when these operators sell pallets, railroad ties, and so on, they compete with large numbers of other similar businesses. Deprived of bargaining power in their sales operations and enjoying total significance in their procurement operations, it isn't difficult to anticipate that the prices for hardwood logs are likely to be somewhat depressed.

It can be seen from Figure 16.5 that the volume of resources produced and sold is constrained under conditions of monopsony as compared with polyopsony. Thus, resources are most probably processed under conditions of less than optimal economic efficiency and very possibly with less than optimal scales of plant. As fixed resources are depleted in the resource production sector, the size of that sector will very likely decline.

Like monopoly, there is nothing inherently evil in monopsony. An agricultural producer who has local access to only one meat packer or grain elevator is much better off than would be the case if he had access to none. A case in point is cotton. During the 1960s, cotton prices were very low relative to other crops, and many areas that had formerly produced cotton shifted land resources to the alternative crops. As a result, many gins were abandoned. Today, no matter how high cotton prices may rise, these areas cannot produce cotton because there is no local place to have the cotton ginned. Transportation costs make moving the seed cotton to alternative areas prohibitively expensive. It must be recognized, however, that while monopsony *per se* may not be evil, monopsony conditions do lend themselves to significant abuse.

MONOPOLY–MONOPSONY ————————————

To complete our analysis of monopoly and monopsony, let's consider a firm that enjoys the luxury of being the only buyer of some resource in a given market and at the same time is the only seller of the good made from that resource (Figure 16.6). If both polyopoly and polyopsony prevailed in that market, the price for the good and the resource (since we are assuming processing costs to be zero) would be P_c and the volume available would be Q_c. But under the conditions postulated, our monopolistic monopsonist would utilize only Q_e, paying P_p for resources and selling the product at P_s. Thus, the economic profits extracted can be identified as to which portion flows from the monopoly conditions and which flows from the monopsony circumstance.

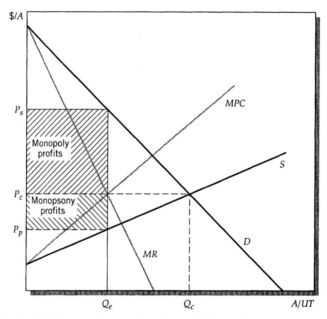

FIGURE 16.6.   Pricing and output under conditions of monopoly and monopsony.

CHAPTER **17**

Market Structure— Oligopoly and Oligopsony

In Chapters 15 and 16, we examined the two extremes of the conditions of competition in the marketplace. The structural conditions of the market circumstance render the individual basic producers of most agricultural goods powerless in the negotiation of prices. Likewise, the individual consumers of the products that those agricultural goods ultimately become are typically powerless in the area of price negotiation, again, as a result of the structure of the market. The purely competitive polyopolist maximizes profits where marginal revenue and marginal cost are equal. Since no individual—buyer or seller—can influence the market price, that market price *is* the marginal revenue with which marginal cost is equated. The market structure, which leads to the lack of individual bargaining power, particularly in the case of producers, also leads to the highest degree of economic efficiency, with products tending to be produced at the lowest possible average total cost and tending to be priced at the average total cost of production.

We recognized that the profit-maximizing position under conditions of monopoly occurs at the point where marginal cost and marginal revenue are equal—the same criterion as for the purely competitive producer. However, since the monopolist is the only seller and therefore faces the market demand function, the marginal revenue function is no longer identical with market price. Rather, as sales increase, the marginal revenue function declines at *twice* the rate exhibited by the market demand function. Thus, under conditions of monopoly (if the market is large enough to accommodate more than one firm), a smaller volume of product is made available and market prices are higher than would be the case under polyopoly, and the degree of economic efficiency is reduced.

In the case of monopsony, with a single buyer of resources in the market, the marginal cost of resource procurement rises at twice the rate as the resource supply function. The result of this circumstance is that fewer resources are utilized and resource prices are lower than would be the case under more perfectly competitive conditions. The monopsony and monopoly market structures both lend themselves to exploitative practices.

The purely competitive market structure of polyopoly is fairly rare except in the case of basic agricultural production. That of polyopsony is typical for virtually all consumer goods. Except in a locational sense, monopoly and monopsony are fairly uncommon. But between these extremes in market structure (polyopoly vs. monopoly and polyopsony vs. monopsony) lies a vast area that might be called imperfect competition. Technically, monopoly and monopsony with a single seller or a single buyer are the ultimate in competitive imperfection. But for purposes of clarity, these have been treated separately.

Imperfect competition on the selling side includes a wide range of conditions such as monopolistic competition, consumer franchises, and oligopoly. Similar distinctions may be drawn on the buying side. But by far the most common of these intermediately competitive circumstances, the most readily recognizable, and the most important so far as agricultural goods are concerned are the conditions of oligopoly and oligopsony. These are the imperfectly competitive circumstances upon which we will focus.

OLIGOPOLY _____

When we use the word *"competition"* in our everyday conversation, we typically view competition in the sense of *rivalry*—every competitor is attempting to out-do his rivals. But when we examined pure competition in Chapter 15, we discovered that competition in the economic context was devoid of emotion. Two competing polyopolists may be the best of friends. It is very common, for example, for two neighboring cattlemen who sell in the same market to share labor when working cattle. Rancher Smith will very readily take his crew to Rancher Jones to assist with branding, dehorning, and so on, this week, and Rancher Jones will return the favor next week. They may occasionally share ownership of some infrequently utilized piece of equipment. One will very willingly share technical production information with the other. If one sells cattle at a lower price, the other may pity the unwisdom, but will in no way resent the cut-throat pricing practices. This lack of emotion and animosity among competing polyopolists is a result of the lack of individual bargaining power. Since neither individual can influence market price, neither perceives the other in any way to be a threat to their personal economic well-being. As a result, intense personal rivalries that are based on business operations are very rare in the case of pure competitors.

The oligopoly market structure is quite a different matter. How many local service station operators who share a market are close personal friends? Does Elanco share technical information with Upjohn? Does Grace and Co. share equipment with Vitagro? If the local Safeway store found itself temporarily short of labor, how likely is it that the manager of A&P would detail the hired help to assist Safeway for a day? Ford tells Chrysler nothing—and Chrysler doesn't ask. That's the reason God made industrial espionage!

The firms that provide farm inputs and those involved in marketing farm outputs (i.e., those contributing to the marketing margin) typically operate under some form of oligopolistic or oligopsonistic arrangement. Under these arrangements, the individual actions of any firm are almost certain to impact upon the profit or loss experienced by competing firms. Thus, any unusual action is very likely to provoke retaliation. Frequently, an oligopsonistic buyer is also an oligopolistic seller, creating the situation in which the business must be prepared to deal with retaliation at more than one level. Since the structure of the markets in the entire agribusiness sector tends toward the oligopoly arrangement, it is important for the agricultural price analyst to be able to anticipate at least the direction of and to recognize the constraints upon price movements associated with these circumstances.

Since the oligopoly arrangement is concerned with the conditions under which products are produced and sold, for purposes of understanding, let's assume for the moment that the oligopolist buys resources under conditions of pure competition. Thus, the cost structure will be of the conventional sort we have used throughout our study of price analysis. There are three general types of oligopoly situations that we will examine: the organized collusive oligopoly, the unorganized collusive oligopoly, and the unorganized noncollusive situation.[1]

Organized, Collusive Oligopoly

The organized, collusive oligopoly situation is fundamentally a cartel arrangement. Thus, this arrangement is essentially a monopoly problem (Figure 17.1). For convenience, let's assume that the members of the cartel are producing a homogeneous product. The summation of that portion of the marginal cost curves, which lie above the average variable cost curves for all of the individual members of the cartel, becomes an umbrella marginal cost curve (ΣMC) for the entire cartel. You will note that there are no average cost relationships shown since the average cost relationships may well lie at very different levels and are of very doubtful relevance to the analysis. The cartel will choose that volume of product that equates the overall marginal cost with marginal revenue (Q_e), establishing the price (P_e) associated with that volume, and will assign shares of that volume to the various members of the cartel on a quota basis.

The quotas assigned to the members of the cartel may be an allocation of market share, with each member of the cartel handling its own mar-

---

[1] The author is indebted to Dr. Richard H. Leftwich, a superb teacher under whose tutelage the author had three courses in microeconomics, for this classification. More detailed discussion may be found in Dr. Leftwich's book, *The Price System and Resource Allocation*, Rinehart and Company, Inc., New York, 1955.

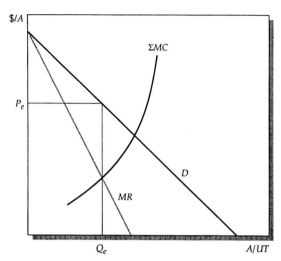

FIGURE 17.1. Pricing and output under conditions of organized, collusive oligopoly.

keting (*a la* the Organization of Petroleum Exporting Countries—OPEC). There are several limitations to this sort of quota arrangement. First of all, there are substantial incentives for cheating, particularly for those firms with the lower cost structures or with strong nonprofit incentives. OPEC learned this lesson when two of its members, Iran and Iraq, found themselves faced with financing a war against each other. Second, there are incentives for other producers (Britain and Norway, in the case of OPEC) to refuse to be members of the cartel. The third problem is that of maintaining discipline among the cartel members. What do you do about those members that do violate their quotas when they are conducting their own independent marketing efforts? The OPEC cartel leaked oil like a sieve during the Iran–Iraq conflict, causing real prices for crude oil to decline to very near the 1973 levels that prevailed prior to the first Arab Oil Boycott.

A second approach that the members of a cartel may use when assigning quotas avoids the problem of cheating. This approach is to assign quotas on some historical volume of production basis, with the cartel actually doing the selling, rebating to the various members their proportionate share of the cartel's sales. The profits of the cartel would be calculated by each member and then totalled since the unique cost structures of the individual members cannot be reflected in the sum of the marginal cost curves.

A third approach to the assignment of quotas could be to assign geographic areas within which the members of the cartel do not compete.

Thus, the individual members of the cartel would function as locational monopolists.

Regardless of the quota approach employed, if a cartel is to be successful, entry into the industry must be at least partially blocked. Entry can be blocked in much the same fashion as under monopoly—through control of essential resources or through some institutional arrangement such as patent ownership. In the case of the United States, organized collusive oligopoly is illegal. This is the anti-Trust law that many people think of as outlawing monopoly.

Unorganized, Collusive Oligopoly

There are several variations of the unorganized, nevertheless collusive, oligopoly. The two most readily recognizable are those industries in which there is price leadership by a large, dominant firm, and those industries with price leadership by a low-cost firm.

Price Leadership by a Dominant Firm   The oligopoly situation of price leadership by a large, dominant firm is illustrated in Figure 17.2. The market demand as shared by the various oligopolists is shown by D_m. The willingness of the several small firms to produce and offer products for sale is represented by the sum of the marginal cost functions (ΣMC) for those firms. The marginal revenue function, so far as the small firms

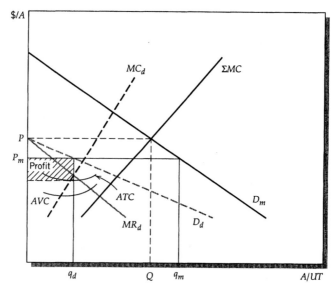

FIGURE 17.2.   Pricing and output under oligopoly conditions of price leadership by a dominant firm.

are concerned, is the price that is ultimately established by the dominant firm, the product from which is vital for supplying the total market. The smaller firms exit the market at prices below their individual average variable cost functions and re-enter when market prices rise to levels above those functions. Thus, ΣMC represents a supply function of sorts for the small firms that operate in essentially the same manner as if they were polyopolists.

In the absence of the dominant firm, the market price and quantity would be established by the intersection of D_m and ΣMC. Thus, at price p, the small firms would be willing and able to provide the entire market volume of Q units of A. Therefore, the demand facing the dominant firm (D_d) at any given price would be the quantity demanded along D_m, less the quantity the small firms would provide along ΣMC *at that price.*

Since the demand faced by the dominant firm is a "residual" demand, the marginal revenue function facing that firm is the function that is marginal to (falling twice as fast as) D_d—or MR_d. The cost structure for the dominant firm is shown by MC_d. The dominant firm will choose to maximize profits by equating marginal revenue and marginal costs, generating economic profits of the magnitude shown by the shaded area in Figure 17.2. The dominant firm will produce and sell q_d, establishing a price of p_m, which the smaller firms have no choice but to accept. The smaller firms will produce and sell the difference between q_m and q_d.

This dominant firm price leadership oligopoly situation is "collusive" in the sense that the smaller firms accept the price leadership of the dominant firm. If MC_d were added to ΣMC—as would be the case under a purely competitive market situation—one can establish that consumers would be able to purchase a bit more product at a slightly lower market price under conditions of pure competition rather than under conditions in which a large dominant firm establishes the price.

Price Leadership by a Low-Cost Firm For convenience, let's assume that there are only two firms with equal shares of the market, producing an essentially homogeneous product (Figure 17.3). Firm A has a higher cost structure (MC_a and ATC_a) than does Firm B (MC_b and ATC_b). Market demand is shown by D_{mkt}. Since the two firms have equal shares of the market, the demand facing each individual firm vertically bisects the area under the market demand function. Thus, $D_{a\&b}$ represents the demand as faced by each firm. The curve marginal to $D_{a\&b}$ ($MR_{a\&b}$) represents the marginal revenue against which these firms would equate marginal cost in their efforts to maximize profits.

It is clear from Figure 17.3 that these two firms have a difference of opinion regarding the "ideal" levels of output and price. If each firm maximized profits by equating marginal cost and marginal revenue, Firm A would want to produce q_a at a price of p_a, whereas Firm B would

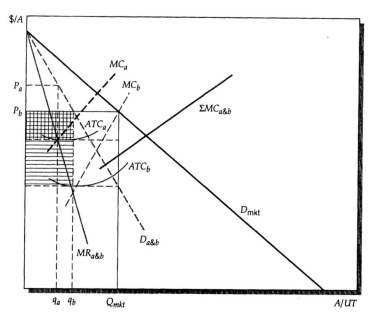

FIGURE 17.3. Pricing and output under oligopoly conditions of price leader-ship by a low-cost firm.

prefer to produce the larger quantity of q_b at a lower price of p_b. But if Firm A attempts to charge p_a, Firm A's customers will transfer their business to Firm B. Thus, Firm A has no choice except to meet the price established by Firm B. That is, Firm A's marginal revenue *becomes* the price established by the lower-cost firm. Under these circumstances, the economic profits extracted by Firm A are shown by the area of Figure 17.3 that is horizontally shaded. The economic profits extracted by the lower-cost firm are shown by the area that is vertically shaded.

The intersection of the market demand function and the line that sums the marginal cost functions for both firms ($\Sigma MC_{a\&b}$) shows the market quantity and price that would occur if this market were purely competitive. This illustrates that while market prices may be lower as a result of price leadership by a low-cost firm, consumers still get less product and pay higher prices than would be the case under pure com-petition.

Figure 17.3 examines the situation of low-cost firm price leadership under oligopoly conditions in which each oligopolist struggles to main-tain market share. But suppose that the higher-cost firm's (Firm A's) marginal cost curve intersects the marginal revenue established by mar-ket price at some output that is *less* than half the total quantity de-manded at that price. If Firm A should decide to sacrifice a part of their market share in the interest of improved profitability, the picture is altered (Figure 17.4).

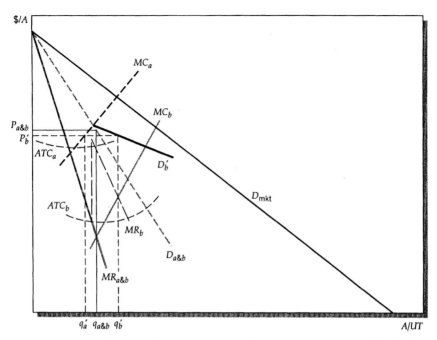

FIGURE 17.4. Pricing and output under oligopoly conditions of price leadership by a low-cost firm when a high-cost firm reduces market share in the interest of improved profitability.

Under these conditions, Firm B faces the equal market share demand curve ($D_{a\&b}$) down to the point at which that demand curve intersects the marginal cost for Firm A. From this point on, the demand facing Firm B is the difference between the market demand and MC_a—or D'_b. That is, there is a "kink" in the demand curve facing Firm B. As a result of this kink in the demand curve, there is a discontinuity in the curve that is marginal to demand curve D'_b. That is, Firm B faces the marginal revenue for the equal market shares ($MR_{a\&b}$) up to the volume of output at which the kink in demand occurs. Because of the reduced slope of this portion of the demand curve, the marginal revenue curve that becomes relevant at levels of output beyond this point (MR'_b) is at a higher level and has a lesser slope than the original marginal revenue function, giving rise to the discontinuity. Rather than the equal market shares of $Q_{a\&b}$, the output is redistributed to q'_a and q'_b. Market prices are marginally reduced and total output is marginally increased as a consequence of the high-cost firm's decision to concede a part of the market share in order to improve profitability. Like the case of price leadership by a dominant firm, the "collusion" in this case occurs when the higher-cost firms accept the prices established by the lower-cost firm.

Unorganized, Noncollusive Oligopoly

The unorganized, noncollusive oligopoly situation typically results in genteel—and sometimes not so genteel—business warfare among competing business firms. The potential for price wars is characteristic, particularly for an immature or a rapidly expanding or declining industry operating under oligopolistic conditions. Some recent examples of these situations include microcomputers, hand-held calculators, microchips, and electronics in general.

Price wars may be touched off by a variety of factors, all of which are rooted in the fact that profits and losses for each firm are impacted by the independent unilateral action of any individual. A firm attempting to gain market penetration in a new geographic area, for example, may touch off a price war. The classic example of gasoline price wars typically occurred when retail gasoline chains attempted to expand into new areas. Similar circumstances have been observed in retail milk markets when milk marketing cooperatives have acquired access to milk processing facilities—either through ownership or lease arrangements—and have used retail milk pricing as a weapon in their efforts to improve fluid milk prices. More recently, the effort to gain market acceptance for compatible clones of certain models of IBM microcomputers generated a series of reductions and counterreductions in price for these machines.

An existing firm that attempts to revive declining sales may touch off a price war. Gasoline price wars may break out when a new superhighway disrupts historical traffic patterns. Or a supermarket that faces a pattern of outward migration of population in its service area may generate a price war when it uses a loss leader such as bread or milk in its efforts to attract enough traffic through the store to maintain sales volumes.

Another circumstance that may create the potential for price wars arises when surplus stocks cannot be sold at existing prices. The price war may take the form of price rebates from the manufacturer, as in the case of automobiles during much of the 1980s, or the form of various other price incentives. In the case of the world market for grains, a price war of sorts has occurred from time to time as various governments have attempted to dispose of surplus stocks through a variety of export incentives, which have effectively reduced the prices ultimately paid by purchasers.

Finally, in a new industry or in one that is experiencing rapid expansion, individual managers not knowing what to expect of rivals may inadvertently promulgate a price war in their scramble to establish their place in the market. This was most probably the case for many of the price wars in the various sectors of the electronics industry that emerged in the 1970s and 1980s.

Regardless of the source of any price war, managers who have been through one typically are dedicated to avoiding a repetition of the experience. As the industry matures, some of the danger of price wars subsides as managers learn what *not* to do. Most of them will very carefully refrain from activities that could result in a price war, which might well prove to be disastrous. A price, or a cluster of prices, with which all of the firms can live from a profitability standpoint will have been established. The risk of price wars typically causes these prices to be rigidly maintained. But some very creative forms of nonprice competition may be undertaken.

While various brands of laundry detergents, toilet soaps, wieners, prepared cereals, cigarettes, cola-flavored soft drinks, blue jeans, or beer are fundamentally the same, the manufacturers of these products will go to great pains through color, perfume, spice blends, form, or packaging to make them appear to be different. The real differences among the competing brands is typically very slight. But the advertising of the apparent differences would lead one to believe that there is absolutely no comparability among products. Oscar Mayer processed meat products, for example, are only slightly different from other high-quality meat products, except for very subtle differences in the spice blend. But the subtle message in Oscar Mayer's use of enormously attractive children in advertising their product is a suggestion to parents that these products make beautiful children—a superbly effective technique. The blatant sexuality of ads focusing on the crotch of a slinky blond model wearing a particular brand of blue jeans allowed a significant volume of that brand to be sold at prices at least 50 percent above the price of other brands of comparable quality. The American consumer's vulnerability and the influence of oligopoly firm advertising has been very clear in the case of athletic shoes that can be pumped, primed, and preened to ostensibly allow the use to leap higher and hang longer while slam-dunking a basketball. Numerous cases of real physical violence have been recorded as have-not adolescents have relieved peers of their high-priced athletic shoes.

Analytically, the circumstance of price rigidity in a mature, noncollusive oligopoly market situation is shown in Figure 17.5. If the oligopolist attempts to elevate the price that rivals have come to perceive to be "normal," competitors do not respond, but his customers desert him, causing the volume of sales to decline very rapidly. If, on the other hand, he attempts to enlarge his normal market share by reducing prices, rivals retaliate with their own vengeful price reductions and his sales expand by no more than his normal share of the increased total market volume that results from generally lower prices. Thus, the demand function facing the oligopolist is "kinked" at the volume and the price that have come to be perceived as normal.

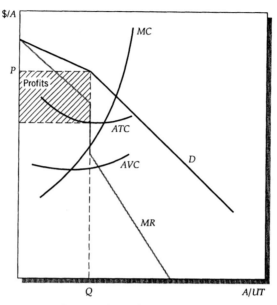

FIGURE 17.5.   Price rigidity resulting from unorganized, noncollusive oligopoly.

The kinked demand curve facing the noncollusive oligopolist is the reverse of that observed for the low-cost firm price leadership situation. The curve that is marginal to the upper portion of this demand curve is different from that which is marginal to the lower portion. As a result, the marginal revenue function facing the oligopolist is discontinuous at the volume of product which is his normal market share.

Because of the discontinuity in marginal revenue, marginal revenue and marginal cost will be equal at the same volume of output over a fairly substantial range of resource costs that may shift the oligopolist's cost structure up or down. Thus, the price charged is maintained. The volume of sales in the total market can expand or decline within a fairly broad range, causing the demand and marginal revenue functions faced by the oligopolist to shift to the right or the left. But the kink in demand still occurs at the normal price level.

If the discontinuity in marginal revenue that is associated with the kink in demand coincides with marginal cost, the oligopolist will not change his price. If resource costs, technological change, growth or decline in the total market demand, or if a low-cost-firm effort to penetrate the market should cause the oligopolist's marginal cost curve to intersect marginal revenue *outside* the discontinuity in marginal revenue, the oligopolistic manager has an incentive to adjust prices. When this is done, he is confronted with the necessity of going through the price war that will reestablish a new market share and a new price that rivals will view as normal.

OLIGOPSONY ————————————————

Oligopsony is the circumstance in which there is a very limited number of firms purchasing a resource that is required for the production of other goods either for investment or consumption. The conditions necessary for the existence of oligopsony in a resource market, and the types of oligopsonies are similar to those observed in the case of oligopoly. There are only a few buyers of the resource. Thus, the independent actions of any one of the buyers will almost certainly impact upon the profits realized by other competing oligopsonists. The resource is typically homogeneous, and entry into the market is at least partially blocked. The blockage of market entry is generally a result of the fact that the economies of scale and size in the resource-processing activities are such that the market simply isn't large enough to accommodate more perfectly competitive conditions.

The rivalries based on business operations that are observed in the case of oligopoly are at least as intense in the case of oligopsony. Packer buyers who call on commercial feedlots or who purchase at livestock auctions, for example, will frequently engage in guerilla tactics of economic ambush in their efforts to gain an advantage over rivals in the procurement of slaughter cattle or hogs. Similar tactics may be observed in the case of competing grain companies in their efforts to procure wheat, corn, or soybeans. The efforts of competing poultry integrators in securing the services of contract growers can be equally cold blooded.

Organized, Collusive Oligopsony

Organized, collusive oligopsony is illegal in the case of the United States. The Consent Decree signed by the four major meat packers (including Swift, Armour, and Wilson) in the 1920s was essentially an admission of collusive fixing of livestock prices and an agreement to cease and desist from these practices. Interestingly, while all of these firms were major players in livestock markets into the 1970s, none of them are major forces in livestock markets in the 1990s. Indeed, none of the three companies cited above are currently engaged in livestock slaughter. Analytically, organized, collusive oligopsony is identical with the monopsony problem discussed in Chapter 16.

Unorganized, Collusive Oligopoly—Price Leadership by a Dominant or Low-Cost Firm

The oligopsony situation of leadership in resource pricing by a dominant or a low-cost firm is collusive in the sense that small firms accept the resource price as established by the dominant or low-cost firm. Since the oligopsony situation is concerned with the conditions under which resources are purchased, for purposes of convenience, let's assume that the oligopsonist sells a product under conditions of pure competition. Thus, the value of the marginal product (VMP) of the resource defines the resource demand for any individual firm. The sum of the VMPs for all firms in the market would define the market demand for the resource (i.e., the *total factor demand*). If the market situation in Figure 17.6 were for a purely competitive market, the intersection of the market supply for resources (S_{mkt}) and the total factor demand would define the level of resources utilized (Q_c) and the market price (P_c) for those resources.

The value of the marginal product for the dominant firm (VMP_d) in Figure 17.6 defines the resource demand for that firm, assuming that the price for the product of the resource is constant. The resource demand for all other firms is shown by ΣVMP_0, with the total factor demand being the sum of VMP_d and ΣVMP_0.

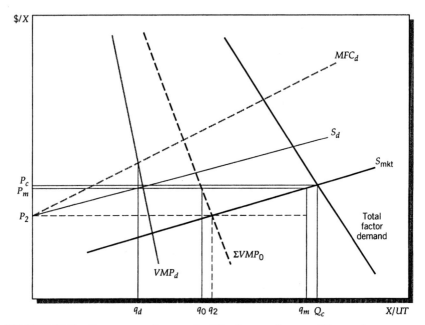

FIGURE 17.6.   Resource prices and utilization under conditions of unorganized, collusive oligopsony with price leadership.

Left to their own devices (that is, in the absence of the dominant firm), the smaller firms would utilize q_2 of the resource at a price of p_2. Thus, the supply function facing the dominant firm at any price above p_2 is the difference in the quantity demanded by the smaller firms and the market quantity that would be supplied *at that price.* That is, at any given price, the quantity defined by S_{mkt} less the quantity defined by ΣVMP_0 would define the quantity available to the dominant firm. Thus, S_d is the supply function faced by the dominant firm.

At prices above p_2, the marginal cost for additional units of the re-source [i.e., the *marginal factor cost* (MFC)] rises twice as fast (i.e., has *double* the slope) as does the supply function facing the dominant firm. Thus, the dominant firm maximizes profits at the level of resource utilization where the marginal factor cost is equal to the value of the marginal product. Market price is established at p_m, which becomes the resource price paid by all firms in the market. The dominant firm purchases q_d, with other firms purchasing q_0 and a total market volume of q_m.

Unorganized, Noncollusive Oligopsony

As in the case of oligopoly, the unorganized, noncollusive situation of oligopsony is fraught with peril for participants in the market. The participants in a new industry in an area may get into bidding wars as a result of simple ignorance regarding the likely response of rivals. The development of a major cattle feeding area in the Plains area during the 1960s, for example, brought about the development of a new beef slaughter industry in the 1970s. There were frequent bidding wars for fed cattle as the new slaughter plants strove to establish their place in the market, and as established plants attempted to maintain their sources of supplies.

A second source of resource bidding wars is a rapid change in the availability of resources in a market. The development of the Plains cattle feeding industry diverted large numbers of feeder cattle from the Upper Midwest, creating a situation of reduced fed cattle supplies in that area. This created a situation of massive overcapacity in the region's beef slaughter industry—again touching off frequent bidding wars for the reduced volume of fed cattle.

Once the various oligopsonists in these types of circumstances have gained enough experience to anticipate the probable response of rivals, the industry will begin to stabilize at least within certain limits. As the industry matures, the supply function facing the individual oligopsonist is "kinked" (Figure 17.7). That is, the oligopsonist can buy up to his "normal" market share (q_n) with only nominal increases in price as the volume of purchases increases. But beyond that normal share, he invites

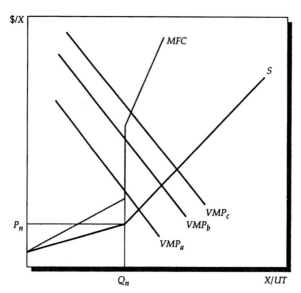

FIGURE 17.7. Price and utilization of resources under conditions of unorganized, noncollusive oligopsony.

retaliation from his rivals, and prices rise much more rapidly as volume purchased is expanded. This situation creates a discontinuity in the marginal factor cost, which is analogous to the discontinuity in marginal revenue for the oligopolist.

So long as *VMP* (which defines the firm's demand for a resource) intersects *MFC* in the discontinuity, resource prices and market shares will tend to be stable at P_n and q_n (as is the case with VMP_a and VMP_b in Figure 17.7). But once *VMP* intersects *MFC* in the more rapidly increasing portion of *MFC*, great instability is introduced. In the case of agricultural commodities that are subject to substantial seasonal or cyclical variation in output, this instability can occur regularly as the resource market supply function (and hence the resource supply function facing the oligopsonist) shifts dramatically from season to season or from one phase of the cycle to another. If the resource supply function facing the oligopsonist in Figure 17.7 should shift only slightly to the left, the discontinuity in *MFC* would likewise shift to the left, causing VMP_b to intersect *MFC* in the more rapidly increasing portion, introducing the resource price instability of which processor nightmares are made.

The kink in the supply curve facing the oligopsonist in the unorganized, noncollusive situation of Figure 17.7 frequently arises from the situation in which the oligopsonist may enjoy virtually total dominance within part of the resource procurement area, but face fierce competition in other portions of the area. Consider, for example, the situation in

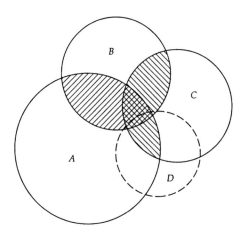

FIGURE 17.8. Resource procurement areas for competing oligopsonists.

which three competing oligopsonists share the resource market in a region (Figure 17.8). Firm A faces very little competition for resources in the unshaded portion of his procurement area that does not overlap with the procurement areas of Firms B and C. The darker the shading in a portion of the procurement area, the more intense the competition for resources.

If Firm A is content with the volumes of resources available within the procurement area that is free of the influence of Firms B and C (up to Q_n in Figure 17.7), the resource supply function Firm A faces has only a moderate slope—modest increases in resource prices will bring forth substantial increases in available resource volume. But once Firm A expands his operation beyond the volume available in the "clear" portion of his procurement area, he can expand *only* by sharply increasing the prices he bids for resources.

Should a new Firm D decide to enter this resource market, the encroachment not only upon the area in which Firm A has previously enjoyed dominance, but also upon the areas of both Firms B and C would be almost certain to touch off a resource price war. Once the four firms had reestablished normal market shares, the market would be expected to stabilize.

OLIGOPOLY–OLIGOPSONY ————————————————

To this point, in order to focus upon the impacts of the market structure, our analysis has assumed that the oligopolist buys resources as a pure competitor and that the oligopsonist sells products as a pure competitor.

These assumptions are obviously at frequent odds with the facts. In the real world, a firm that is of sufficient size to influence resource prices will be large enough very frequently to influence product prices as well. This is especially true for agricultural products.

Meat products are typically sold under oligopoly conditions, and the livestock resources required for producing those products are at best purchased under conditions of oligopsony. The same is true for most grain products, most canned or frozen fruits and vegetables, and most dairy products. Therefore, we need to relax our simplifying assumptions and examine the circumstances of the oligopolist who is also an oligopsonist in the area of resource procurement. In order to simplify the analysis, let's assume that the in-plant cost structure is essentially zero in order to focus upon the impact of the market structure without the complication of the in-plant operating cost issues.

The case illustrated in Figure 17.9 shows the situation in which the kinks in the demand and supply occur at the same quantity and the discontinuities in MR and MFC coincide. In this serendipitous situation, resource prices are stable at P_r. Product prices are stable at P_p, and the quantity of the resource utilized is stable at Q. The profits earned in this situation would be defined by the difference between P_p and P_r, multiplied by Q.

The circumstance in which the oligopolistic share of the product market captured by an agricultural processing business coincides precisely with the oligopsonistic share of the resource market captured is fairly uncommon. More frequently, because of differing degrees of emphasis on activities such as sales forces and advertising the market shares for an

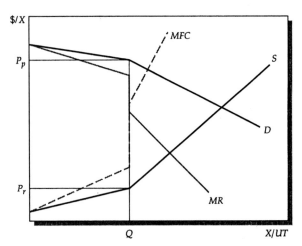

FIGURE 17.9.   Oligopoly–oligopsony with stability and price rigidity.

individual business at these two levels do *not* coincide. As a result, the "ideal" magnitude of the business from the resource procurement standpoint is different from the ideal magnitude from a sales point of view. Businesses that are oligopsonistic in resource procurement and are also oligopolistic in product sales are typically organized functionally into divisions or departments, with the resource procurement and the sales divisions each having their own profit and loss responsibility. The internal corporate conflicts that can arise from this situation can be awesome to behold.

Figure 17.10 shows the situation in which the ideal resource market share exceeds the volume that is ideal or accepted for a share of the product market. The profit-maximizing condition of equating marginal revenue and marginal factor costs occurs in the discontinuity of the marginal factor cost function, allowing a reasonable degree of stability in the resource markets. But this profit-maximizing situation occurs *beyond* the discontinuity in marginal revenue—in the more rapidly declining portion of the function. Operating in this portion of the marginal revenue function invites enormous instability in the product market. Thus, the sales division of this firm must inevitably be in a continuing state of anxiety unless top management administratively decrees that there will be no more than Q_p of resources purchased. But such a decree would force the procurement division into a position of sacrificing market share and profitability. Further, a portion of the total potential profitability of the firm will have been sacrificed in the interest of stability. Thus, it is obvious that the potential for internal, corporate conflict is enormous.

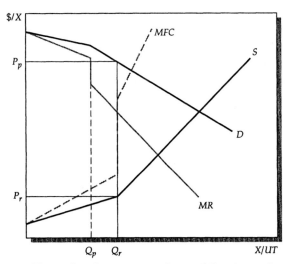

FIGURE 17.10. Oligopoly–oligopsony with instability in product marketing.

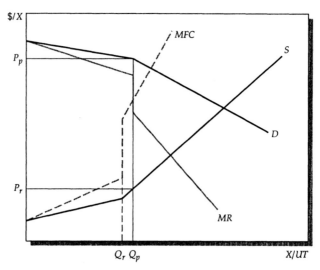

FIGURE 17.11.   Oligopoly–oligopsony with instability in resource markets.

Conversely, Figure 17.11 illustrates the situation in which the established product market share exceeds the share that has been established in the resource market. The profit-maximizing position occurs at a volume of output that permits stability in the product market, but at a volume of resource utilization that invites bidding wars in the resource market. Again, the only way the conflicting objectives of the sales and procurement divisions can be resolved is through administrative decree. The volume of Q_r will lower average resource procurement costs and will allow greater stability in resource markets. But the loss of market share and profits will be difficult for the sales division to accept. Further, the reduction in overall corporate profits may be equally difficult for the stockholders to accept.

A third circumstance that may arise occurs when the established market shares for procurement and sales may be quite comparable, but the nature of the demand and supply functions facing the oligopolistic oligopsonist is such that the profit maximizing position occurs at a volume that is greater than either of the established market shares (Figure 17.12). Under these circumstances, life would be a great deal more comfortable for both the procurement and sales divisions if the operation were limited to a volume of Q_i. But the potential for the increased profitability offered by Q_a creates an enormous temptation for the more aggressive members of both divisions.

In the case of agricultural products, all of these oligopoly–oligopsony situations can be enormously complicated by the normal seasonal or cyclical patterns of production. A firm may regularly face a situation of

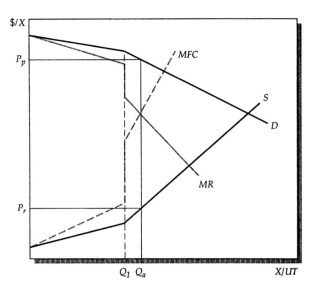

FIGURE 17.12. Oligopoly–oligopsony with instability in both product and re-source markets.

instability in product markets in one quarter of the year as a result of seasonal gluts in raw material production. During another quarter, this firm may face a situation of instability in resource markets as a result of seasonal shortfalls in production. This same firm may find itself confronted with cyclical instability in **both** product and resource markets during certain phases of the cycle. The use of models such as those in Figures 17.09, 17.10, and 17.11 should assist the price analyst to antici-pate at least the probable direction of the impact on prices.

Index

Page numbers preceded by n refer to footnotes.

Printed in the United States
151029LV00003B/5/A

9 780471 304470